Praise for *Asserting a Culture of Child Safety*

This book is a must-have for every early childhood professional's bookshelf. Nicole takes a confronting topic and turns it into something real, something tangible, something not so scary. The way Nicole is able to inspire a passion and commitment for child safety through her writing should be commended. Full of practical examples, links to reputable resources and opportunities for reflection on current thinking and practice makes this book a useful resource for early childhood professionals at all stages of their career.

Sarah Louise Gandolfo
Professional learning project coordinator,
Early Childhood Australia

Having met Nicole Williams aged 17 at Melbourne University, I vividly remember her passion and her handwriting as she wrote lots of notes and used her highlighter! I like the way you can flick to the parts you need more information on, as obviously the content is quite heavy. The topic has so many layers to unpick, so everything in it is important. I would definitely use it as a resource when needing further clarification. So very proud of the passionate and hardworking advocate she has become and continues to be as she explores and gains new knowledge to share with us all. Can't wait to purchase and come to your book signing.

Karryn Grunden
Early childhood teacher

Congratulations on your phenomenal book. The early years sector will really benefit from your hard work. We must start teaching protective education from the age of three at the latest, and your brilliant book will definitely help.

Holly-ann Martin OAM
Child abuse prevention education specialist

The most valuable resource an early childhood educator can have right now is this book. A powerfully written text that provides not only a detailed yet easy-to-read summary of all Child Safe Standards, but cleverly and importantly a working document. This book allows educators and all those within our community to understand, to reflect and to be better when considering best practice. Congratulations to Nicole on her tireless efforts to not only bring these Standards to the forefront of planning within services, but taking the extra step to ensure meaningful dialogue occurs and, importantly, is actioned.

Michelle Smith
Early childhood teacher

I really enjoy your writing style and choice of language and expression. I only had to google one word to find its meaning! I loved it. You write beautifully.

Susie Rosback
Owner early childhood centre

What a splendid and informative read your book is! I want you to know that I went through it meticulously. What I found was that the entire book was set out in a manner that will assist my director colleagues with implementing the Standards. I believe that everyone will benefit from reading this and working through the suggestions, ideas and helpful/practical supports you have provided. As I read through your book, I created an extended version of a Quality Improvement Plan for Child Safe Standards. You have supported me to achieve a quality benchmark to implement all of the Standards. Thanks from your number one cheerleader and fan!

Lorrelle Orrman
Early childhood director

Asserting a Culture of Child Safety

Offering children the protection and care that they deserve

Nicole Talarico

Copyright © Nicole Talarico 2023

All rights reserved. No part of this book may be reproduced or transmitted in any form or by any means, electronic or mechanical, including photocopying, recording or by any information storage and retrieval system, without prior permission in writing from the publisher.

First published in 2023

Published by Amba Press
Melbourne, Australia
www.ambapress.com.au

Cover designer – Tess McCabe
Editor – Rica Dearman

ISBN: 9781922607485 (pbk)
ISBN: 9781922607492 (ebk)

A catalogue record for this book is available from the National Library of Australia.

DEDICATION

To my partner, John Talarico, and my four inspiring children, Tuscany, Morrissey, Valen and Rome

CONTENTS

About the author	ix
Acknowledgements	xi
Preface	xiii
Introduction	1
Part one	
Chapter 1: Child abuse – the actualities	7
Chapter 2: Child abuse – terminology and indicators	27
Chapter 3: Child protection – unpacking sector regulators	35
Chapter 4: Child protection – responding and reporting	61
Part two	
Chapter 5: Child safety – working in the forefront mitigating risk	97
Chapter 6: Child safety – children championing their safety and wellbeing	123
Chapter 7: Child safety – auditing your space	153
Chapter 8: Child safety – governance and leadership	179
Conclusion	219
Appendices	223
References	243
Support services	255

ABOUT THE AUTHOR

Nicole Talarico is the founding director of Talarico Consulting and Medical Action Bag. She has been involved in consulting in the early childhood sector for more than 20 years, supporting children's services with high-quality practice and ongoing improvement, specialising in exceeding service provision. Best known as an advocate for professionalism and children's rights with a social justice lens always present, Nicole is personable and knowledgeable. She assists services with governance, administrative systems and change management to align with professional and ethical standards, helping teams to create and maintain a positive workplace culture and community engagement. Nicole's mentoring strategies have been outlined in a range of early childhood sector publications, with her insight being shared at conferences both nationwide and overseas. Nicole is a valued and respected member of many network groups and has a prominent presence on social media and virtual communication platforms. With a long-term commitment to supporting sector growth, Nicole has a strong focus on the prevention of child abuse and neglect.

Nicole is grateful to live on unceded Wurundjeri land, work on many lands and acknowledges Aboriginal and Torres Strait Islander people as the Traditional Custodians of the land, paying respect to their Elders, past, present and future. She celebrates, values and includes people of all backgrounds, genders, sexualities, cultures, bodies and abilities.

Aboriginal acknowledgement

I acknowledge Traditional Owners of Country throughout Australia. I am grateful to live on unceded Wurundjeri land and respect Aboriginal and Torres Strait Islander and their Elders past, present and future. I support a continuing connection to land, sea and community, honouring cultural and spiritual connections to country. I acknowledge the ongoing leadership role of the Aboriginal community and join with our First Peoples to respect cultural heritage, customs and beliefs of Aboriginal people to enhance all communities.

Victim survivor acknowledgement

I acknowledge the impact of violence on individuals, families and communities, and the strength and resilience of the children and adults who have – and are still – experiencing violence. I pay respects to those who did not survive and to their family members and friends.

> **Forewarning:** The content within this book can be confronting, so please reach out to support services if you need to at www.respect.gov.au/services/#nat. You can also talk to your GP or another allied health professional, and report experiences of abuse to police. Another option is to contact Lifeline on 13 11 14 or chat to someone online at lifeline.org.au

ACKNOWLEDGEMENTS

SARAH LOUISE for seeing my professional capacity and channelling me to consider this challenge. Thank you for celebrating 'in advance' before every single writing stint and constantly keeping me inspired and motivated to be professionally fierce in this sector.

LORRELLE ORRMAN for always telling me you are *"my biggest cheerleader, number one fan"* and showing me this by nominating me for awards for the past 20 years!

MICHELLE SMITH for capturing my attention with your successful community-minded business model and career mindset. Thank you for pushing me both personally and professionally to not only reach new goals but to smash them with GRIT every single day. I fondly recall messages of *"How you going?"* and *"You done?"*, as you knew the time frames I wanted to 'stay in the writer's vortex'! For these, I thank you, they kept me going so I could share progress.

DEANNE TOLLEY for the laughter and caffeine starts to every day to boost our own, as well as the community, spirit.

JAYNEEN SANDERS for your time reading my book, I thank you.

RINA BULIC for your close presence, hand on the shoulder and understanding that I have to be busy, while caringly asking, *"Are you OK, though?"*.

JOHN TALARICO for always admiring and valuing my work enough to partner with me in our family commitments. **TUSCANY**, **MORRISSEY**, **VALEN** and **ROME**, my children, who I have wanted to role model a hard work ethic and strong advocacy to. Thank you for waiting in our parked car until I finish writing a Post-it note to myself before I resume driving, for not removing stationary from my desk – especially the highlighter – and accepting that I spend many hours glued to my computer chair. I know my drive is visible when your friends comment and call me 'woke queen' (greatest compliment ever!).

And in this space, to **ALICIA COHEN**, my publisher, for believing in me to be an author to trust that I could channel what I know into a concise format. For teaching me, at the beginning of this process, that I'm working on my book when I am thinking, reading, highlighting and photographing because the research is valid and necessary. For recognising, after our first meeting, that I will absolutely meet a deadline without the need to micromanage me.

PREFACE

Advocating children's rights means proactively safeguarding them from harm. It is my goal to see the education and care sector take a great leap forward, to be working from a position of prevention, as well as earlier identification. We are not customary to considering the likelihood of abuse occurring while children are in our care. It is time for early childhood professionals to step into a new paradigm of protection, one that asserts a culture of child safety.

Better safeguarding children is not an idealism. This book is your practical tool, to give clarification and confidence about what to do to create and maintain a culture of child safety at your service. At the conclusion of this book, you will know how to work from a strategic position, because there is no room for complacency. A lot of these strategies can be adopted to help protect children in all environments, not just in education and care settings.

Preventing harm to children is not a new phenomenon. The UN Convention on the Rights of the Child is a global treaty that Australia ratified in 1990. (Find out more at www.unicef.org.au.) Australia has constitutional protections, preserving the public's civil liberties and rights, but it has been three decades since we signed this commitment. Our methodologies do not stand out for surpassing this agreement, and it is time we truly take action. Children have a right to protection because of their vulnerability to exploitation and abuse.

We, as educators, working directly with children, are often best placed to identify signs and behaviours that may indicate a child has been subject to harm, but we need to become conscious in our everyday. For many children, warning signs pass by unnoticed. Safety and wellbeing need to be at the forefront of thoughts, values and actions to facilitate earlier detection. How do we become cognisant when our sector is working in a climate of fatigue due to illness and staff shortages?

Why isn't children's safety against abuse powerful enough to override our emotional states and lassitude? How do we defeat the current status quo and shift children's wellbeing to the top of the priority list?

By knowing who has to report child abuse?

The answer is: technically, everyone. As citizens, we all have an ethical obligation to report concerns to children's welfare. In addition to this, there are some of us who, due to our roles, are mandated to report in society. If you suspect something, you need to say something.

By knowing legislation?

There is a wealth of guiding documentation to support educators to ensure children are protected; some is regulatory, others developed as tools to assist practice. It seems that the large volume of advice has created confusion when it comes to what we should, could and must do.

The directive of punishment for non-compliance is certainly not motivating individuals to uphold their professional obligations – it's just not a motivator, especially not for those who habitually fall into the human services sector, who are generally not driven by administrative tasks and legislature. As a successful mentor for more than 20 years, I have proven that to successfully drive change, you need to emotionally connect with someone, and it is only then that they are inspired to be more accountable.

By collaborating?

We need to utilise a framework of consultation with others to facilitate a holistic understanding of the best ways to prevent harm. This means we need to reinvent what 'connection' to families and community looks like and consider pragmatic language to ensure social and cultural safety. It's more than establishing a conduit for relaying information to families, especially when this can now be done at the push of a button. This is about true stakeholder consultation, inclusive of children. Children need to know they have a right to be informed of, and partake in, any decision-making that affects them. "*We need to be unapologetically passionate about advocating children's rights in our curriculums.*"

Self-advocacy is necessary in your blueprint, to establish a strong culture of child safety. For children to know how to champion their own self-worth and safety, and that of their peers, educators need to be well-informed about risks to children. Preventative education is a key element of teaching and learning.

If we are going to change the narrative, we need to provoke an emotional connection to this topic.

Educators who have (and continue to) weather the storm affecting the early childhood sector, give yourself permission to go back to the educator you envisaged yourself being, when you first took on this career. Re-envisage yourself as the professional who first and foremost holds children dear, children who are innocent and who naturally connect with others. It's that magic that, when we see it, drives our innate need to co-learn with children and in turn co-teach with them, too.

If we become present with children again, we will reignite the emotional spark in us. When that glisten comes back, from reconnection, we will inevitably project children's safety against abuse to the forefront of our vocation.

Making the most of this book
- Use this preface as an invitation to go back to the professional educator who values children and their ability to thrive.

- Use the rest of the content in this book as knowledge building to support the rationale for why creating a culture of child safety is of the upmost importance.
- Use this book as a prescription for how to create an environment that is committed to proactively minimising harm to our youngest citizens.

This book is your step-by-step guide to champion children's safety and wellbeing.

(Note: 'Educator' is the term that will most frequently be used throughout this book to refer to teaching and education and care professional roles, in both a paid as well as voluntary capacity.)

INTRODUCTION

The multilayered nature of child protection in Victoria is echoed in similar and different ways throughout Australia and overseas. There is a common factor: children are vulnerable and need protecting. We uphold children's rights through policies, procedures and practices, but these need to be child focused, trauma informed and culturally appropriate. Only by working together as partners, families, practitioners, professionals and with children themselves will we be able to offer children the protection and care they truly deserve.

Abuse and neglect are a global issue, proliferated since the world has been affected by the latest pandemic. The ill treatment of children is prevalent in all societal groups, more so in those marginalised, but let's be clear – abuse does not discriminate, and every child can become a statistic.

So, why is it then, that professions such as those in the early childhood sector are not excelling in this area of health and safety? The National Quality Standard (NQS) (Australian Children's Education and Care Quality Authority, 2018) is a component of the National Quality Framework (NQF) that Australian children's services are required to work towards. In Quality

Area 2.2, under the standard of Safety 'Each Child is Protected', there are three elements: Supervision (2.2.1), Incident and Emergency Management (2.2.2) and Child Protection (2.2.3).

To ensure *"children are protected from harm and hazard, adequate supervision and reasonable precautions"* are necessary. Preventing physical injury is a fundamental focus for educators, however:
1. Are we allowing our gaze to include the possibility of abuse?
2. Are we considering how to prevent abuse occurring?

This is a concept educators may not have considered when assessing risk within their environments.

Incident and Emergency Management focuses our attention on plans and procedures in case unforeseen situations arise. Once we develop these protocols, we make them clear to all stakeholders, however:
- Are we, as an organisation, making arrangements clear to everyone of how abuse will be managed? What will the consequences be?

This is something educators may not have made known to the centre community, even if there is a Reportable Conduct Scheme sanctioned for the jurisdiction in which the centre operates.

Annual training updates for child protection are designed to help educators ensure that services fulfil their obligations, so *"Management, educators and staff are aware of their roles and responsibilities to identify and respond to every child at risk of abuse or neglect."* However, many educators are still not confident with traits of abuse and who they actually contact if concerns arise, both within the service and beyond.

When identifying children who might be at risk of abuse or neglect, customary thinking is that harm is coming to them when away from the children's service. We need to realise that:
- Every child is at risk.
- All children are vulnerable to exploitation and abuse, but there is the prevalence of those children who are disadvantaged, who are so often more exposed, such as Aboriginal and Torres Strait Islander children, those who are home-schooled or living in under-resourced households, children living out of home, children with disabilities, children from

culturally and linguistically diverse backgrounds and lesbian, gay, bisexual, transgender, intersex, queer, asexual (LGBTIQA+) children and young people, and other sexually or gender-diverse people.

We need to be trying to identify all the possible circumstances where children could be in a position where they could be taken advantage of when they are in the care of the children's service.

Risk assessing the possibility of abuse occurring within a service is a concept that educators find confronting. Guilt is felt for not realising there were potential dangers present while undertaking their daily routines and transitions in their children's service. There is, however, great relief through eliminating these risks, which is doing more to protect children in care and education settings.

The existing state of affairs:
1. When I undertake professional development training sessions on this subject matter, it is not uncommon that educators are not familiar with *abuse indicators*, and many are surprised that neglect actually constitutes abuse.
2. Educators often fail to differentiate the locality of their reporting department – is it the details of the one in which the children's service is located? Or is it the one where the child resides if they are not living local?
3. The prospect of reporting suspected abuse of a child is distressing for educators. The fear of being wrong no doubt slows down a response rate, but I question: whose wellbeing is taking precedence? Is the discomfort associated with revealing harm of a child a deterrent for making queries in the initial stages? The sureness of needing to action *making a report* is often impeded by wondering who should be notified first.
4. Educators also grapple with whether they are mandated to report.

During Quality Assessment and Rating (to determine a service's competence against the NQS), it is common practice for educators to be asked (Quality Area 2 Children's Health & Safety, Quality Area 7 Governance and Leadership) what the difference is between *child protection* and how their service provides a *culture of child safety* (NQS, 2018). Consequentially, educators fail to differentiate the two-part question, the child protection information is hazy and then the latter part of the question is confusing, rendering them speechless. This status quo is not acceptable, so again, we need to do more to uphold our professional responsibility towards children.

All these reasons have prompted me to collate the information in this book, so it can be used as a practical tool for all educators to use as a guiding light towards improving outcomes for children.

Early childhood professionals need to know and be confident in:
- Knowledge about what abuse actually is
- When to seek advice
- Where to obtain guidance
- Who to contact to make a report
- Who can report

The first part of this book is made up of the following:
1. Child abuse – the actualities
2. Child abuse – terminology and indicators
3. Child protection – unpacking sector regulators
4. Child protection – responding and reporting

The second part will provide what you need to know to create and maintain a strong culture of child safety. It is made up of the following:
5. Child safety – working in the forefront mitigating risk
6. Child safety – children championing their safety and wellbeing
7. Child safety – auditing your space
8. Child safety – governance and leadership

Our services must be regarded as grounds for perpetrators, or else we will neglect children in our care, and we will fail in our responsibility towards providing adequate supervision. We must take our ethics of care more seriously so that our actions execute the policies we have in place to keep children safe. This angle of thinking about what could go wrong has to saturate our considerations when assessing our places of education and care. This attitude goes against the dominant discourse of having a positive view and lens of seeing. Unequivocally, child safety isn't a subject where we avoid offending and assume the best in people.

This frame of thinking encourages us to see far-reaching, and be open to, possibilities, because we can no longer work with blinkers on when it comes to the safety of children. The truth is, if you continue to clear the way for these painfully defining moments in children's lives, you will be operating in a deficit approach to your service provision, in regard to child safety. By using an appropriate range of transformative pedagogies and learner-centred curricula, you can be working with a positive model of protecting children.

Your thoughts and ideas to make your setting the safest place possible need to be consuming and deeply considered. Be obliged to have your procedures and experiences meticulously planned and executed if you are going to be attentive to your service provision in its entirety.

This book will give insight into being astute – mitigating risk and developing a long-lasting capacity for safety. Discover how to act with perception so that 'children's wellbeing is at the forefront of all your thoughts and decision-making', and therefore the organisational culture takes on a zero tolerance to abuse and neglect.

There are National Standards that states and territories have aligned with when creating their own Child Safe Standards, however, the same variable surrounding these mandates is that educators need to be interested in children's safety, rights and their wellbeing. As Liana Buchanan, Principal Commissioner for Children and Young People, described in a communities of practice meeting I attended by the Victorian Commission for Children and Young People (CCYP), new standards allow you to broaden your understanding, with a *"refresh, rev up and deeper push for child safety"*.

There needs to be a strong force of proactivity for minimising risk of harm coming to children with better accountability for the quickest and most effective response, and for providing children with the tools to know their own self-worth.

Interestingly, the Commissioner for Children and Young People in Western Australia (Jacqueline McGowan-Jones) spent the initial few months of her appointment in the role on a 'listening tour' and will continue this endeavour. Valuing the voices of children has also been resonated through a Western Australia publication called *What can adults learn from children?*, which you can find at www.ccyp.wa.gov.au. I think this is the perfect way of thinking if we are going to get the underpinning right for a strong culture of child safety. Children must be, in every respect, included in the development and maintenance of our culture of child safety.

Nicole

Nicole Talarico
Early childhood professional and child advocate

PART ONE
CHAPTER 1

Child abuse – the actualities

Insight for educators/practitioners:

- The mindset of an educator to better protect children

Chapter elements:

- Why is abuse prevalent?
- A global problem
- Environments to thrive
- Marginalised groups
- Child and community impact

Why is abuse prevalent?

If you suspect abuse, then you must report it to authorities. This might seem obvious, but people do not adhere to this guiding statute. As living, feeling beings, it is intrinsic for us to oppose heinous acts. We have a predisposition to revolt at inhumane accounts. We believe that, for people to undertake evil actions, they must have been conditioned to behave in this destructive manner.

If this is the case, how can abuse be so widespread in the world? One of the significant explanations for why is because of dangerous stereotyping. We instinctively divert our thinking to *'it's only disturbed people who hurt children'.* We believe we would easily recognise such people and therefore we would protect children from them. Perhaps we, as a society, are organically delusional?

Emma's Project is a newly released undertaking by the Australian Childhood Foundation that personifies the impact of gender stereotyping. Emma Hakansson was a victim by a female perpetrator who had been trusted, but blindsided their family. **Emma's mother says the "biggest blind spot was, I didn't count that it could be a woman that could hurt you".**

"Child abuse makes us uncomfortable. How our children end up in our worst nightmares for them is too painful to think about. But it's always more painful for them... survivors" (Hakansson, 2022).

We have been propagandised through the television and movie industry, which depict characters as 'good', 'evil' or 'good turned bad'. Storylines lean towards male offenders, with little to no light shed on other types of offenders. We could be functioning from a posterior position due to our good nature and exposure to media.

The reality is that abuse is deeply rooted in cultural, social and economic practices (United Nations, 2018). Across time (historical comparison) and different cultures (comparative cultural analysis), children have been treated in a variety of ways in relation to issues such as safety and risk, sexuality, the age of consent, marriage, legal rights and working age. Some forms of activity and behaviour recognised as abuse or neglect today would not have been seen as such in the past.

There are many forms of abuse, which are gradually being developed into sets of types, typologies. As recognition and identification of abusive practices increase, there is a greater awareness socially and legally of these, along with increased law-making and criminal justice consequences. Many organisations are committing to *safeguarding* in a drastic attempt to minimise harm to children.

Early childhood professionals

That being said, why is it that we, in the early childhood sector, are not leading the way in the capacity of child safety and prevention?

It is instinctive for early childhood professionals to care for others. We have, after all, chosen to work in the human services sector. It is fair to say that it is a difficult task to fathom how harm could be enforced upon others, especially children. Alas, we need to acknowledge the reality that people do immoral things.

Understanding key concepts in abuse and safeguarding with youth in a global context is one of many topics researched by PAPYRUS, which is a European project team focused on improving youth work for young refugees and asylum seekers in Finland, Italy, Malta, Serbia and the United Kingdom. Its website (www.papyrus-project.org) has resources for educators from an international perspective and it references Australian Government resources to inform its work, with specific reference to: "*The organisation does everything possible to minimise risk and address concerns and incidents appropriately when they arise. Integrate safeguarding measures into all areas of the organisation*" (PAPYRUS, 2017).

The true fact, regardless of your location in the world, is: "*Just because someone works in a profession that is supposed to help young people, it cannot be assumed a. they will do so, and b. that they themselves are not an abuser*" (PAPYRUS, 2017). A perpetrator aims to be near children, so it is naive to assume they wouldn't take on roles to grant closer proximity.

People working with children and young adults – whether they be professionals or volunteers – need to be reflective and challenge their own assumptions of abuse; this is a difficult task for reasons that I will explore further below.

Even adults with no personal experiences of child abuse or sexual trauma will often have instant, gut-wrenching reactions to hearing or seeing anything about the abuse of a child, particularly sexual abuse. Such unpleasant and unwanted reactions make many people very resistant to paying attention to anything that might trigger such responses again (Hopper, 2022).

We must rise above our own disbelief and discomfort if we are going to work attentively in our settings. After all, it is children who are central to our chosen profession, so we should have a greater level of alertness towards their safety.

What is 'child abuse'?

If we have these descriptors, and we know we must consider our own biases, why don't more people know what child abuse includes? One of the reasons is that the simple phrase 'child abuse' is an 'umbrella' term that covers a wide range of activities that harm children. It is a form of 'shorthand' and as such has advantages and disadvantages: "*The use of a short and simple label allows us to communicate without the need to repeatedly define and redefine our terms. The disadvantage is that by using such an umbrella phrase we inevitably lose something*" (Goddard & Tucci, 2006).

Abuse and neglect are complex – and typically involve many connected factors. All forms of child abuse and neglect are perilous acts, regardless of their nature – there is not one form that has less impact than another. Abuse can be intentional or unintentional and can include acts of omission (for example, neglect) and commission (for example, abuse).

There is confusion about what abuse actually is – therefore, there is disorder encompassing systems if and when children and families are coupled with relevant organisations. Definitions that impact legal implications vary in different countries, which prompts further indistinctness. For example, assaults during pregnancy are ruled 'double intentioned violence' due to abuse of the mother as well as the child.

There are global definitions of abuse – there are also country-specific characterisations. The World Health Organization (WHO) defines child abuse and neglect as: *"All forms of physical and/or emotional ill treatment, sexual abuse, neglect or negligent treatment or commercial or other exploitation, resulting in actual or potential harm to the child's health, survival, development or dignity in the context of a relationship of responsibility, trust or power"* (WHO, 2006).

Types of abuse, following categorisation, are always progressing. We know that technology has advanced online abuse (grooming and cyberbullying) as well as expediated the transmission for human trafficking. The Australian Government Safety Commission's website (www.esafety.gov.au) offers a range of support for those experiencing tech abuse as it, too, is prevalent in society.

In Australia, we have both national and state-developed conventions that are always developing and changing, considering forms of abuse that emerge as our understanding develops. It is important to check in with online policy documents in your own area to see how these are transforming with emerging issues.

This means we need to be *"working towards national definitions of the different forms of violence to inform and support programme and policy design across the public and private sector, as well ensuring that all Australians have equal access to support and justice"* (Women's Agenda, 2022). To be able to determine whether a child is at risk, a national guide for continuity would help analysis.

Victoria Legal Aid says the law states: *"A child or young person at risk of harm or neglect, as a result of a single incident or a number of ongoing incidents, must be protected"* (Victoria Legal Aid, n.d.).

We are often inundated with material about the importance of acting on the signs of child abuse, even though there is a much lesser volume of tools to understand triggers to recognise the signs (we will cover warning signs in Chapter 2).

The early childhood sector is largely not well informed to notice the early-warning signs – I can confidently say this from working with many different service types. The majority of educators tell me they would not know forewarnings and therefore lack confidence in their ability to respond early to suspicions of abuse.

So, why don't people delve deeper to find out this information so they can do something at the first inclination of concern?

A global problem

As adults, we all have a societal obligation to report concerns about children's welfare, but there are reasons why people don't speak up. People who are supposed to keep children safe are, like all of us, imperfect and complicated individuals. This does not excuse the failure to act protectively, it just offers possible explanations for why.

The defectiveness to protect children has been known for decades. The WHO's *World Report on Violence and Health*, back in 2002, described child abuse as a *"serious global health problem"*, and this gut-wrenching fact was outlined once again in The State of Child Protection by emphasising the *"Lack of good data on the extent and consequences of abuse and neglect has held back the development of appropriate responses in most parts of the world. Without good local data, it is also difficult to develop a proper awareness"* (Goddard & Tucci, 2006).

The sad truth is that millions of children are abused every year in this country. *"Many of them believe, correctly, that someone else knows or should know about their situation, but does little or nothing to protect them"* (Hopper, 2022).

"Community recognition and understanding of the problem of child abuse and neglect and their subsequent willingness to act to protect children or support families remains elusive" (Australian Childhood Foundation and Child Abuse Prevention Research Australia, 2008).

It is tricky to detect abuse, but if we become familiar with *what* harm/mistreatment is, as well as signs and symptoms of abuse, it raises the likelihood that someone may recognise an aggregate of related signs suggesting someone could be at risk. As a society, if we raise awareness of warning signs, we are going to build competence to safeguard children.

Australia's NQF came into effect on 1 January 2012 with an objective to ensure the safety, health and wellbeing of children attending education and care services with a guiding principle *"the rights and best interests of the child are paramount"* (Australian Children's Education and Care Quality Authority, 2012).

Most notably, it is a legal requirement that every reasonable precaution must be taken to protect children from harm and any hazard likely to cause injury. Child safety is a mantra we ought to be embracing. There is a pressing need to upscale our quality to include abuse detection if we are going to pride ourselves in having the highest standards of service provision.

Commonwealth and State Royal Commissions highlight serious failings in the way institutions across Australia protect children and young people, and the ways they deal with reports of abuse when it occurs (Department for Child Protection, 2021). Victoria's new Child Safe Standards (effective from 1 July 2022) are encouraging services to see their breaches as *"systemic failures"* and work to mend the unsafe gaps in education and care services. Access the information sheet under the resources section of www.ccyp.vic.gov.au.

Commitment to safety

By investing in a commitment to safety, we can build on the strengths of families and communities to support the continuing care of children in a way that offers the best long-term prospects. Attention also needs to be given to deliver targeted and timely support to vulnerable families.

The inauguration of the *National Framework for Protecting Australia's Children 2021-2031* (Commonwealth of Australia, 2021) reveals a shared *vision* that children and young people in Australia have the right to grow up safe, connected and supported in their family, community and culture. They have the right to grow up in an environment that enables them to reach their full potential. Our shared *goal* is to make significant and sustained progress in reducing the rate of child abuse and neglect and its intergenerational impact.

Victoria leads the way when it comes to placing more Aboriginal children with kin or an Aboriginal carer, at 79.1% compared with the national rate of 64.3%. Reasoning for this higher statistic is partly due to the Victorian Aboriginal Children and Young People's Alliance embrace *Wungurilwil*

Gapgapduir: Aboriginal Children and Families Agreement strategic action plan (Victorian Government, 2018). The alliance has a serious responsibility to ensure the Victorian Government and key stakeholders hear the voice of not only Aboriginal children and young people, but the inclusion of local Aboriginal communities in policy and programme design and delivery to improve safety and wellbeing for vulnerable Aboriginal children and families. Aboriginal-led teams respond to child protection reports in partnership with the Department of Health and Human Services, and help local families who may become involved in the child protection or care services system.

Connecting children and their families with Aboriginal Community Controlled Organisations early is vital in improving self-determination for Aboriginal communities and works to address the over-representation of Aboriginal children in out-of-home care.

The National Principles for Child Safe Organisations outline 10 elements that are fundamental for making an organisation safe for children. Dissemination of this initiative of the Council of Australian Governments is encouraged so that information in the publication can be used as a tool to promote awareness and safeguard Australia's children.

The National Office for Child Safety worked in partnership with the Secretariat of National Aboriginal and Islander Child Care (SNAICC) – National Voice for our Children to create resources that support organisations working with Aboriginal and Torres Strait Islander children, young people and communities to implement the National Principles for Child Safe Organisations (National Principles). SNAICC, with the help of Victorian Aboriginal Child Care Agency, has created the *Keeping Our Kids Safe* resources, which apply a cultural lens to the National Principles to help organisations think about how to make themselves more child safe in a culturally safe way:

- An animated video, *Keeping Our Kids Safe: Understanding Cultural Safety in Child Safe Organisations*, gives viewers an introduction to the National Principles through a cultural lens.
- A guide, *Keeping Our Kids Safe: Cultural Safety and the National Principles for Child Safe Organisations*, gives practical advice on how to implement the National Principles in Aboriginal and Torres Strait Islander organisations and communities.

REFLECTION ACTIVITY

Why might it be problematic for some people to address abuse issues in their workplace?

The reasons or causes include:

1. **Workers may have experienced abuse themselves**, either as targets or bystanders.
2. **Explicit descriptions of abuse may be distressing** to engage with for some staff members, including those who have experienced, or are experiencing, abuse. A professional culture of safety for a team is a climate that maintains a guaranteed level of support when having difficult conversations. The latest Victorian Child Safe Standards indicate the need to offer support to anyone who may need emotional assistance. There is a need to offer support to those triggered by training content, being affiliated with reporting concerns or who are experiencing violence themselves.
3. **Beliefs and cultural issues**, plus confusion caused by incorrect stereotypes about what kinds of people sexually use and abuse children. Complex cultural backgrounds can permeate ideas about abuse, which are reinforced by social, media and subcultural assumptions. What abuse is, who carries it out, how it can be identified, who is to blame for it and what should be done about it are issues that shape ideas, views, attitudes, experiences and understandings. Sometimes there is victim-blaming, gender-biased, racist or xenophobic (hating of newcomers or strangers) that clouds speaking up
4. **Physical, emotional and financial dependency** on an individual or group that would be lost if such concerns are raised.
5. **Fears of various consequences** (for example, of acknowledging betrayal by a trusted and respected person, of being wrong, of being right). Workers may not have

experienced abuse themselves, but they may still fear dealing with it in their work. The anxiety over how to help people who have experienced abuse can be a preventative factor for raising concerns. The aftereffects might involve engaging with highly charged emotions of the abused person, no emotions (detachment), mental health issues and so forth; the range of issues that might occur is wide, because abuse survivors engage with the world post-abuse in different ways.

6. **Workers may have been perpetrators of abuse in the past.** This could take many forms. If they have engaged in abusive behaviour previously, such as bullying others at school or in the workplace, they may struggle to deal with abuse at work.

Other reasons people don't follow up on suspicions is because they are 'paralysed and prone to second-guess themselves'. This self-doubt is a normal response when you are confronted with something that makes you uncomfortable.

Some people are reluctant to make a judgement about others' relationships: "*I might not have the accurate picture here*"; "*It's not my child so it's none of my business*"; or "*Someone else will do something*".

Every child is our business if it involves child abuse and neglect. Adults will happily take part in the success of every child, but we are distant when it involves protecting a child.

As a sector, we need a stronger commitment to make a difference. By investing in professional development and the utilisation of tools to better inform individuals within teams, we will be better equipped to cope with this crisis.

When you know what signifies abuse, what the warning signs are, as well as support networks that are available, then you have an opportunity to prevent abuse or neglect re/occurring. The ability to act on knowledge makes us better able to make informed decisions, with logical and ethical grounds considered in the process.

Environments to thrive

Before you can assess whether a child is at risk, you are compelled to know what constitutes a safe environment for children. Having a thorough understanding of what contributing factors make environments deemed safe and nurturing for children gives you a point of reference for evaluating a child's situation.

There are many factors that contribute to the wellbeing and safety of children, including those relating to the child themselves, their family, and the supports and services to which they have access in their community. Indicators that a child's environment is safe and nurturing across these different factors include...

For the child:
- Optimal antenatal and infant development
- Optimal physical health
- Health professionals accessed appropriately for preventive and interventional health needs
- Optimal social and emotional development
- Optimal language and cognitive development
- Adequate exercise and physical activity
- Positive child behaviour and mental health
- Success in literacy and numeracy
- Safety from injury and harm
- An ability to rely on supportive adults

Communities that support a child to be safe and nurtured:
- Enable parents, children and young people to build connections and draw on informal assistance
- Support cultural connections, especially for Aboriginal families
- Are inclusive of diversity and embrace marginalised groups such as culturally and linguistically diverse (CALD), those with a disability, those who are unable to live at home, and LGBTIQA+ children and young people
- Have local recreational spaces, activities and community facilities
- Have low levels of crime in the community
- Are safe from environmental toxins

When the environment is not optimal, many factors influence a child's wellbeing and safety. Children need stable, sensitive, loving, stimulating relationships and environments to reach their potential. Adults who can hold a safe space for children and can help them back to calm are healthy influences.

Clinical therapists using child and family trauma informed practice will consider the positive relationships a child has had, and currently has, in their life when understanding the child's relational health. Relationships are the key to healing from disrupted attachment and trauma. These act as a buffer because when there are stronger attachments present in a child's life, children can cope with adversity better and the impact is reduced because they know they have stable connections. In addition, trauma can also dissipate over time (Berry Street, 2022).

To provide an environment in which children can thrive, capable parents and carers must:
- Meet physical needs, by providing food, shelter, clothing and hygiene
- Ensure the child's safety is appropriate to their age and development
- Provide emotional warmth and responsiveness
- Provide behavioural support and boundaries
- Be consistent and reliable

The absence of these factors does not necessarily mean a child will be adversely affected – some people are capable of great resilience. However, the absence of factors is likely to have a greater impact the earlier they occur, the more severe they are and the longer they last.

Theoretical models

Berry Street, one of Australia's largest independent family service organisations – with a history of over 140 years – has a model of practice for clinical intervention that aligns with the Dr Bruce D Perry MD, PhD model. Dr Perry is principal of the Neurosequential Network and his work over the past 30 years has been in relation to the impact of abuse, neglect and trauma on the developing brain. His research has impacted clinical practice, programmes and policy across the world, informing the development of innovative clinical practices and programmes working with maltreated and traumatised children.

Most prominently, the Neurosequential Model© is a developmentally sensitive, neurobiology-informed approach to clinical work (NMT), education (NME), inclusive of early childhood (NM-EC) and caregiving (NMC). Berry Street's Education Model (BSEM) provides strategies for teaching and learning that enable teachers to increase engagement of students with complex, unmet learning needs. Pedagogical strategies incorporate trauma-informed teaching, positive education and wellbeing practices.

Building the capacity of educators to understand the impact of childhood trauma and how to engage in a trauma-informed way with infants, children and families, we can repair trauma and build relational health. *"Current level of relational health will be a stronger predictor of wellbeing – even considering trauma history"* (Berry Street, 2022).

American psychologist Urie Bronfenbrenner's Ecological Systems Theory supports the notion of environments influencing a child's growth and development. This 'social ecological' model focuses on the quality and context of the child's environment. Bronfenbrenner states that as a child develops, the interaction within these environments becomes more complex. This traditional theory, founded in the 1970s, identified four key systems within which children exist that would combine to have an impact on how they grow and develop. He uses the terms microsystem, mesosystem, exosystem and macrosystem. The microsystem is the most influential level of the ecological systems theory. This is the most immediate environmental settings containing the developing child, such as family and school (education and care services included).

In Australia, our approved learning frameworks incorporate a range of guiding ideologies to support educators to help children to thrive, forcing us to be concerned about children's welfare – the undeniable key influencer being the extent of the interrelation between a child's influencing environments.

The Victorian Early Years Learning and Development Framework (VEYLDF) was created with strong consideration for Bronfenbrenner's perspective. *"This model illustrates the strong network of community, services and programs that support children's learning and development"* and more notably includes the statement: *"Each adult around the child learns, leads, supports and actively invests in the child's success. Each professional who engages with a child and their family has a part to play*" (Department of Education, 2016).

The VEYLDF outlines the principles of early childhood pedagogy that underpin practice (Department of Education, 2019). Educators draw on a rich repertoire of pedagogical practices inclusive of adopting "*holistic approaches*" and "*being responsive to children*". It is imposed that educators pay attention to children's physical, personal, social, emotional and spiritual wellbeing, as well as cognitive aspects of learning. We simply need to align our practices more closely with these guiding documents as a strong point of reference for improved practice.

Relational health and wellbeing look at the quantity (duration and frequency) and quality (health) of relationships, so perhaps we need to reconsider our priorities as educators. Stop ticking off our to-do list and (re) commit to connections with children as a top priority.

Marginalised groups

As early childhood professionals, our role is not only responding to and reporting any incidents, disclosures or suspicions when children are experiencing abuse or neglect. We can also have a significant impact by identifying vulnerabilities within families and by providing links to early support and intervention. A collaborative approach to care and education of children is what is required to simultaneously share knowledge, observation and provide feedback. Relationships need to be reciprocal for us to work authentically with children and their families.

Taking an intersectional approach means race, gender identity and expression, nationality, culture, fertility, mental health, ability, political affiliation, language, religion, class, location, marital status, education, ethnicity, hobbies, physical health, age, culture, personality, appearance, ability and no doubt there are more worthy for sustainable movements for change due to systemic injustice in your own context. Intersectionality is a prominent word at the Better Together National LGBTIQA+ conferences, a term coined by American civil rights advocate Kimberlé Crenshaw 30 years ago. She argues that "*A robust understanding of Intersectionality is needed to know what a community needs to thrive*" (Coaston, 2019).

Recognising vulnerable children: a precursor for detection

Awareness and action is a collective responsibility between families, services, Government and the community to help keep children safe. This connection is often not established, and if it is, it is frequently not maintained.

This prompts a rethink for how you welcome prospective members of the community into your setting – is your message of equity explicit? Furthermore, is it well informed? Have team members and all other stakeholders been consulted before placing 'safe symbols' to ensure everyone will be supportive of those considered marginalised in society? Training and more information may be needed to facilitate a commitment before you can truly welcome and include all members of society through the door of your service. I recall Deanne Carson, founder of Body Safety Australia, stating: *"How dangerous it can be to place visual tools (such as signage and flags) that state acceptance when, if not representing everyone's mindset, there could in fact be dangerous pockets in your service provision."* If this is the case, you then set children and their families up to fail, because they were in fact not safe.

Standard 5.1 in Victoria's new Child Safe Standards highlights: *"The organisation, including staff and volunteers, understands children and young people's diverse circumstances, and provides support and responds to those who are vulnerable."*

How is diversity recognised among your families and are they genuinely supported? Do you have a sharper lens on some children?

Victoria's new Child Safe Standards are mandatory in Victoria, but are extremely beneficial to all services nationwide. These new standards greatly align with the National Principles for Child Safe Organisations and guide high-quality practice for creating a culture of child safety within children's services. For example:

Standard 5.2: Children and young people have access to information, support and complaints processes in ways that are culturally safe, accessible and easy to understand.

Standard 5.3: The organisation pays particular attention to the needs of children and young people with disability, children and young people from culturally and linguistically diverse backgrounds, those who are unable to live at home, and lesbian, gay, bisexual, transgender and intersex children and young people.

Standard 5.4: The organisation pays particular attention to the needs of Aboriginal children and young people and provides/promotes a culturally safe environment for them.
(*CCYP, 2022*)

Accessibility
Have you considered how practical your avenues are for gathering feedback and ideas? Have you ensured these methods are considerately contextual to your service community?

How can families, inclusive of children, be consulted about policies and practices if the forums are adult oriented and information is only communicated via complex English language? For instance, are you modifying your policies to accommodate the viewpoints of people who may not be able to read? Is your information only in English? Have you considered printed material in languages applicable to your local community? Have you considered simplified and even audio versions of documents supporting your governance? For example, to better communicate your Commitment to Child Safety or your Code of Conduct.

We need to rethink what is respectful and inclusive engagement in our settings for those we are wanting to consult with.

Here are some things to consider, particularly when working with people considered marginalised (we expand on these ideas in Chapter 5):
- Do we need translated material?
- Would audio be better for children/adults who cannot read?
- Is there a choice about where to meet? (Offices can be intimidating for some people.)
- Can a Zoom meeting be an option? People can be more comfortable and responsive in an environment they have chosen.

Child and community impact

Detection of abuse as early as possible helps communities because it means support and recovery can commence for the child, the abuser and their families. We are living in unpredictable, confronting and damaging times. Early childhood professionals have a significant role in the lives of children and therefore need to deploy critical awareness of their wellbeing. Recommit to your role as a professional to notice, be present, engage with children and families, and know how to take appropriate action if concerns arise.

Children's exposure to domestic/family violence can result in profoundly damaging impacts on children's psychological, emotional and physical safety and wellbeing, as well as compromising their educational and social development by interrupting their attendance at school/children's services and their opportunities to socialise with peers.

Australia's first Royal Commission into Family Violence was completed in 2015. The Commission made 227 recommendations to reduce the impact of family violence in our community. It would also provide a national view of what is and what isn't working, given that states and territories report on domestic and family violence in their own ways.

Domestic and family violence is a significant social problem, which has become the focus of increased community concern. The seriousness and prevalence of domestic and family violence has been recognised nationwide. Forecasts for Australia, predicted in 2009 for 2021–22, indicated the need for preventative action due to the increase of violence quashing human rights and the national economy.

More than a decade later, Australia is still creating action plans in response to WHO recommendations. In a national plan to end violence against women and children 2022–32, a Federal Family, Domestic and Sexual Violence Commission will be the latest strategy to address domestic and family violence in a bid to bring rates down *"toward zero"* (Women's Agenda, 2022).

Australian law reforms

In May 2022, the Fair Work Commission granted working Australians the right to seek 10 days of **paid domestic violence leave** each year. *"This historic decision aims to provide greater flexibility and support in the workplace with respect to domestic violence survivors as well as better resources for maintaining safety in the workplace and at home"* (Gardoce, 2022).

Over the past decade, workplaces have been referenced as safe partners against domestic violence. It is not until perhaps now that Australian law reforms have really shown up in early childhood sector governing documents. The latest release of Child Safe Standards in Victoria has a strong inclusion of compassion for those affected by violence.

"<u>Domestic and family violence</u> *is a longstanding issue in Australia. In the recent ruling, the Fair Work Commission noted that 'from the age of 15, 1 in 4 women, compared to 1 in 13 men, experienced at least one incident of violence by an intimate partner"* (Gardoce, 2022).

Together, these reforms create a more collaborative, integrated system that will help improve outcomes for children and families.

Recommendations have been made by the Royal Commission into Family Violence (Victoria) because *"Many victim survivors may not yet have reached out to specialist family violence services but are in regular contact with universal health and education services such as early childhood services"*, *"these workforces are crucial in the response to family violence"*, however, *"universal services often lack the knowledge and expertise to identify and respond when people are experiencing family violence"* (Victorian Government, Family Violence Reform Implementation Monitor, 2022).

Disclosures and suspicions of child abuse need to be acted upon, of course, if legislation mandates professionals to do so, but also because ethically, we owe it to children to try and prevent the abuse happening to them.

Challenges to educating and empowering people to overcome such barriers to action is what many organisations are addressing in their efforts to prevent and end this real-world complexity, the sexual exploitation and abuse of children.

In summary

After reading this chapter, you should now know that:
- Children and young people in Australia have the right to grow up safe, connected and supported in their family, community and culture.
- Raising concerns is essential if we are going to truly put children's wellbeing before our own.
- The impact of one's abuse is inimitable and can vary.
- Some children are more vulnerable to abuse happening due to their life circumstances.
- A connected and responsive environment can give support to children so they can thrive.

Chapter 1 reflection questions

- Are you aware of possible marginalised groups within the context of your service?
- How do you currently determine if a child/family are considered vulnerable?
- Does your record-keeping system allow for all staff members to confidently record information about the safety of a child's environment?
- Have you considered the quality and quantity of positive relationships in individual children's lives?
- Would family violence be taken into consideration when assessing a child's need for protection?

CHAPTER 2

Child abuse – terminology and indicators

Insight for educators/practitioners:

- Guide to help assess individual situations
- Warning signs/child abuse indicators

Chapter elements:

- Abuse and neglect terminology
- Risk of harm abuse indicators

(Note: This content can be confronting. Please reach out to help services at www.respect.gov.au/services/#nat if this content triggers you in any way).

In Chapter 1 we touched on the impact abuse has on communities and the reality that family violence is a major contributor. Many people do not realise that *family violence and neglect are considered abuse*. Children hearing or witnessing family violence is sometimes misjudged because children may not be the main target of the violence. Whether children experience violence themselves or witness this behaviour, the violence can have long-lasting impacts on them.

Neglecting children impacts on their ability to grow and develop – they may have been limited in having their fundamental needs met: food, shelter and regular, all-encompassing connection (positive relationships).

Abuse and neglect terminology

You need to know what abuse includes, as well as repercussions of it, so you are better able to ascertain the aftereffects and prevent it from occurring in your domain. This content will help you to be able to recognise signs of child abuse and includes definitions plus physical and behavioural indicators.

Child abuse is any behaviour that harms a child (in this case anyone under the age of 18). It can take many forms, including:
- Physical
- Sexual
- Emotional
- Neglectful
- Financial
- Exploitation
- Spiritual and cultural

Refer to Appendix 1: Glossary of key terms and definitions.

Risk of harm abuse indicators

Children may experience a range of emotional, psychological and physical difficulties due to being harmed, including:
- Increased fear, anxiety, guilt and self-blame
- Shame
- Fear of trusting people

- Disrupted attachments with those who are meant to keep them safe
- Anger towards the abuser
- Mental health disorders (such as anxiety, attachment, post-traumatic stress and depression disorders)
- Mood swings
- Fear of – or an inability to talk about – what happened
- Sadness, confusion and low self-esteem
- Flashbacks, nightmares, sleeping difficulties and reliving the abuse
- Denial that it happened
- Self-harming or suicidal thoughts
- Learning disorders (including poor language and cognitive development)
- Developmental delay, eating disorders and physical ailments
- Permanent physical injuries or death
- Trouble in education services with learning new things and socialising with others
- Violent, aggressive or other behavioural problems
- Later drug and alcohol abuse and high-risk sexual behaviour
- Regression to an earlier stage of development (such as thumb sucking and bedwetting)
- Withdrawal from people and events
- Becoming a victim or perpetrator of bullying
- Cruelty to animals
- Stress-related illnesses (such as headache or stomach pain)
- Speech difficulties (such as stuttering)

Effects of abuse

Substantiation effects can include:
- Impacts on the brain's neural pathways, affecting cognitive development and stress-response systems
- Low self-esteem and difficulties at school affecting their long-term employment and financial security
- Mental health problems, including anxiety, depression, symptoms of trauma, eating disorders and, for some, suicide attempts
- Increased aggression, antisocial behaviour, likelihood of substance abuse, teenage pregnancy

It should be noted that, for some children who have been abused, the impacts may not be evident in their behaviour – aftereffects that can be present after abuse can include...

Abuse/neglect effects impacting social interactions, which could look like:
- Indiscriminate affection
- Lacking trust and empathy
- Inability to form age-appropriate relationships with adults/peers
- Chaotic interactions with others

Abuse/neglect effects impacting cognitive/development, which could look like:
- Delays in reaching developmental milestones (for example, speech)
- Loss of previously acquired developmental milestones

All family violence abuses children

Domestic and family violence impacts upon the fundamental human rights of children and families to live in safety and security. Domestic and family violence is characterised by patterns of abusive behaviour in an intimate relationship, or other type of family relationship, where one person assumes a position of power over another and causes fear. It is also known as 'domestic violence, family violence or intimate partner violence', according to the National Sexual Assault, Family & Domestic Violence Counselling Service. In recent years, the experiences of children and young people witnessing violence have been increasingly understood through the lens of complex trauma.

Trauma

Trauma is pervasive throughout the world, commonly understood as *"a distressing or life-threatening situation"*. Complex trauma is cumulative, repetitive and interpersonally generated. *"Trauma overwhelms an individual's ability to cope, causes feelings of helplessness, diminishes their sense of self and their ability to feel a full range of emotions and experiences"* (Unyte, 2022).

When identifying child abuse, it is critical to remember that: "*Aside from the immediate physical injuries children can experience through maltreatment, a child's reactions to abuse or neglect can have lifelong and even intergenerational impacts*" (Child Welfare Information Gateway, 2018).

This resonating message appears in *Child protection in early childhood*: "*The trauma associated with child abuse can be catastrophic to the wellbeing and development of a child, and can continue after the abuse has ended*" (Victorian Government, 2016). Child abuse is a form of trauma, and a person's response to that trauma can show up in different ways. Harm experienced in childhood can have significant and lasting effects, and children can respond differently to what has occurred.

Children and violence

Children do not become used to violence – they adapt. When there's violence in the home children are always affected, even if they are asleep or not in the room when the violence occurs. The longer children live in a violent situation, the more difficult it will be for them. When violence occurs, children may feel scared and ashamed, or they may even think that they caused the problem. Children are egocentric and therefore cannot fathom how they couldn't have induced the violence. This comes with the ramifications of poor self-worth, believing they are unlovable and a bad person.

Early childhood educators need training "*to equip them to recognise family violence may be occurring and know what to do when it is identified*".

Victoria's *Building from strength: 10-Year Industry Plan for Family Violence Prevention and Response* includes universal services as widespread family violence capability building. It will provide avenues for training so that universal services – inclusive of early childhood educators – can feel confident to identify and respond to all forms of family violence. Access more information on the three rolling action plans for implementing this plan at www.vic.gov.au/building-strength-10-year-industry-plan

Perpetrators and those using violence are also often in regular contact with children's services. As emphasised by the Victorian Royal Commission, staff in these services have a unique opportunity to identify family violence early to support the safety of victim survivors.

REFLECTION ACTIVITY

Education services can assess their own capacity to identify and respond to family violence by examining:
- How well staff can recognise the signs of family violence among stakeholders
- Access to resources/tools in the workplace to support identifying and responding to family violence
- Whether appropriate monitoring and feedback loops have been put in place to measure progress in building family violence capability within the children's service
- Whether there will be ongoing training opportunities (post-induction) in the children's service about abuse, inclusive of family violence

A child's response to repeated family violence depends on several factors, including their age, gender, personality and family role.

Impact on behaviour

Research over the past 10 years has begun to pinpoint the impact of complex trauma on brain structure and chemistry. An understanding of the changes in the brain has given insight into behaviours by children and young people that may otherwise be misunderstood as 'defiant', 'naughty', 'unmanageable', 'not paying attention' or even 'spaced out'.

As well as abuse impacting on health, wellbeing and education, growing up with family violence can affect relationships in later life.

Domestic Violence Victoria states that many children who experience family violence do not go on to use violence as adults, but research shows that boys who have been exposed to family violence are more likely to become perpetrators themselves. Meanwhile, girls may be more accepting of intimate partner violence than those who hadn't experienced family violence as children. Family violence is not solely a gendered problem, but also an intersectional problem driven by complex hierarchies of power, privilege and oppression with far-reaching impacts that reinforce structural disadvantage and marginalisation.

Research demonstrates that the populations most impacted by family violence are younger women, children, older people, people with disability, people from culturally and linguistically diverse backgrounds (including people with temporary residency status), LGBTIQA+ people, people in rural and remote communities, people with mental health issues and/or substance misuse problems, people from socioeconomically disadvantaged areas and Aboriginal and Torres Strait Islander peoples (Australian Institute of Health and Welfare, 2019).

Emerging evidence also shows that the rates of intimate partner violence within same-sex relationships are as high as the rates experienced by cisgender women in heterosexual relationships, and possibly higher for bisexual, transgender and gender-diverse people (Victorian Government, Department of Health, 2017).

What constitutes abuse and neglect

Turn to Appendix 2 at the back of this book for a table showing examples of indicators of abuse and neglect. This table should be used as a guide only to help determine if your suspicions of abuse are well-founded and should be reported via the reporting process in your governing jurisdiction. Keep a record of any observations. Information recorded greatly enhances the quality of any subsequent reports of child abuse. Consider consultation with a professional with expertise in child/youth protection if you are uncertain.

In summary

After reading this chapter, you should now know that:
- Perpetrators are not always easy to distinguish.
- A child's exposure – or risk of exposure – to the determining factors increases their vulnerability to abuse and neglect.
- Abuse constitutes several varying factors and warning signs.
- The impact of trauma is individual and lasts longer than the period/s of abuse and/or neglect.

Chapter 2 reflection questions

- Are there training opportunities at your service to ensure every member of the community is familiar with details of each abuse type?
- Would warning signs be noticed when educators are implementing children's programmes?
- Is there opportunity to share information and undertake dialogue among your colleagues regarding individual children's wellbeing, inclusive of concerns (warning signs)?
- Would all staff, inclusive of those not working directly with children, know what risk of harm indicators are?
- Do you inform families about abuse and indicators at your children's service?
- Do you provide a range of opportunities for families to build their parenting skills at your service?
- Do you have strong links with local maternal and child/community health centre organisations?
- Have you reflected on your community attitudes? Is violence accepted in the community? For example, community values racism, gender equity.
- Does your governance system at your children's service accommodate families facing financial hardship?
- Can community members at your service access support contact information without having to ask staff members?

CHAPTER 3

Child protection – unpacking sector regulators

Insight for educators/practitioners:

- Who are the governing bodies for the nation?
- What regulators oversee me in my service?

Chapter elements:

- A global commitment
- Our national commitment
- The professional commitment
- Jurisdiction in states and territories
- What are Child Safe Standards?
- Reportable Conduct Schemes
- Code of Conduct
- Violence reforms – Victoria is leading the way

A global commitment

Child abuse and neglect is an international problem. It is a national priority that requires a national solution. Everyone has a role to play to better safeguard children and young people:
- All levels of governments
- Private and not-for-profit organisations
- Communities, families and individuals
- Child-related organisations must have children and young people's safety and their rights at the foundation of their organisations' operation and purpose

"The most widely ratified human rights treaty in history has helped transform children's lives around the world" – the United Nations Convention on the Rights of the Child (UNCRC) (2022). All countries – except South Sudan and the United States – have signed this international agreement. *"[It] is an important agreement by countries who have promised to protect children's rights. The Convention on the Rights of the Child explains who children are, all their rights, and the responsibilities of governments. All the rights are connected, they are all equally important and they cannot be taken away from children."* Even though there are 54 articles in all, the later focus on adult and Government collaboration, to ensure children receive all these rights. For more on this, visit the United Nations Treaty Collection website at treaties.un.org

If we focus on taking action, to respond and report concerns for children's welfare, then it is very easy to pinpoint a range of related rights, for example:
- All organisations concerned with children should work towards what is best for each child (Article 3).
- Children have the right to live a full life. Governments should ensure that children survive and develop healthily (Article 6).
- Governments should protect children from sexual abuse (Article 34).
- Children should be protected from any activities that could harm their development (Article 36).
- Governments should make the Convention known to all parents and children (Article 42).

The extensive version of the UNCRC Article 19 relates strongly to the work in our early childhood sector and states:

1. *"Parties shall take all appropriate legislative, administrative, social and educational measures to protect the child from all forms of physical or mental violence, injury or abuse, neglect or negligent treatment, maltreatment or exploitation, including sexual abuse, while in the care of parent(s), legal guardian(s) or any other person who has the care of the child.*

2. *"Such protective measures should, as appropriate, include effective procedures for the establishment of social programmes to provide necessary support for the child and for those who have the care of the child, as well as for other forms of prevention and for identification, reporting, referral, investigation, treatment and follow-up of instances of child maltreatment described heretofore, and, as appropriate, for judicial involvement."*

The UNCRC *"emphasises respect for the inherent human dignity of all children, the importance of recognising diversity – including learning styles, abilities, gender, family circumstances and geographic location – and the principles of non-discrimination, best interests of the child, participation, survival and development".* The full convention has been translated into several languages and there are child-friendly versions that simplify language to aid communication and interpretation.

Find a simplified version of the UNCRC at www.unicef.org.au/upload/unicef/media/unicef-simplified-convention-child-rights.pdf and children's text versions on the UNICEF website (www.unicef.org), plus another child-friendly language version at www.ccyp.wa.gov.au. I encourage education and care services to use these documents to inspire the creations of their own versions so that these rights are explored and portrayed in a meaningful way with children.

Do we, as a sector, need to be prioritising the creation of alternative tools such as translated child-friendly versions of children's rights, inclusive of audio? Perhaps even video versions?

Interestingly, we, as an education and care sector, have predominantly focused our attention on identification of maltreatment through child protection training. It is only in very recent times that we are considering creating a *culture* of child safety, which in essence is leaning towards *prevention* with a strong motivation being children's rights.

This book provides knowledge to support prevention and detection. It will also guide you to consider avenues of support for the victims as well as those involved in disclosure of abuse and neglect.

Our national commitment

What role does the National Children's Commissioner play in the safety of children? Since Australia took on obligations in relation to children's rights by ratifying the UNCRC in December 1990, there were calls to establish a National Children's Commissioner. Legislation establishing the position was passed by the federal Parliament on 25 June 2012 – albeit 22 years later. An inaugural National Children's Commissioner (Megan Mitchell) was appointed on 25 February 2013 and in November 2020, Anne Hollonds was appointed (Australian Human Rights Commission, 2020).

It is part of the National Commissioner's role to liaise with departments and authorities of the Commonwealth and of the states and territories; non-governmental organisations; international organisations and agencies; and other organisations, agencies or persons considered appropriate.

To ensure we respond justly to children, the National Commissioner must have regard for the following human rights instruments:
- Universal Declaration of Human Rights
- International Convention on the Elimination of All Forms of Racial Discrimination
- International Covenant on Economic, Social and Cultural Rights
- International Covenant on Civil and Political Rights
- Convention on the Elimination of All Forms of Discrimination Against Women
- Convention on the Rights of the Child
- Convention on the Rights of Persons with Disabilities

While the Convention is not incorporated as a whole into Australian national and state laws, its principles *inform* and *guide* components of various legislation, policy, service provision and practice.

Initially, *Supporting young children's rights: Statement of intent (2015-2018)* gave a strong explanation of 'how Australia would uphold its commitment to children's rights' in accordance with the UN Convention, seeing as we have responsibility as signatories of this international human rights treaty. The UNCRC *"formally and explicitly outlines the rights of children in international law including basic human rights such as the right to be free from abuse, neglect and exploitation, the right to an education and healthcare, and the right to be free from discrimination of any kind"* (Australian Human Rights Commission, 2015).

National Principles for Child Safe Organisations

The Royal Commission into Institutional Responses to Child Sexual Abuse (Royal Commission) uncovered shocking abuse of children within institutions in Australia. It recommended taking action to make organisations across the country safe for children. The development of the National Principles for Child Safe Organisations (Australian Human Rights Commission, 2018) is a key national reform in response to these recommendations. The Council of Australian Governments (COAG) endorsed these on 19 February 2019 so that all Commonwealth, state and territory governments had a national approach to utilise in order to embed child safe cultures within organisations that engage with children. The implementation of these National Principles acted as a vehicle to give effect to all Royal Commission recommendations related to Child Safe Standards.

The National Principles are not currently mandated under legislation, and state commissions do not enforce compliance with them (Child Safe Standards present in individual states are what mandate compliance).

The 10 National Principles are as follows:

1. Child safety and wellbeing is embedded in organisational leadership, governance and culture.
2. Children and young people are informed about their rights, participate in decisions affecting them and are taken seriously.
3. Families and communities are informed and involved in promoting child safety and wellbeing.

4. Equity is upheld, and diverse needs respected in policy and practice.
5. People working with children and young people are suitable and supported to reflect child safety and wellbeing values in practice.
6. Processes to respond to complaints and concerns are child focused.
7. Staff and volunteers are equipped with the knowledge, skills and awareness to keep children and young people safe through ongoing education and training.
8. Physical and online environments promote safety and wellbeing while minimising the opportunity for children and young people to be harmed.
9. Implementation of the national child safe principles is regularly reviewed and improved.
10. Policies and procedures document how the organisation is safe for children and young people.

SNAICC is the national peak body in Australia, representing the interests of Aboriginal and Torres Strait Islander children and families. The National Office for Child Safety worked in partnership with SNAICC to develop the *Keeping Our Kids Safe* resources, which applies a cultural lens to the National Principles to help organisations think about how to make themselves safer for Aboriginal and Torres Strait Islander children.

The 'Keeping Our Kids Safe: Cultural Safety and the National Principles for Child Safe Organisations' resources build on the existing guidance materials available to support the National Principles. It applies a cultural lens to the National Principles and can help organisations think about how to make themselves safer when implementing the National Principles for Child Safe Organisations (Secretariat of National Aboriginal and Islander Child Care, 2021).

It is informed by, and aligns with, the United Nations Declaration on the Rights of Indigenous Peoples – this was adopted by the General Assembly on 13 September 2007. For more information, visit the UN website (www.un.org) and search 'Indigenous Peoples'.

Cultural safety is the positive recognition and celebration of cultures. It is more than just the absence of racism or discrimination and more than 'cultural awareness' and 'cultural sensitivity'.

The professional commitment

Our country also declares commitments in key professional groups, inclusive of the early childhood sector.

Early Childhood Australia *Code of Ethics*

The Early Childhood Australia (ECA) *Code of Ethics* (ECA, 2016) is especially for early childhood education and care environments and is based on the principles of the UNCRC (first developed in 1988 and the third version was approved in 2016). Download it from the ECA website (www.earlychildhoodaustralia.org.au).

The ECA *Code of Ethics* reflects current pedagogical research and practice, providing a framework for reflection about the ethical responsibilities of early childhood professionals who work with or on behalf of children and families in early childhood settings. It states:

"Professionals who adhere to this Code of Ethics act in the best interests of all children and work collectively to ensure that every child is thriving and learning.

"Being ethical involves thinking about everyday actions and decision-making, either individually or collectively, and responding with respect to all concerned. The Code of Ethics recognises that childhood professionals are in a unique position of trust and influence in their relationships with children, families, colleagues and the community, therefore professional accountability is vital."

The National Quality Framework

The articles within the UNCRC are embedded within the objectives and guiding principles of the Education and Care Services National Law (Australian Children's Education & Care Quality Authority, 2010) and National Regulations (NSW legislation, 2011), and both operate under an applied law system: the NQF – see the *Guide to the National Quality Framework* (Australian Children's Education & Care Quality Authority, 2020). Keep an eye out for future, updated guides.

The purpose of the NQF is to set a national standard for children's education and care across Australia. In effect, it means the same law is applied in each state and territory, but with some varied provisions as applicable to the needs of each state or territory.

The NQF introduced a new quality standard in 2012 to improve education and care across long day care, family day care, preschool/kindergarten, outside school hours care services. It includes:
- National Law and National Regulations
(www.acecqa.gov.au/nqf/national-law-regulations)
- National Quality Standard
(www.acecqa.gov.au/nqf/national-quality-standard)
- Assessment and quality rating process
(www.acecqa.gov.au/assessment/assessment-and-rating-process)
- National learning frameworks
(www.acecqa.gov.au/nqf/national-law-regulations/approved-learning-frameworks)

Australian Children's Education & Care Quality Authority

The Australian Children's Education & Care Quality Authority (ACECQA – pronounced *a-see-kwa*) is an independent national authority that assists governments in administering the NQF for children's education and care. ACECQA works with the Australian and state and territory governments to:
- Implement changes that benefit children from birth to 13 years of age and their families
- Monitor and promote the consistent application of the Education and Care Services National Law across all states and territories
- Support the children's education and care sector to improve quality outcomes for children

ACECQA is an independent national authority based in Sydney, Australia. It is guided by a governing board whose members are nominated by each state and territory and the Commonwealth, and the board is accountable to Education Ministers.

Jurisdiction in states and territories

"*All Australian states and territories have Children's Commissioners and/ or Guardians. The legislative functions of these Children's Commissioners and Guardians differ between jurisdictions. Some have a broad focus, which includes all children, whereas others have specified responsibilities relating to children who are at risk or who are vulnerable. Their primary focus is state laws, programmes and issues affecting children*" (National Children's Commissioner, 2019).

Human rights guidance for child protection is also applied in some state and territory legislation, including:
- *Human Rights Act 2004* (Australian Capital Territory)
- *Human Rights Commission Act 2005* (Australian Capital Territory)
- *Human Rights Act 2019* (Queensland)
- *The Charter of Human Rights and Responsibilities Act 2006* (Victoria)

The Australian Capital Territory is unique to most jurisdictions in Australia. All its legislation is grounded within a human rights framework. The Australian Capital Territory *Human Rights Act 2004* (HR Act) imposes direct obligations on Australian Capital Territory public authorities to act compatibly with the human rights protected in the HR Act, and to take relevant human rights into account in decision-making.

Regulatory requirements are specific for jurisdiction. Victoria passed the *Education and Care Services National Law Act 2010*, and other jurisdictions adopted that law through an Application Act or passed corresponding legislation.

For example, there are two regulatory schemes for early childhood services that operate in Victoria:
1. The NQF, which consists of the Education and Care Services National Law (National Law) and the Education and Care Services National Regulations (National Regulations)
2. The Children's Services Act 1996 and Children's Services Regulations 2020

Both schemes aim to ensure children attending early childhood services are protected from harm, and that their opportunities for learning and development are maximised. The regulatory requirements under both schemes are aligned, where appropriate.

Refer to Appendix 3 for information on where to find child protection legislation across state and territory jurisdictions in Australia.

Turn to Appendix 4 to view a table that indicates the legislation that applies in each state or territory, and if applicable, the corresponding Application Act.

What are Child Safe Standards?

In Australia, statutory child protection is the responsibility of state and territory governments. Some individual states, such as Western Australia, have also decided to individually interpret the National Principles, creating guides to assist organisations to embed them. States such as New South Wales and Victoria have taken a stronger preventative, proactive and participatory approach to child safety by endorsing their own Child Safe Standards and created a comprehensive suite of resources to aid in adopting them. Victoria has in fact reviewed and redeveloped its initial seven standards, modifying them, under the Victorian Child Wellbeing and Safety Act 2005, to 11. The new Victorian Child Safe Standards align more closely to the National Principles and explicitly include priorities such as needing to have a Child Safety and Wellbeing Policy, having a strong focus on the safety, rights and wellbeing of Aboriginal children.

Victorian education and care services will be assessed in their efficacy of implementing all 11 Child Safe Standards using an assessment summary against every compliance indicator, and marked with a result:
- N/A
- Met
- Partially met
- Not met
- Opportunity
- Undetermined/not assessed

Evidence and comments are collated on an Evidence Mapping Assessment Template, initially with a section for Organisational Overview, which includes the education and care services':

- Vision and mission
- Organisational structure
- A chart (suggested helpful)
- Number of staff
- Key roles and responsibilities, and governance
- Locations
- Services delivered

There is an Actions Recommendations Section on the assessment template sheet and opportunity to create an action plan with agreed actions, assessor recommendations, the responsible person, due date and assessor recommendations.

National Quality Standard

In the NQS, the aim of Quality Area 2 is to safeguard and promote children's health and safety, minimise risks and protect children from harm, injury and infection. Standard 2.2 specifically looks at *'Each Child is Protected'*: *"Children have the right to experience quality education and care in an environment that safeguards and promotes their health, safety and wellbeing"* (ACECQA, 2018).

We are customarily led to thinking about safeguarding children or protecting them from physical injury that may result from accidents happening. The simple fact is that our preventative approaches, and how we must act in response to an incident, need to include the possibility of *abuse transpiring.*

Element 2.2.3 of Standard 2.2 requires service personnel to be aware of their roles and responsibilities to identify and respond to every child at risk of abuse and neglect. You cannot adequately meet Element 2.2.3 Child protection if you do not consider Supervision (Element 2.2.1), as well as Incident and emergency management (Element 2.2.2). See the table overleaf.

Table 1: The elements of NQS Standard 2.2: *'Each Child is Protected'*

Supervision	Element 2.2.1	At all times, reasonable precautions and adequate supervision ensure children are protected from harm and hazard
Incident and emergency management	Element 2.2.2	Plans to effectively manage incidents and emergencies are developed in consultation with relevant authorities, practised and implemented
Child protection	Element 2.2.3	Management, educators and staff are aware of their roles and responsibilities to identify and respond to every child at risk of abuse or neglect

You can download a revised A4 poster from the ACECQA website (www.acecqa.gov.au). It includes components of the revised NQS from 1 February 2018 and further amendments to the National Regulations 2020.

The Snapshot report can also be accessed via the ACECQA website. It provides analysis and information on the profile of the sector and the quality ratings of services against the NQS. The NQF Snapshot Q2 2022, which is ACECQA's 38th national report on children's education and care services operating under the NQF, was published in August 2022.

Australia has 16,986 approved children's education and care services operating under the NQF. That is a lot of children to be accountable for and uphold the rights of. The proportion of services rated 'Meeting NQS' or above by overall rating and Quality Area (QA) indicates that, in 2013, only 75% met QA2, which rose to 88% in the later part of 2022. The alarming statistics indicate the proportion of services rated 'Exceeding NQS' or above by overall rating and QA in 2013 for QA2 was only 21%, but this dropped to only 18% throughout 2022.

Australia's education and care sector must better to protect children.

National Law and National Regulations

The table below highlights the legality according to National Law and National Regulations underpinning Standard 2.2. You will see that many *can* and *should* absorb protection of children.

Table 2: National Law and National Regulations specific to children's health and safety

Element	National Law and National Regulations underpinning Standard 2.2	
2.2.1	Section 51(1)(a)	Conditions on service approval (safety, health and wellbeing of children)
	Section 165	Offence to inadequately supervise children
	Section 166	Offence to use inappropriate discipline
	Section 167	Offence relating to protection of children from harm and hazards
	Section 170	Offence relating to unauthorised persons on education and care service premises
	Section 171	Offence relating to direction to exclude inappropriate persons from education and care premises
	Regulation 82	Tobacco, drug and alcohol-free environment
	Regulation 83	Staff members and family day care educators not to be affected by alcohol or drugs
	Regulation 99	Children leaving the education and care service premises
	Regulation 100	Risk assessment must be conducted before excursion
	Regulation 101	Conduct of risk assessment for excursion
	Regulation 102	Authorisation for excursions
2.2.2	Section 51(1)(a)	Conditions on service approval (safety, health and wellbeing of children)
	Regulation 97	Emergency and evacuation procedures
	Regulation 98	Telephone or other communication equipment
2.2.3	Section 51(1)(a)	Conditions on service approval (safety, health and wellbeing of children)
	Section 162 A	Persons in day-to-day charge and nominated supervisors to have child protection training
	Regulation 84	Awareness of child protection law

(acecqa.gov.au/sites/default/files/2020-09/NQS_AssessmentRatingInstrument.pdf)

The following could also unquestionably correlate to child protection and therefore influence requirements for responding to and reporting (which we explore in Chapter 4):

Regulation 85	Incident, injury, trauma (and illness) policies and procedures
Regulation 87	Incident, injury, trauma (and illness) record
Regulation 161	Authorisations to be kept in enrolment record
Regulation 166	Children not to be alone with visitors
Regulation 168	Education and care service must have policies and procedures
Regulation 177	Prescribed enrolment and other documents to be kept by approved provider

In 2021, Victoria published a new Code of Conduct and Code of Ethics specific to teachers. The purpose of *The Victorian Teaching Profession's Code of Ethics* is to:

- State the values that guide our practice and conduct
- Enable us as a profession to affirm our public accountability
- Promote public confidence in our profession

(Victorian Institute of Teaching, 2021)

The Victorian Institute of Teaching (VIT) has an overarching function of providing for child safety and wellbeing, and this underpins the principles set out in the Code of Conduct. "*The Code of Conduct recognises that the teacher-learner relationship is not equal; teachers hold a unique position of influence and trust with learners that should not be violated or compromised.*" It applies to all teachers and early childhood teachers registered with the VIT. This Code of Conduct is complementary to any other relevant policies, procedures or codes of conduct used by a sector or education setting in which a teacher works.

An early childhood teacher's professional and personal conduct reflects on the standing of the entire profession. In taking on the responsibilities of a teacher, including providing for the safety and wellbeing of children and young people, teachers – like other professions of public trust – are held to a high level of accountability.

The Code of Conduct clearly states the expectations placed on teachers by the profession and the community. The VIT may consider a departure from the Code of Conduct to be grounds for an allegation of misconduct or serious misconduct, or call into question a teacher's fitness to teach. Whether it does will largely depend on the individual circumstances and the context in which the conduct occurred.

Any regulatory measures should always be viewed within the context of what is considered necessary to protect the safety and wellbeing of children and young people.

This brings us to reportable conduct – *Information sheet 1 About the Victorian Reportable Conduct Scheme* (CCYP, n.d.).

Reportable Conduct Schemes

Reportable Conduct Schemes hold employees in organisations big or small accountable because they solely focus on the behaviour of *employees*. They do not focus on child protection matters that occur within a family (unless the parent is also a teacher, doctor, childcare worker or any other profession covered under the scheme). Reportable conduct includes allegations, offences or convictions relating to child abuse or misconduct, including:

- Ill treatment of a child (including emotional abuse and inappropriate use of force or physical restraint)
- Neglect
- Psychological harm
- Misconduct of a sexual nature
- Sexual or physical offences and convictions where a child is a victim or is present

Many organisations create their own strict protocols if there is not an established Reportable Conduct Scheme. In Victoria, the *Child Wellbeing and Safety Act 2005* has enabled a Reportable Conduct Scheme to be designed, to ensure that CCYP will be aware of every allegation of certain types of misconduct involving children in relevant organisations that exercise care, supervision and authority over children. It provides a clear directive for heads of organisations.

Victoria's background

The *Betrayal of Trust Report* 2012 (Victorian Government, Department of Justice and Community Safety, n.d.) looked at the inquiry into the handling of child abuse allegations within religious and other non-government organisations. It included a range of recommendations (tabled in Parliament 2013), including:
- The need to better protect children from child abuse when they access services provided by organisations
- Child Safe Standards and the Reportable Conduct Scheme (CCYP, 2022) are the ways the Government implemented these recommendations. You can access information on the new Child Safe Standards for Victoria at the CCYP website (www.ccyp.vic.gov.au)
- Imposes new obligations on heads of organisations that are within the scheme
- Must have in place systems to prevent child abuse
- If child abuse is alleged, to ensure allegations can be brought to the attention of appropriate persons for investigation and response
- Ensure that the Commission is notified and given updates on an organisation's response to an allegation

The Commission can share information where appropriate, including with the Working with Children Check Unit, relevant regulators and Victoria Police, to better prevent and protect children from abuse.

A finding that a person has engaged in reportable conduct can trigger an assessment of whether that person is suitable to continue to work or volunteer with children. In turn, this may lead the Working with Children Check Unit to revoke a person's Working with Children Check card.

Table 3: A snapshot of a head of organisation's obligations under reportable conduct

Notify	You must notify the Commission within three business days of becoming aware of a reportable allegation
Investigate	You must investigate an allegation – subject to police clearance on criminal matters or matters involving family violence You must advise the Commission that is undertaking the investigation You must manage the risks to children
Update	Within 30 calendar days, you must provide the Commission detailed information about the reportable allegation and any action you have taken
Outcomes	You must notify the Commission of the investigation findings and any disciplinary action the head of entity has taken (or the reasons no action was taken)

(CCYP, 2017)

"After five years, our regulatory functions designed to keep children safe from abuse and harm within organisations are becoming increasingly embedded. This is reflected in a record number of notifications received this year under the Reportable Conduct Scheme (1,006 in total), which gives the Commission oversight of how complaints and disclosures about inappropriate conduct against children are managed. These reports serve as a confronting reminder that harms within trusted organisations are not problems of the past, and that the ongoing work of building and maintaining child-safe cultures cannot be overlooked" – Liana Buchanan, Principal Commissioner (CCYP, 2021).

A Reportable Conduct Scheme/Policy needs to be read in conjunction with an organisation's Code of Conduct.

Code of Conduct

A Code of Conduct should outline:
1. Behaviour that is expected – this will align with your Commitment to Child Safety and Child Safety and Wellbeing Policy
2. Behaviour/actions that will not be tolerated (with explicit consideration and consequences for racism, discrimination and bullying)

By establishing what behaviours/actions are not acceptable, and are considered offences (in breach of the organisational Code of Conduct), the Code should also outline what the consequences will be (this may include reporting to authorities).

With so many documents available to convey ways to best protect children from harm, are we limited to what our state or territory imposes?

As a professional, it is important that, as part of your role, you make sure you are familiar with the individual service policies and procedures that underpin your practices and inform decision-making, in addition to the centre philosophy (there could be mission/vision statements as well).

We are certainly not restricted in the measures we put in place to promote children's safety and wellbeing. High-quality practice is recognised by advisors who are assessing and rating children's services against the NQS. Additional methods and practices can certainly be included as evidence of exceeding themes of standards and could even contribute to an individual service's model of excellence.

You want to set a high-quality benchmark. Regulatory authorities keep a record of any issues that need rectifying. In fact, before an assessment and rating visit, authorised officers complete a Desktop Review, making *"notes relevant to each particular standard or quality area based on the review of the service's compliance history and current Quality Improvement Plan, including items to check at the visit".*

Assessors will recognise high-quality practice and will:
- Refer to and consider the exceeding themes included as a reference point for each standard
- Record evidence for the standard where the service practice goes above the standard to further enhance outcomes for children

To ensure you have the most up-to-date information, it is suggested educators view the online version of the *Guide to the National Quality Framework*. The guide is not legal advice and should be read in conjunction with the National Law and Regulations, which take precedence over any guidance.

Any changes to the guide are added to the ACECQA website and will also update amendments to National Regulations. There is ongoing monitoring, review and modifications to improve practices as a nation as well as in the individual states and territories.

Violence reforms – Victoria is leading the way

Victoria is strongly committed to early identification of family violence within universal services. The Victorian Government and its agencies deliver the family violence reforms outlined in the Government's implementation plan: *Ending Family Violence – Victoria's 10-year plan for change*. The commitment to implement all 227 recommendations from the Royal Commission into Family Violence provided the basis for this reform.

In response to recommendations made by the Victorian Royal Commission into Family Violence, the laws regarding how information about perpetrators, victims or third parties involved in family violence have changed.

Victorian Government reforms

The Victorian Government has introduced three reforms that will be integral to promoting the wellbeing and safety of children (aged 0–18 years) and reducing family violence. These are:
1. The Child Information Sharing Scheme (CISS), which enables prescribed organisations and services to share information to promote the wellbeing and safety of children
2. The Family Violence Information Sharing Scheme (FVISS), which enables prescribed organisations and services to share information to facilitate assessment and management of family violence risk to children and adults

3. The Multi-Agency Risk Assessment and Management Framework (MARAM) sets out the responsibilities of different workforces in identifying, assessing and managing family violence risk across the family violence and broader service system

The Child Information Sharing Scheme

The CISS allows authorised organisations to share information to support child wellbeing or safety. The scheme has expanded legal permissions for professionals to share and request information from other professionals. This ensures that professionals working with children, young people and families can gain a complete view of the children and young people they work with, making it easier to identify wellbeing or safety needs earlier, and to act on them sooner.

Victoria has three reforms, and prescribed organisations in children's education and care service type include the following (all types are prescribed under all three schemes):
- Schools
- Kindergartens
- Long day care
- Out-of-school-hours care
- Child protection
- Youth justice
- Maternal and child health
- Public hospitals
- Victoria Police

The Family Violence Reform Implementation Monitor

The Family Violence Reform Implementation Monitor (2022) was formally established in 2017 as an independent statutory officer of the Parliament after the Royal Commission into Family Violence released its report in 2016.

As a result, the FVISS was created by Part 5A of the *Family Violence Protection Act 2008* (www.legislation.vic.gov.au). The FVISS supports effective assessment and management of family violence risk.

Multi-Agency Risk Assessment and Management Framework

Family Violence Protection Regulations 2018 enabled a legislative basis for departments to initially begin implementation of Victoria's Family Violence MARAM (Victorian Government, 2019).

Education professionals have been recently brought into these reforms under Phase 2, and include long day care, kindergartens and schools (see table below, which highlights the large range of education professionals now included).

Table 4: Health and education organisations prescribed for MARAM and information-sharing legislation (FVISS and CISS – this is not an exhaustive list and is illustrated to highlight the Department of Education organisations)

Rollout of MARAM	What the Department of Education organisation includes
Phase 1 of MARAM and information sharing commenced in September 2018 across 850 organisations, covering approximately 37,500 professionals	• Maternal and child health services • Victoria Police • Courts • Family violence services • Child protection • Mental health and alcohol and drug services
Phase 2 of MARAM came into effect in April 2021 across 5,800 Government and non-government organisations, covering approximately 370,000 additional professionals	• Government and non-government schools • Kindergartens • Long day care • Relevant non-government school system bodies • Out-of-school-hours care • Student disengagement and wellbeing services and programmes funded by the Department of Education (www.education.vic.gov.au/Pages/default.aspx), for example, LOOKOUT, Navigator, School Focused Youth service, National School Chaplaincy Programme • Child health and wellbeing services, for example, student support services, incident support and operations centre, education justice initiative, area-based regional staff • Doctors in schools

(*CCYP, 2017*)

The MARAM, together with the FVISS and the CISS, combine as a suite of interrelated reforms that work to reduce family violence and promote child wellbeing and safety. Many of the authorised organisations under the FVISS are also prescribed under the CISS (www.vic.gov.au/child-information-sharing-scheme).

So, Victoria has three reforms, and prescribed organisations in children's education and care service type include the following (all types are prescribed under all three schemes):
- Kindergartens
- Long day care
- All schools (Government and private)
- Before and after-school care (not if vacation care only)

Once you know your service is on the ISE list (Victorian Government website), you use reform tools together, according to what you are prescribed.

Access further information about the Information Sharing Schemes and who can share information at www.vic.gov.au

Under the scheme, ISEs (key organisations and services) can share information related to assessing or managing family violence risk. The purpose of the scheme is to:
- Keep perpetrators in view and accountable
- Promote the safety of victim survivors of family violence

Additionally, the Orange Door Network – replacing Child First – was due to be established in all 17 Department of Families, Fairness and Housing regions in Victoria by the end of 2022; it is designed to be a clear point of contact for referrals and secondary consultations (www.orangedoor.vic.gov.au).

Together, these reforms create a more collaborative, integrated system that will help improve outcomes for all Victorian children and families, from agencies being able to work together. Many organisations already work together, but the schemes have expanded legal permissions for professionals to collect, use, share and request information from other professionals. This ensures that professionals working with children can gain a complete view of the children they work with, making it easier to identify wellbeing or safety needs earlier, and to act on them sooner.

Reform activity

A Family Violence Reform Rolling Action Plan has guided Victoria through years of the reform. It is delivered through a web portal as a digital product setting out the focus of activities to 2023 in the context of the 10-year plan to end family violence (2019). By presenting the Rolling Action Plan as an interactive digital product, it enables people to read about the plan and use links to see the range of reform activity across Government departments and agencies.

One example of reform activity in Victoria is a digital tool called Child Link, launched on 31 December 2021. This web-based platform displays information about a child to authorised key professionals – key staff in early childhood education settings, for example, early childhood education and care services and funded kindergartens, who both have responsibility for child wellbeing and safety. Child Link shows limited but critical information, such as a child's participation in key early childhood and education services. When a child and the child's family engage with these services, the service creates a record of the engagement in a 'source system' of that relevant service, with the information that the child or their family has provided.

Child Link may display the following information in relation to a child:
- Their name, date and place of birth, and sex
- The names of their siblings
- The names and the relationship of persons who have parental responsibility and/or day-to-day care of the child
- Whether the child is identified as Aboriginal and/or Torres Strait Islander
- Their participation and engagement in Government childhood services and the contact details of those services
- If they or their sibling has a past or current child protection order, and if the order placed the child or their sibling in out-of-home care

Read more about Child Link at www.vic.gov.au

Part 7A of the *Child Wellbeing and Safety Act 2005* and regulations made under that Act allows Child Link to draw information from Victorian Government source systems.

Part 5A of the *Family Violence Protection Act 2008* (Victoria) and Part 6A of the *Child Wellbeing and Safety Act 2005* (Victoria), with their supporting regulations, permit key organisations to share current and previously collected information relating to family violence risk and the wellbeing or safety of children – to keep people safe and perpetrators of violence in view.

Universal Services Report

In May 2022, the latest Universal Services Report was released, which examines the implementation progress strengthening universal health and education workforces to identify and respond to family violence early to support the safety of victim survivors. In undertaking monitoring, the following cross-cutting themes are examined across all topics:

- Intersectionality
- Children and young people
- Aboriginal self-determination
- Priority communities such as LGBTIQA+, people with disabilities, rural and regional, criminalised women, older people and refugee and migrant communities
- Data, evaluation, outcomes and research
- Service integration

Both FVIS and CIS schemes recognise the importance of seeking the views and promoting the agency of children and adults (who are not perpetrators of family violence), wherever appropriate, safe and reasonable to do so.

The Family Violence MARAM must always be applied to identify and guide the assessment and management of family violence risk – for children and adults. This is to ensure that information is shared safely and lawfully, so as not to escalate family violence risk.

Under the FVISS, some ISEs are also prescribed as Risk Assessment Entities (RAEs). RAEs include all specialist family violence services, Victoria Police and child protection.

Victoria's commitment in the protection of children is no doubt extensive. Victorian children's services, inclusive of schools, have the new Child Safe Standards (effective 1 July 2022). These 11 standards are mandatory and foster a long-term approach to systemic change and continuous improvement. The indicators prompt deeper thinking and proactivity, and compliance will be determined by all stakeholder involvement. The Child Safe Standards, mandatory reporting and child protection training combine to require a stronger duty of care that is both preventative and responsive. Mitigating, identifying and responding to all forms of child abuse, including family violence, is the expectation.

In summary

With this chapter complete, you should now know that:
- There is a global commitment to protecting children.
- There is a national agenda to reduce violence.
- Professionals have commitments and ethics they must adhere to.
- Victoria has a number of schemes to action its Plan for Change.
- Reportable conduct and a Code of Conduct can be implemented into any organisation.

Chapter 3 reflection questions

- Do you know what child protection legislation you work under in your state or territory?
- Do you have Child Safe Standards in your jurisdiction?
- Are you familiar with the five groups that early childhood professionals have a commitment to in the ECA Code of Ethics?
- Do you utilise a child-friendly version of the UNCRC in your curriculum?
- Did you know there was an additional guide created that outlines how to implement the National Principles for Child Safe Organisations through using a cultural lens?
- Have you heard of Reportable Conduct Schemes?
- Are you familiar with Victoria's Violence reform schemes that enable information sharing among professionals?
- Do you offer ongoing training to ensure all team members are up to date with legislation, and how changes affect them in their role?
- Would your entire team know about the responsibilities of their co-educators' roles to facilitate a collaborative approach to information sharing?
- Have you accessed the suite of resources on the ACECQA website lately?

CHAPTER 4

Child protection – responding and reporting

Insight for educators/practitioners:

- Responding to abuse and neglect
- Reporting to authorities
- How to report concerns
- What to do if a child discloses
- The need for a cultural lens for accurate child protection evaluations

Chapter elements:

- Responding to and reporting abuse
- Data and statistics
- Voluntary and mandatory reporting
- Communicating concerns to authorities
- Responding to a child
- National reporting process
- What to include in a report
- Professionals working together

'Too much red tape' or 'they do nothing, you're wasting your time' are common phrases heard not just among early childhood professionals, but general members of the public, too. We are in a *violence crisis*. It is a reality – there are understaffed and overworked child protection units. You just have to take note of the copious alerts, struggles to fill vacancies or the many news reports that blame 'the system' – and it doesn't matter what country, state or territory you are in. There are laws in every jurisdiction that stipulate strict processes be followed, but in the meantime, all this turbulence hurts children. We, as a society, don't get to decide it's all too problematical and give up.

The Australian Federal Police-led Australian Centre to Counter Child Exploitation has linked a spike in reports to better detection and greater community awareness. In the financial year 2021-22, the centre fielded 36,600 online child abuse reports – up more than 60% from the previous year's 22,600 (Morgan, 2022).

However, University of Melbourne research fellow Dr Gemma McKibbin, an expert leading the Disrupting Child Sexual Exploitation project, says reports are *"just the tip of the iceberg; we're facing a tsunami of child exploitation online".*

Looking away is not going to stop perpetrators abusing children (Haynes, Blair-West, 2022). *"Perpetrators have really worked out how to use social media and other kinds of networking platforms to target children"* (Morgan, 2022).

Responding to and reporting abuse

All concerns about the safety and wellbeing of a child – or the conduct of a staff member, contractor or volunteer – should be acted upon as soon as is practicable. Early intervention can save lives. Early childhood professionals need to be more attentive and persistent in our *responding* and *reporting* duties than ever before.

"The pandemic has exposed profound inequality in our community and the precarious circumstances too many live in. The broader social, physical and psychological impacts of prolonged lockdowns are yet to unfold" (CCYP, 2021).

The onus is unequivocally on us to pay attention to all children, but with an even sharper lens on children who are at risk or vulnerable. This means all jurisdictions working together in areas such as disability, early childhood education and care, health and mental health, alcohol and other drug treatment and prevention, domestic and family violence, justice, housing and employment.

"*We want all children, young people, families and communities in Australia to be safe and resilient and to have the opportunity to thrive*", which means there has been a vital shift in the way governments are working, recognising that "*Aboriginal and Torres Strait Islander Peoples have the right to self-determination*" and therefore "*need to lead the decisions that impact their lives*". The National Framework for Protecting Australia's Children, 2021, can be found on the Australian Government website (www.dss.gov.au).

To best protect children, and to support them to thrive, we need to be confident about our core work for children's education and care. Educators need to be well acquainted with the multitude of foundational documents (we explored in Chapter 3) of the early childhood sector, as these prompt the professional obligations you have towards children to keep them safe. We need to lead, in our local contexts, to honour the national commitment to child safety.

Duty of care

'Duty of care' is a legal concept that refers to your responsibility to adequately protect children in your care from harm. It applies to all staff members within any early childhood service. It's usually expressed as a duty to take *reasonable steps* to protect children from injury that is reasonably foreseeable.

The courts will objectively determine what constitutes 'reasonable steps'. This will depend on the individual circumstances of each case, including the nature of the service and your role within it. "*The courts have found that the standard of care owed by early childhood service providers to children is high*" (Victorian Government, Department of Education, 2022).

You may breach your duty of care towards a child if you fail to act in the way a reasonable or diligent professional (Commitments in Code of Ethics discussed in Chapter 3) would have acted in the same situation.

In relation to suspected child abuse, examples of reasonable steps within an early childhood service will vary depending on the nature of the service, but a thorough example is outlined in the dot points below. These actions are to direct educators working under regulators in Victoria, but you can adjust them to suit the jurisdiction you are in:

- Acting on concerns and suspicions of abuse quickly and in a child's best interests
- Seeking appropriate advice or consulting when unsure
- Reporting suspected child abuse to Department of Families, Fairness and Housing (DFFH), Child Protection and/or police
- Sharing information, upon request, to assist DFFH, Child Protection or police to investigate the suspected child abuse and protect and/or promote the wellbeing and development of a child
- Notifying the regulator where appropriate or required

Four critical actions

To make sure that you fulfil your duty of care obligations for all children who are involved in, or affected by, suspected child abuse, it's strongly recommended that you follow the four critical actions set out on the Victorian Government's Department of Education website (www.education.vic.gov.au) – search for 'Report child abuse in early childhood'.

These four actions include:
1. Responding to an emergency
2. Reporting to authorities
3. Contacting parents/carers
4. Providing ongoing support

Development, cultural and social support

Staff and volunteers in early childhood services need to be sensitive to a child's individual circumstances and consider diverse family compositions. We also need to tap into our own unconscious biases and call out oversight by others who compromise the wellbeing of any child. Do we overlook children's wellbeing without realising? Are we upstanding, not bystanding, when it comes to children's demeanour? Is cultural safety recognised as a significant contributor to wellbeing? Justin Mohamed, Commissioner for Aboriginal Children and Young People Victoria, outlined in his 2020-21 annual report that *"racism not only exists in society, but also taints its systems of protection".*

When working with LGBTIQA+ families who have been impacted by child abuse, it is important to connect affirmative counselling services delivered by LGBTIQA+ friendly mental health practitioners.

Complaints or concerns

You should make a complaint to your regulatory authority if you have any concerns; contact details for all states and territories can be found on the ACECQA website (www.acecqa.gov.au). You can also access contact details for each state and territory on the Australian Government's Australian Institute of Family Studies website (www.aifs.gov.au).

States and territories

As early childhood professionals, we need to be confident in all facets of our legal obligations and the processes for reporting. We need to be concerned about all types of abuse, regardless of where it occurs. We are directed by our states and territories. For example, Queensland practice is guided by the *Safe and Together* model and is underpinned by the *Strengthening Families: Protecting Children Framework for Practice* (Queensland Government, Department of Communities, Child Safety and Disability Services, 2015). The Queensland Department of Child Safety, Youth and Women wrote a paper on this in 2018.

Why do children's services need to consider family violence in their service provision? *"Victim survivors emphasised the importance of universal services being properly skilled in this area. They talked about the power of a GP, teacher or nurse planting the seed that helped them realise that their experience was family violence, even when they were not ready to address it at that moment. Conversely, how disempowering it was to have their situation minimised or missed"* (Victorian Government, Department of Justice and Community Safety, 2022).

Recognising the signs of abuse

The only way to stop perpetrators abusing children is by knowing the signs, paying attention and listening when a child tries to speak up.

Jeni Haynes is a remarkable survivor of horrific, ongoing childhood abuse at the hands of her father. *The Girl in the Green Dress* is Jeni's brave account of her extreme trauma, co-written with her psychiatrist. One of the imperative aspects I believe is worth making clear, is that Jeni needs you to *"understand the words and descriptions a child might use to try to disclose abuse"* (Haynes, Blair-West, 2022). The power of connection resonates here, highlighting an educator's need to be present with children to notice and understand a child communicating.

The *"current level of a child's relational health"* is determined by quality and quantity (frequency) of relationships. This is a strong predictor of wellbeing – even when considering trauma history (Berry Street, 2022).

Information Sharing and Family Violence Reforms Toolkit and Contextualised Guidance

The Information Sharing and Family Violence Reforms Toolkit and Contextualised Guidance were developed in close consultation with education and care professionals. They were designed to help organisations prepare their workplaces for implementation, and provide guidance on information sharing.

Codes of Conduct

To support you to comprehend your roles and responsibilities, as part of your professional duty of care, employers will outline these in your position description, which will align with the organisation's Code of Conduct.

Codes of Conduct seek to improve organisations' responses to allegations of child abuse and neglect by their workers and volunteers. A Code of Conduct will:

- Require organisations to *report*, *investigate* and *respond* to allegations of child abuse made against their workers or volunteers
- Report allegations of reportable conduct (explained below) by an employee or volunteer, including the ill treatment of a child (such as emotional abuse or use of force)
- All organisations should be able to demonstrate that the behaviour and conduct of all staff and volunteers promotes cultural safety throughout your organisation and its direct practices

The Victorian Government introduced new criminal offences to protect children from sexual abuse. Under those reforms, a failure to report or act in relation to suspected child sexual abuse can constitute a criminal offence, including the failure to disclose and failure to protect. The Victorian Government also introduced compulsory minimum standards for all organisations providing regulated or funded services for children that have now been revised and new Child Safe Standards are in place (as of 1 July 2022) for all early childhood services, as well as schools and other organisations. You can access a thorough outline of these 11 Standards at www.ccyp.vic.gov.au/child-safe-standards/the-11-child-safe-standards

Reportable Conduct Schemes

We touched on Reportable Conduct Schemes in Chapter 3. In Victoria, they require organisations involving children to notify the CCYP of any alleged abuse by people employed by:

- The organisation
- Volunteers
- Contractors

- Office holders
- Ministers of religion
- Officers of a religious body
- Foster and kinship carers in a formal care arrangement

There are five types of 'reportable conduct':
- Sexual offences (against, with or in the presence of a child)
- Sexual misconduct (against, with or in the presence of a child)
- Physical violence (against, with or in the presence of a child)
- Behaviour that causes significant emotional or psychological harm
- Significant neglect

Find more information at the Reportable Conduct Scheme page of the CCYP website (www.ccyp.vic.gov.au/reportable-conduct-scheme).

If there is no official Reportable Conduct Scheme in place where a service is located, organisations can outline their own internal systems for how they report and address harm to children – organisations create their own internal Reportable Conduct Scheme.

Facilitating wellbeing

One of the biggest professional obligations for yourself and co-workers is facilitating wellbeing. Stress is an important dimension to consider when addressing impacts on you/your service. Understanding stress markers so you can do something about it and share responsibility is vital. What has stress and your wellbeing got to do with children's safety? Stress impacts how you function in your role, assess information and make decisions around risks posed to children.

Joe Tucci, CEO of the Australian Childhood Foundation, talks about the need to monitor your own reactions to help you to detect blind spots. The Australian Childhood Foundation gifts the public a wealth of resource material. The advice given at a practical level is to look after yourself and make sure stressors of work counterbalance enjoyment and fun in your personal life.

A healthy routine, inclusive of sleep and a balanced diet, contribute to your capacity to deal with the stresses families and children bring into the dynamics that you work with. Knowing how to deal with one's own stress, how to calm oneself through responding to needs of the body are vital. The mind is open to information/nuances of what is going on for children and families, however, "*it is OK to not be OK, because it's distressing*".

Knowledge, processes and systems for reporting don't help with the emotional side. Teams need to support team members; this is a culture of wellbeing. External allied health supports may need to be utilised, to deal with the impact of what you have been exposed to. Management needs to understand emotional state and needs of staff and volunteers, and respond positively to build capacity for teams and communities, to safeguard children. It is critical that wellbeing is an explicit value because it impacts community resilience and development.

Support strategies

Would you know what support strategies you could tap into at your place of work? A great strategy to facilitate team environments to be more responsive is to list what works for individuals to unwind in their personal life and try and find commonalities within the team. This blend of personal and professional creates a third space, which is ultimately the unique formula for the team's wellbeing. Every team's 'third space' will look different because of the people and the environment. A commitment to values-based quality improvement is essential for all education and care services because there is great healing in the power of connectivity.

Paying attention to stressors

Identifying ways we can reduce stress is a protective factor for mental health and a self-care strategy. Protective factors can reduce the impact of negative stress and increase your window of tolerance. Beyond Blue's national mental health in education initiative Be You has a wealth of tools specific for educators, and it suggests *being and feeling connected to others* is a protective factor for mental health. Be You suggests a Stop, Reflect, Act process for considering how you can support yourself while supporting others. You can access these tools at www.beyou.edu.au

If you are going to create a wellbeing plan, the following questions may be useful:
- What are my stress behaviours and how do they affect others and me?
- What stressors (biological, emotional, cognitive, social or prosocial) trigger my stress behaviours?
- What protective factors can best support my wellbeing?

Be You plans suggest wellbeing strategies for each of the following:
- Biological
- Emotional
- Cognitive
- Social
- Prosocial

Culture of transparency and openness

To be proactive in responding and reporting, a culture of transparency and openness in organisations is the best mechanism for protecting children. Joe Tucci suggests you deliberate the following:
- Your commitment (to child safety)
- Policies/procedures (to support the safety of children in your organisation)
- Your educators being the early-warning system
- Reliability from an organisation – quality responses/support when concerns raised and not holding on to information
- Concerns taken seriously and investigated/effective actions to protect children
- Engaging with the idea that there's no right or wrong (trust your gut)
- Speaking up – talk to a colleague or manager

Data and statistics

While most children in Australia grow up in families that provide them with environments where they are safe, happy and healthy, we know historical trends in data reveal many children are the subject of maltreatment (any abuse and/or neglect).

The 2016 Australian Bureau of Statistics (ABS) Personal Safety Survey estimated that about 2.5 million Australian adults (13%) experienced physical and/or sexual abuse during childhood (ABS, 2019). In 2017-18, approximately 26,400 children aged 0-12 had one or more child protection notifications substantiated (excluding New South Wales, as data was not available).

Australian Institute of Health and Welfare's (AIHW) most recent reports and data (2020-21) confirm that state and territory child protection services supported more than 178,800 children in 2020-21. This has increased from about 168,300 in 2016-17 and 170,200 in 2018-19. Of these 178,800 children, 68% (around 120,800) were the subject of an investigation of a notification of abuse or neglect and about 49,700 children were the subject of substantiations in 2020-21. At 30 June 2021, more than 46,200 children were in out-of-home care, with 91% in a home-based care placement. Between 2016-21, emotional abuse remained the most common primary type of substantiated abuse or neglect.

A substantiation indicates cases where there is sufficient reason to believe the child has been, is being or is likely to be harmed in some way. The rate of children who were the subject of substantiations has remained stable over this period at nine per 1,000 children.

These are the statistics that strike you when you access the AIHW website (www.aihw.gov.au). Released in March 2022, the calculations are reflective of the period between 2020-21. Pandemic lockdowns no doubt affected these figures, so they may not reflect the true volume of incidents.

Refer to Appendix 5 to view the statistics for children receiving child protection services by state or territory during 2020-21.

Notifications appear to have fluctuated immediately in response to COVID-19 restrictions; the impacts on substantiations and out-of-home care may take longer to manifest. Previous findings suggest that children are at increased risk of violence during emergencies and natural disasters.

Kids Helpline experienced a 24% increase in contacts between March and July 2020 (yourtown, 2020). At early September 2020, Kids Helpline was receiving around 10,000 contacts per week (yourtown, 2020). The service provided 33% more duty-of-care interventions for child abuse between 1 January and 31 July 2020 compared with the same period the previous year.

Aboriginal and Torres Strait Islander Children

Aboriginal and Torres Strait Islander children were almost five times more likely to be placed in out-of-home care compared with non-Indigenous children, according to SNAICC in its collaborative project with the Australian Institute of Family Studies' (AIFS) *Indigenous responses to child protection issues* (Higgins & Butler, 2007).

Despondency is still the status today. According to The Conversation (Bhathal et al, 2021), *"First Nations children are still being removed at disproportionate rates."* In an account of the fact that many Australians have been trying to acknowledge and apologise for the traumatic 'Stolen Generation' history, child protection systems continue to operate on assumptions about race and class that increase inequalities and injustices against First Nations families.

We can collectively do better. *How We endUP* puts forth ideas about how we can, in community, improve support and care for children, youth and families as we move towards abolition of family policing. Family policing is *"The child welfare system is predicated on the subjugation, surveillance, control, and punishment of mostly Black and Native communities experiencing significant poverty"* (upEND Movement, 2021).

Here in Australia, educators can work with the intention of adopting a cultural lens to our assessments and offer proactive, culturally appropriate support to best protect Aboriginal and Torres Strait Islander children. *"We can contribute to work already occurring and provoke new actions and innovations from others"* (upEND Movement, 2021).

The Aboriginal and Torres Strait Islander Child Placement Principle (ATSICPP) is designed to reduce the over-representation of Indigenous children in the child protection system. ATSICPP practices relating to Indigenous children in out-of-home care include:

- Preferred placement with Indigenous or non-Indigenous relatives or kin, or other Indigenous carers
- Support to maintain or re-establish connections to their family, community, culture and country

Key findings from *The Aboriginal and Torres Strait Islander Child Placement Principle* indicators report include:

- About 18,900 Indigenous children were living in out-of-home care as at 30 June 2020 (a rate of 56 per 1,000).
- Nearly two-thirds (63%) of Indigenous children in out-of-home care were living with Indigenous or non-Indigenous relatives or kin, or other Indigenous caregivers.
- 69% of Indigenous children in out-of-home care had current, documented and approved cultural support plans as at 30 June 2020, which include details such as the child's cultural background and actions taken to maintain their connection to culture.
- 15% of Indigenous children in out-of-home care during 2019–20 were reunified with family.

(AIHW, 2022)

How does Australia compare internationally?

Child abuse and neglect is a pervasive public health problem, impacting one in seven children in the US. The global unrest has inspired a plethora of research surrounding the impact of the pandemic on children experiencing abuse and neglect.

We should be sure of narratives before we put them out there; we now have statistics that many journalists and child advocates have noted that there may be a lack of data showing the purported increase in child abuse because, due to school closures and stay-at-home orders, there have been fewer 'eyes on children'.

The National Library of Medicine in the US has published reports from early in the COVID-19 pandemic, which demonstrated a decrease in reports of suspected child abuse and neglect by 20–70%. In addition, national data indicated a decrease in the total number of emergency department visits for child abuse and neglect in 2020 compared to 2019, but also noted an increase in hospitalisations due to child abuse and neglect. There is some concern that this decrease reflects a lack of interaction between children and mandated reporters, rather than a true reduction in abuse and neglect, particularly in light of increased hospitalisations.

Elizabeth Bartholet, faculty director of the child advocacy programme at Harvard Law School, says, *"Such findings may be misleading—they may simply reflect the inability or unwillingness of under-resourced child protection agencies to actually respond to, investigate and substantiate the allegations that come in."*

However, as reported on the not-for-profit journalism site about criminal justice, The Marshall Project, *"Many child welfare experts and officials told The Marshall Project that losing hotline reports [notifications] amid the pandemic is not the catastrophic problem it has been made out to be in news reports—because they do not identify and prevent most child abuse anyway"* (Hager, 2020).

This upsets me as a child safety advocate, and I am left infuriated, questioning *why the hell not?* We don't need statistics or scholarly articles to reframe the *why* behind the reasons to report. We simply need to articulate that we are promoting *healthy brain development* by responding. Perhaps child protection training be duty-bound to include explicit reminders about the *neurological effects* of *not* reporting child abuse and neglect.

Childhood trauma

Monash University educational and developmental psychologist Dr Emily Berger has examined key research and articulates how exposure to trauma affects child development. *"When children are exposed to trauma, the effects can be widespread and long-lasting, not only on behavioural and social skills, but also in the classroom"* (Berger & Martin, 2020).

We know that *"Trauma-induced changes to the brain can result in varying degrees of cognitive impairment and emotional dysregulation that can lead to a host of problems, including difficulty with attention and focus, learning disabilities, low self-esteem, impaired social skills, and sleep disturbances"*, not to mention the *"significantly increased risk of developing several mental and behavioural health issues"* (Child Welfare Information Gateway, 2018).

There are multiple sources available to outline the research to indicate the effect of trauma on brain development of children (Hager, 2019).

Many professionals corroborate the reality that childhood trauma physically damages the brain by triggering toxic stress. A google of 'trauma and brain development' will showcase many pyramid-style images. One that is adapted often is that of Holt & Jordan, Ohio Department of Education, which shows trauma causing the brain to be overridden by its survival mode.

Strong, frequent and prolonged toxic stress rewires several parts of the brain, and it spends a large portion addressing survival and less on cognitive development mode. When prefrontal lobes are full and functional (executive state), the child is learning and therefore benefitting positively from their experiential environments. If the survival state predominates, then it hijacks feelings of love (emotional state), because the child's brain will automatically try and assess if they are safe. If a child has major adversity in early childhood, it can weaken their brain development and permanently set the body's stress response on high alert. A brain damaged by toxic stress will have far fewer neuron connections (Radley et al, 2004).

I stand in solidarity with Dr Lori Desautels when she says we must continue to share the *"research and knowledge of what we now know and understand through science, attachment theory, and how trauma and adversity compromise and detrimentally affect the developing brain, stress responses, behaviours and wellbeing"* of children. This neuroscience-informed and compassionate perspective provides optimism for a world where children can thrive in our education and care environments (Desautels, 2020).

The importance of reporting

What can we, as educators, do to make the importance of reporting clearer? Adverse Childhood Experiences (ACEs) build up under one's skin by way of toxic stress. Excessive activation of the stress response system is from ACES, inclusive of racism, discrimination and community violence that vulnerable groups experience. Barbara Sorrels is a child development specialist, educator and consultant with a heart for *"children from hard places".* In her work she adds to the traditional ACEs, suggesting the prevalence of screens and a preoccupied culture in addition to racism, discrimination and relational poverty. To reduce the number of ACES/toxic stress a child has, supportive adults are needed to meet children's basic needs, which may require reporting. Perhaps, alongside the poster with the details of how to report, we should have a poster that includes:

The most common-known source of notification for investigated child protection cases was:
- Police – 30%
- School personnel – 19%
- Medical/health personnel – 14%
- Cases where the child involved was the source of notification accounted for less than 1%

Other categories include friend/neighbour, departmental officer, childcare personnel and cases where the source of notification was anonymous and may include the person responsible (AIHW, 2020).

It is unclear whether our education and care teachers are embedded into the statistics for 'school' or 'childcare personnel'; regardless of the grouping, the fact remains that we make up a low percentage of those who notify authorities. Educators relinquish responsibility and *this must change* – and is the reason for this book!

It is a requirement for adults – both Government and other professionals – to ensure these rights are upheld according to the UN Global Treaty, in addition to commitments by states and territories of Australia, however, it is still a common question: Who must report child abuse? The answer is: Technically, everyone. As citizens, we all have a societal obligation to report concerns about children's welfare. In addition to this, there are some groups of professionals who are mandated to report, due to our roles, in the community.

Voluntary and mandatory reporting

Let's take the guesswork out of categorising whether someone is voluntarily or mandatory reporting. If you are not sure, the simple fact is: as citizens, anyone *can* and *should* report child safety concerns. Your moral obligation will provide you with the reassurance you need to know that you can, and are, doing the right thing by notifying authorities. While mandatory reporters are required by law to report in relation to significant harm – the laws are not the same across all jurisdictions – *anyone* is able to report concerns about any type of child abuse or neglect.

Voluntary reporting

Voluntary reporting is conducted by any person who is concerned. It includes a report of an unborn child if it is believed or suspected that this child may be at risk after birth – this is also called prenatal reporting.

Mandatory reporting

Mandatory reporting legislation generally contains lists of particular occupations that are mandated to report cases of suspected child abuse and neglect. The groups of people mandated to report range from persons in a limited number of occupations (Queensland) to a more extensive list (Victoria and Western Australia) to a very extensive list (Australian Capital Territory, New South Wales, South Australia and Tasmania), through to every adult (Northern Territory).

The occupations most named as mandated reporters are those who deal frequently with children in the course of their work: teachers, early childhood education and care practitioners, doctors, nurses and police. Mandatory reporters are people who deliver the following services, wholly or partly, to children as part of their paid or professional work:

- Healthcare (for example, registered medical practitioners, specialists, general practice nurses, midwives, occupational therapists, speech therapists, psychologists, dentists and other allied health professionals working as sole practitioners or in public or private health practices)
- Welfare (for example, psychologists, social workers, caseworkers and youth workers)
- Education (for example, teachers, counsellors and principals)
- Children's services (for example, childcare workers, family day carers and home-based carers)
- Residential services (for example, refuge workers)
- Law enforcement (for example, police)

Access the AIFS at www.aifs.gov.au for more information on mandatory reporting of child abuse and neglect, which sets out the various mandatory requirements for all Australian jurisdictions.

All mandatory reporters *must* make a report to police and/or their department of child protection *as soon as is practicable* if, during the course of carrying out their professional roles and responsibilities, they form a belief on reasonable grounds that:

- A child has suffered, or is likely to suffer, significant harm because of physical injury and/or sexual abuse.
- The child's parents have not protected, or are unlikely to protect, the child from harm of that type.

What types of abuse and neglect must be reported?

The AIFS states that: *"Differences exist in the types of abuse and neglect that must be reported. In some jurisdictions (for example, NSW and NT) it is mandatory to report suspicions of all five recognised types of abuse and neglect (i.e. physical abuse, sexual abuse, emotional abuse, neglect and exposure to family violence). In other jurisdictions it is mandatory to report only some of the abuse types (for example, WA, Qld, Vic and ACT).*

"In most jurisdictions the legislation generally specifies that, except for sexual abuse, it is only cases of significant *abuse and neglect that must be reported. While not required by the legislation, suspicions of less severe child abuse and neglect may still be referred to child and family welfare agencies.*

"As sexual abuse should always create a suspicion of significant harm… all suspicions of sexual abuse must be reported."

It is a criminal offence not to report in these circumstances. It's recommended that mandatory reporters follow the four critical actions that we explored on page 64 to fulfill their legal obligations.

Communicating concerns to authorities

In all jurisdictions, the legislation provides that as long as the report is made in good faith, the reporter cannot be liable in any civil, criminal or administrative proceedings. In addition, the legislation protects the mandatory reporter's identity from disclosure. Anyone making a voluntary (non-mandated) report is also protected with regard to confidentiality and immunity from legal liability.

It is an offence to knowingly make a false or misleading report.

"*To make a report to child protection a person needs to have formed a reasonable belief that a child has suffered or is likely to suffer significant harm as a result of abuse or neglect, and that their parent has not protected or is unlikely to protect the child from harm of that type*" (Victorian Government, Department of Families, Fairness and Housing, 2021).

However, we need it to be common knowledge that "*a reasonable belief does not require proof*". This is not common knowledge, and therefore creating a hiatus in the safety of children, it could even be a betrayal to children's right to safety if you do nothing or impede the sharing of information.

What about consent?

In Victoria there is an importance of seeking views of children and adults, however, consent is not required to share information relevant to keeping a child safe. The family violence response reforms include:

- The Child Information Sharing Scheme (CISS)
- The Family Violence Information Sharing Scheme (FVISS)
- The Family Violence Multi-Agency Risk Assessment and Management Framework (MARAM)

Kindergartens, long day care and before- and after-school care are prescribed as ISEs under all three reforms. This expands circumstances in which professionals can share information and promotes earlier and more effective intervention. It supports collaboration in service provision to:

- Improve outcomes for children
- Strengthen families
- Prevent harm wherever possible

It is very likely that a child may never disclose in words, so we cannot wait for clear language. Statistics reveal that fewer than 1% of children involved in abuse are the source of notification.

Responding to a child

The Government of the Australian Capital Territory has the following information to help you when a child has disclosed sensitive information to you.

How to respond to a child who discloses:
- Remain calm and in control of your feelings.
- Avoid specific questioning, which can be confusing or intimidating, especially as a child might feel they have done something wrong or that their parents may get in trouble.

What you should do:
- Listen to the child.
- Control your expressions, verbal and facial.
- Tell the child you believe them.
- Let them know they have done the right thing by telling you.
- Say that it is hard to talk sometimes.
- Reassure the child that they are not to blame.
- Inform them of what you will do – reassure them that you want to protect them and will need to tell someone else who will be able to help.
- Assure them that you are there for them and that they can trust you.
- Write notes about what the child told you and contact Child and Youth Protection Services (CYPS).

What you should not do:
- Show anger about the alleged abuser – they may be someone the child loves.
- Confront the alleged abuser.
- Make promises you are unable to keep (such as you will not tell anyone).
- Demand further information from the child.
- Ask for more details than what they freely want to say.

Before you make a report:
- Have a gentle conversation with the child and tell them you are worried there may be something wrong; by offering to listen, you can help them open up about any issues they may be having.

- Talk to the parents about your concerns, depending on the situation. You might be able to work with them to resolve any issues – this could be you being actively involved, connecting them with other services or just letting them know you are there if they want help. You can help to build trust and expand the parents' support network when you engage with them in a positive and supportive way with consideration to cultural safety.

    You can refer back to Chapter 2 – terminology and indicators to help you.

Still not satisfied?

If you believe abuse or neglect may be happening even after you've spoken with the parents, you must not conduct your own investigation or interfere with CYPS processes. Note down the parents' responses along with any observations and comments, as these can be included as part of your report to CYPS. You could also consider contacting one of the many support services that specialise in providing help to parents and their children.

There are many step-by-step guides to ascertain the direction to take when responding to concerns, but the process will include:
1. Forming a belief
2. Making a referral to a support organisation
3. Making a report to authorities

Checklist

Use this checklist to help you decide if you should make a report to CYPS or the police:
- I have formed a reasonable belief that a child is being, has been or is at significant risk of being abused or neglected.
- I am clear on what basis I have formed this belief.
- I understand the definition of abuse and neglect.
- I am responding to a behaviour that may have many causes, or a pattern of behaviours, that point to abuse or neglect.

- I believe the abuse or neglect is occurring within the family.
- The abuse or neglect has not yet been reported to CYPS or the police by anyone else.
- I have sufficient information that will enable CYPS or the police to identify the child my report relates to.

When CYPS receives a Child Concern Report, it is legally required to find out more about the child's situation to determine if they are in need of care and protection. It will carry out a Child Concern Report Risk Assessment to analyse the child's exposure to risk and their potential needs. The focus is whether the reported behaviour meets the criteria of abuse or neglect as required by the legislation upholding the particular region the child resides in.

If the child is not staying in the one location, contact the region in which you are located to seek further advice.

National reporting processs

Regardless of what type of abuse or neglect you are reporting, when making your report you will be asked to provide detailed information.

How to report

Call triple zero (000) if you believe a child is in immediate danger. Where your concerns relate to an alleged perpetrator of abuse who may pose a risk more generally to all children, you should inform the police.

Contact the Child Protection Intake Service that covers the region in which the child lives if you have concerns that a child is at risk of *significant harm* as a result of abuse or neglect. There are after-hours child protection emergency services available.

Intake practitioners do most of their work via the telephone and in some cases email. They do not go out and see clients; intake is the 'entry point' for the statutory child protection service. Response teams receive notifications assessed at Intake as requiring face-to-face follow-up and an investigation. Response staff also provide short-term protective intervention, which may include application to the court for legal orders where necessary.

Child safety assessment

Where the assessment indicates there is a reasonable suspicion of abuse or neglect, the child protection authority considers whether there is a parent both willing and able to protect the child. To establish this, the child protection authority, i.e. CYPS, reviews information it already has about the parents and contacts other parties for relevant information – this includes schools, doctors and you, asking for your experience and opinion of the parents or other significant primary caregivers.

After conducting the assessment, the child protection authority will determine if more detailed investigation should happen – this is an appraisal, if a support response is more appropriate or no action is needed. If there is no evidence of abuse or neglect to the child, and they are assessed as being in a safe environment, the case will be closed.

The onus on an educator, to determine whether a child's situation and circumstances could be compromised and move from 'a wellbeing concern' to being 'at risk of significant harm and in need of protection', is a task we are not trained to gauge. We must reach out to those who are more skilled. Knowing what to look for and when to act is something we should seek guidance about if unsure.

While you may need to gather the information to make a report, remember it is not the role of educators to investigate abuse – leave this to the police and/or child protection units.

Child protection

The child protection contact points are not generally appreciated as support avenues. Child protection intake has been depicted as more like a place to formalise the process of indorsing abuse, to steer towards a probable conviction. The perception of child protection intake services must change. Child protection allied health providers need to be perceived as advisors who can guide and help determine whether a child needs immediate protection, as opposed to officers who will deliver, through you, a hard line towards a guilty verdict.

Referring to a divisional child protection intake service would be appropriate where families:
- Are experiencing parenting problems that may be affecting the child's development
- Are experiencing family conflict or breakdown
- Are under pressure due to the physical or mental illness within a family member, substance abuse, disability or bereavement
- Are young, isolated or unsupported
- Are experiencing social or economic disadvantage that may impact on a child's care or development

Where longer-term protective intervention is required, responsibility for planning to meet the best interests of the child is transferred to members of one of the Case Management teams or Out of Home Care and Adoptions Services, which will provide support to children in need of placement away from their birth family.

Child protection process flowchart

To help understand the sequence that occurs in the child protection system, the following flowchart outlines the process of child protection in Tasmania. Although taken from the Tasmanian Government website, it highlights a common flow for most child protection systems.

	Child protection process in Tasmania
Step 1	Someone is concerned about the safety or wellbeing of a child – they make a **notification**
	⇩
Step 2	Child Protection Intake carries out an initial **assessment** of the notification
	⇩
Step 3	If the notification is assessed as serious and requiring further assessment through contact with the child or family, it is referred to Child Protection Response for an **investigation** OR If it is assessed that there is no risk – or that the risk is being managed and the child is safe – there will be **no further action**
	⇩
Step 4 (if an investigation is necessary)	The matter is discussed with the family, the child will be seen and other services and agencies will get involved; it will be decided whether or not the risk is **substantiated**
	⇩
Step 5 (if the risk is substantiated) and the child is still at risk	**Short-term protective intervention and support** may be necessary
	⇩
Step 6	If the child remains at risk or needs ongoing care and protection, **longer-term protective intervention and support** may be necessary

Who to report to

In Victoria you must report to protective interveners or other appropriately delegated officers. If you are concerned about the wellbeing of a child but do not believe they are at risk of significant harm, and where the immediate safety of the child will not be compromised, a referral to Child FIRST (family information, referral and support teams) now called The Orange Door may be appropriate.

The Orange Door

Child FIRST is the entry point into family services; its teams are located across Victoria and its services are delivered by community service organisations. As the access point for family services, Child FIRST has transitioned to The Orange Door.

It was set up by the Royal Commission into Family Violence and the Roadmap for Reform in Victoria, which recommended the establishment of support and safety hubs because:

- Many people often didn't know where to go for help.
- Fragmented and uncoordinated service responses meant people had to repeatedly tell their story.
- Children and families were not always getting the right support at the right time due to services being overwhelmed, plus family violence was a major driver of child vulnerability.
- Efforts across the service system to hold perpetrators to account were not sufficient – this left victim survivors with the burden of managing risk.
- There was not enough effort in preventing harm and early intervention.
- Practitioners undertaking risk assessments did not have the best information or tools to adequately address people's experiences of family violence and children's wellbeing.
- The type of response people received could be dependent on their point of entry to the service system as well as the capacity of that entry point to respond effectively.

The Orange Door operates in all 17 Department of Health and Human Services areas across Victoria. Women, children and young people who are experiencing family violence, or families who need assistance with the care and wellbeing of children, are able to access the services they need to be safe and supported. The Orange Door holds perpetrators to account by planning interventions to address their level of risk and challenging their abusive behaviour.

The Orange Door provides an integrated intake pathway to women's and children's family violence services, services for men who use violence and family services. It keeps the entire family in view, with expert support tailored to each family member's needs. It welcomes people of any age, gender, sex, sexuality, culture, religion and ability and provides:
- A visible contact point so people know where to find support
- Support and advice for victim survivors, families and children, with a strong focus on perpetrator accountability, based on the best available information and risk assessment tools
- A coordinated and integrated service response where practitioners draw on specialist expertise
- A connection to a wide range of supports across the spectrum of prevention, early intervention and response

The Orange Door is a key part of the ongoing reform of the family violence and children and families services systems. It aims to strengthen responses for victim survivors and devise better outcomes for children and families, while also addressing perpetrator behaviour.

State and territory councils

Authoritative information about state and territory councils is available to access online so that you can:
- Understand any statutory requirements of your role
- Understand and advocate for the human and cultural rights of Aboriginal and Torres Strait Islander people, particularly children

If you refer to *Australia's Children* (2020), which is the report that cumulates the data and statistics by the AIHW, there are snapshots that reveal measures of child abuse and neglect.

The report says: "*Children are considered to have been the subject of child abuse and/or neglect if a child protection notification has been investigated and subsequently substantiated. Not all notifications are investigated and not all investigations are substantiated.*"

It goes on to describe:

Notifications – these are contacts made to an authorised department by those reporting child abuse, neglect, maltreatment or harm. One notification involves one child only; where more than one child is concerned, each child is counted as a single notification. More than one notification about the same event involving a child is counted as one notification. But more than one notification for the same child relating to different events is counted as separate notifications.

Investigation – this is where the relevant department gains more detailed information about a child that is the subject of a notification. The degree of harm to the child as well as their protective needs are assessed during an investigation, which includes interviewing the child where it is practical to do so.

Substantiations – these occur where an investigation concluded there was reasonable cause to believe a child has been, is being, or is likely to be abused, neglected or harmed. Substantiations might occur where there is no suitable caregiver, as a child may have been abandoned or their parents are deceased.

It is important to accurately record relevant specific and general circumstances surrounding risk of harm in accordance with state legislation, service policies and procedures and ethics.

Other information to consider:
- Services involved with the child/family, if known
- Culture/principal language of the family and whether an elder or interpreter for spoken or signed language is required
- Whether a parent knows of the report and their response
- If a child or young person knows about the report and their views

Once a report is made to child protection services, no further report needs to be made – unless new information comes to hand. Child protection departments will undertake a risk assessment to professionally analyse the child's exposure to risk and their potential needs.

What to include in a report

If you devise a template of your own, aim to provide as much information as possible, because the information will be critical to any reports and may be sought at a later date if the matter is the subject of court proceedings. These notes may also later assist you if you are required to provide evidence to support any decisions.

Information provided to child protection when a report is made needs to be sufficiently detailed for child protection to identify the child at risk of harm – documentation is critical.

Refer to Appendix 6 to see what to include in a child protection report.

Use non-judgemental writing in reports

Reports need to make sure they give the reader enough information to support the cause of the writing. In the case of the protection of children and young people, it is vital these kinds of reports have clarity, objectivity, accuracy and facts to bring about credibility.

CLARITY assists the reader to understand your message through the information you provide.

OBJECTIVITY is essential when writing details for documenting concerns and reports. It is important to ensure you remain objective, which means awareness of any potential biases that may relate to a child, young person, the child's family, gender, race, ethnicity, religion, sexual orientation, disability, cultural/community child-rearing practices or socioeconomic status. Formulating reports as a professional means you will be adhering to the ethical framework the sector commits to. There are boundaries that are grounded in principles of social justice to ensure respect and fairness is granted to all groups you engage with. Your actions and decision-making need to be non-judgemental with a non-biased response, which will be the best care for the child/ren and/or young people. Despite distress you may feel towards a child or young person's abuse or neglect, you may be faced with dilemmas that require you to ensure you act within the parameters of your professional role. To support you with responsibilities as a professional, the service will have comprehensive systems and processes to ensure you succeed in facilitating the required help and support to everyone involved. Assistance may be required for immediate families, extended families, co-educators and, of course, yourself.

ACCURACY/FACTS ensure the correct information is given in a sequential manner. Writing a report in a professional manner will mean that you will have relevant, skilfully sound responses, which will be critical elements of a dependable report.

CREDIBILITY is what you want a report to be to ensure it is effective in maximising opportunities for the safety, wellbeing and development of children or young people who have been harmed or who are at risk of harm. The report needs to be impartial and free of any opinion and presumptions. Accuracy, clear and thorough detail will facilitate a credible report because the quality of the information gathered and recorded will form the basis of your reasonable suspicion.

To show your writing is objective rather than subjective – if something has happened and the writer or speaker is simply relaying that information, they are making simple statements of fact. Be explicit in expressing yourself, for example, 'three' instead of 'a few'; 'in 2020' instead of 'a while ago'. Use controlled language, instead of opinionated, prejudiced or emotional language, for example, instead of writing 'Parents who smoke abuse their children', write 'Research indicates second-hand smoke has some harmful effects on children's health'.

To help determine the relevance of information, think of *why* you think the information is relevant and you will see if it fits reasonable grounds for inclusion:

- Avoid words that appear to exaggerate.
- Avoid 'intensifying adverbs' that tend to give this impression, i.e. 'very', 'awful'.
- Avoid excessive use of pronouns, i.e. he, she, they, etc; use people's names more frequently.
- Words like 'probably' or 'possibly' do not create confidence for the reader.
- Avoid generalisations and evaluative words that are based on non-professional judgements and feelings, such as 'badly', 'disappointment', 'amazing', etc.
- Hearsay, information from a third party that is not directly witnessed is not noteworthy.
- Stay factual, as conclusions based on inkling or opinion are not significant.

Be specific and factual because opinions allow room for others to disagree:

- Avoid the personal pronoun 'I' – write more impersonally, for example, 'I have observed' or 'I have been informed', instead of 'I think' or 'I believe'. Stating 'I believe' or 'In my opinion' infers expertise or specialisation you may not have and knowledge you may not possess. Adding such personal comments almost seems to emphasise that the writing is just your opinion or interpretation, rather than positions that are supported by the evidence.
- Avoid such things as 's/he did not want to', 'she thought', 'he feels' or 'they were trying to'. This form of writing supposes the writer knows the feelings of the person as opposed to what they have expressed.

You must notify the regulatory authority for your jurisdiction within 24 hours of becoming aware of a serious incident.

Table 5: Process for heads of organisations to notify and report in Victoria

Term	Meaning
Injury	You must notify the Commission within three business days of becoming aware of a reportable allegation.
Notifiable incident	You must investigate an allegation – subject to police clearance on criminal matters or matters involving family violence. You must advise the Commission who is undertaking the investigation. You must manage the risks to children.
Serious incident	Within 30 calendar days, you must provide the Commission detailed information about the reportable allegation and any action you have taken.
Trauma	You must notify the Commission of the investigation findings and any disciplinary action the head of entity has taken (or the reasons no action was taken).

Ensure maximum effectiveness of the report

Work collaboratively with relevant agencies to ensure maximum effectiveness of the report, by exploring appropriate support services for the child/young person and their family.

Access the National Office for Child Safety website, as it is useful for accessing a range of resources and tools, such as *Speak up and make a complaint* (see www.childsafety.pmc.gov.au). This includes a written guide and videos containing examples of how to respond when a child raises a concern. Guidance is also available to support organisations to understand their important role.

Be as detailed as possible. The information you provide is central to the decision-making process, further action and help to the child and family.

(Note: You can exchange information about the safety, welfare and wellbeing of a child or young person (or a class of children or young people) with prescribed bodies such as colleagues or with other workers that you know are also working with the child/young person or family. Care and protection acts in your jurisdiction will support the sharing of information under professional circumstances.)

Professionals working together

The benefit of professional networking is:
- To help build and change your understanding about the level of risk and protective factors for the child/young person and their family
- Planning how any known risks to children and young people may be minimised and monitored
- Identifying what resources and services could be offered to the family
- Finding who is best placed to further discuss the concerns with the family and offering them referrals and support
- It can assist with coordinated service delivery and decision-making
- Providing advice on exchanging information about the safety, welfare and wellbeing of children and young people with others to coordinate services and supports

Information may be shared to make an assessment, coordinate decision-making or planning, initiate or conduct any investigation, or provide any service. Discuss with all clients as early as possible that you may need to share information with other service providers to work together to address the safety, welfare or wellbeing of the child or young person.

Collaborating with agencies enables responsiveness to children and families. Support agencies understand that every family is different; they are experienced in catering to the diverse needs of local communities. Support providers will take time to talk to families and understand their situation. A family can ask for an interpreter if they need one. If needed, the family support agencies can develop a plan in partnership with the family to help connect them to the right services at the right time and will often stay connected with the family if there's a wait for services.

Aboriginal children, young people and families are a priority for programmes. Aboriginal families can ask to be connected with an Aboriginal worker or referred to an Aboriginal service.

If you are aware that a child/young person is already participating in intervention but the current intervention is not having a positive impact, a Child Wellbeing Unit in your jurisdiction should be made aware. For example, the University of Melbourne has a Child and Community Wellbeing Unit that has a primary focus to:

"Build evidence about systemic and service-based opportunities to promote positive health and wellbeing for children and their families; and to support communities to thrive in times of stability and to adapt and grow in response to disruption" (Tarpey-Brown 2022).

Early intervention can save lives. There is strong reasoning for identifying abuse. Despite major impacts on children's brain patterns from violence, the brain is always changing and evolving according to what it is learning. The neuron pathways in the brain *can* be changed over time, through awareness, practice and patience. But it takes speaking up to begin the journey of repair.

In summary

With this chapter complete, you should now know that:
- Acting on abuse indicators is significant.
- Neurological effects increase from not reporting child abuse and neglect.
- All concerns about the safety and wellbeing of a child should be acted upon as soon as is practicable.
- All concerns about the conduct of a staff member, contractor or volunteer should be acted upon as soon as is practicable.
- Anyone can report – there are no restrictions encroaching on who can communicate concerns to authorities for children's welfare.
- You contact Child Protection Intake covering the local government area where the child lives.

Chapter 4 reflection questions

- Does your service have readily available the *National Framework for Protecting Australia's Children 2021–2031*?
- Are you a professional who is mandated to report?
- Are you familiar with your Code of Conduct? Does it include unacceptable behaviour?
- Do you work in a jurisdiction that has a Reportable Conduct Scheme? Does your organisation have a clear process for reporting concerns about fellow employees?
- Is your service aware of Information Sharing Schemes?
- Do you have multiple ways to report concerns, such as email, template and phone and to document concerns?
- Could you sensitively initiate a conversation about suspicions and respond appropriately (i.e. seeking secondary consultations, referring clients and sharing information)?
- Would you know the best way to react if a child discloses abuse to you?
- Do you know who your local support networks are to support all families?

PART TWO
CHAPTER 5

Child safety – working in the forefront mitigating risk

Insight for educators/practitioners:

- How to build capacity to be child safe
- Individually contextualising a child safe framework

Chapter elements:

- What is a culture of child safety?
- How does child safety differ from child protection?
- Intentions, statements, policies and practices
- Human resource practices
- Physical environments
- Online environments

Children's safety and wellbeing is what we should be manifesting, but that requires advocacy in our inner thoughts, as well as our actions. We are talking about needing organisations to take on a leadership model that truly values children – but one that is flexible. Organisations that continuously strive to enhance procedures and acknowledge that systemic changes are critical will have a greater chance at mitigating risk.

'Tactile infiltration' is how Grace Tame, advocate for survivors of sexual assault, describes abuse, and we need to eradicate the prevalence of such acts. To effectively do this, Grace highlighted the need to *"Know your perpetrators because they are sophisticated, calculated criminals, who can look like anyone and offenders can get into your 'ecosystem' and use it to abuse"* (2022).

As early childhood professionals, we want to act in good judgement, especially if we are part of the management team of a children's service, because persons in charge often set the trajectory taken towards children's welfare. Regardless of the role we are appointed to, whether it be an approved provider and/or nominated supervisor of a children's service, a room leader, casual relief person or volunteer, we are all pledged to uphold the rights and safety of children.

What is a culture of child safety?

This means that protection against abuse is principally considered in all facets of service provision – by everybody. Having a zero tolerance of child abuse means that keeping children safe is the top priority if a service is committed to being a child safe organisation. If we are adhering to this responsibility as an individual within a team of people, it makes sense that the *entire* centre community acts with children's wellbeing dominating thoughts and decision-making, and therefore the organisational culture will take on a *zero tolerance* to abuse and neglect. Furthermore, the new Victorian Child Safe Standards require children's services to make explicit a zero tolerance to racism, which of course means a zero stance on bullying and discrimination.

All children and young people who attend services, events, programmes and spaces in the community have the right to feel and be safe, and to be heard. Children have a right to safety – emotionally, physically, culturally and even spiritually. *"In a child safe organisation, children, young people, family and community members feel that their culture and identity are respected"* (SNAICC, 2021).

"Everyone has a role to play in keeping children safe from harm. Harm can take many forms, such as accidental injury, exposure to physical hazards, bullying by peers, neglect, emotional abuse, physical abuse and sexual abuse" (Australian Human Rights Commission, 2021).

When you are aiming to create and maintain a culture of child safety, your attitude to children's welfare becomes first and foremost, and from that your governance must reflect this ethos as your first and foremost priority. Working in the forefront means taking the reins and being proactive in making a commitment to children's safety and wellbeing. Putting policies and procedures in place, embedding them, reviewing them, adjusting and creating more, are all part of the ongoing journey for quality improvement.

According to the Australian Human Rights Commission, a child safe organisation is one that actively *"creates an environment where children's safety and wellbeing are the centre of the organisation's inspiration, values and actions".*

How does child safety differ from child protection?

To put it simply, if an organisation has a culture of child safety, it works in a proactive way to anticipate potential harm and investigates activeness, instead of reacting in damage control once suspicions have arisen. This means there is an informed approach to:
- **Safeguard** against the risk of child abuse
- **Respond** effectively if abuse is suspected or confirmed

Child protection training

Child protection training informs educators about what to do if they suspect a child is being abused and/or neglected – understanding obligations, knowing how to identify signs of abuse, responding to concerns about the wellbeing of a child and knowing how to report abuse. This content is instructing educators on how to pick up on child abuse and neglect, and what actions need to be taken. Essentially, this information is vital, but it is information in retrospect, meaning after incident/s have transpired. What we want to do is reposition ourselves to be proactive and work fiercely from the forefront.

The Australian and New Zealand Children's Commissioners and Guardians meet regularly to promote and protect the safety, wellbeing and rights of children and young people in Australia and New Zealand. In their initial establishment, a series of actions were created so that organisations could use the principles as a framework for embedding a culture of child safety into their environments. Now, both Australia and New Zealand have their own 10 principles to help increase awareness and understanding around safeguarding.

The National Principles are underpinned by a child rights, strengths-based approach to child safe organisations, and are designed to be flexible so that all sectors that engage with children and young people, and organisations of different sizes, can implement them.

The National Principles collectively show that a child safe organisation is one that:
- Creates a culture of safety
- Adopts strategies and takes action
- Promotes child wellbeing
- Prevents harm to children and young people
- Creates an environment where children's safety and wellbeing are at the centre of inspiration, values and actions
- Places emphasis on genuine engagement with, and valuing of, children
- Creates conditions that reduce the likelihood of harm to children and young people
- Creates conditions that increase the likelihood of identifying any harm
- Responds to any concerns, disclosures, allegations or suspicions
- Creates child-friendly mechanisms for a child's voice to be heard

(Australian Human Rights Commission, 2021)

Refer back to page 39 for Australia's National Principles for Child Safe Organisations.

Clearly defining and clarifying roles and responsibilities between different levels of the organisation will improve internal processes and enable people to interconnect. This keeps the workings within organisations transparent. When you are aware of the ins and outs of the entire organisational flow, it is easier to detect systemic faults and failures, and work together to improve them. These gaps are danger zones, which could be things like a poorly written Code of Conduct, a Commitment to Child Safety that doesn't include online environments or failing to have an anti-bias approach to interviewing potential employees – these are just a few of what could be many examples. A collaborative approach to operations means more people working together to identify and eliminate these pockets of potential harm.

Intentions, statements, policies and practices

Children's wellbeing depends very much on their ability to feel safe – and be safe. Principles and standards are certainly useful to lay down the fundamentals for safer organisations. It is, however, up to individual children's services to articulate these measures into their policies and practices and execute them in the context of their own service type. Good intentions won't keep children safe. Reconsider the opportunties for all stakeholders to give feedback and ideas to facilitate true consultation.

Commitment to Child Safety

To set the scene for your ethos around child safety and formalise one of the underlying foundations of your organisational philosophy, a Commitment to Child Safety should be created (with all stakeholders, inclusive of children) and placed on display in order to make your declaration explicit to the public.

The individual service can outline safety measures as part of its service protocols in other governing documents, such as the Code of Conduct and Child Safe Environment and Wellbeing Policy, but this Commitment document should be inclusive and succinct – it's a statement. If we refer to dictionary definitions, a statement is short, sharp and concise.

How to write a statement

1. Identify your ultimate objective, what you want to accomplish with your statement: a message to the public that explicitly states the organisation's commitment to children's safety and wellbeing and mitigation of harm.
2. Write an introduction.
3. Write the body.
4. Create a strong conclusion, which may include a zero tolerance for abuse, bullying, discrimination and/or racism.

To see an example of a Commitment to Child Safety, refer to Appendix 7, where you will see a universal commitment statement that I wrote for an organisation that has children's services across Australia in varying states and territories, and therefore uses key phrases to encompass the range of legislative requirements as well as wording that would promote best practice.

In addition, you could go to the NAPCAN website (www.napcan.org.au) and read its Commitment Statement to Children and Young People. This example outlines how NAPCAN enhances child wellbeing and safety within its organisation. This concise statement echoes children's rights to feeling and being safe with a strong reference to the UNCRC (NAPCAN, 2020).

I am contemplating how we can action ideas for making Commitments to Child Safety an organisation's message that can be universally understood. I'm thinking that visuals could, and should, accompany the Statement of Commitment.

In the new Victorian Child Safe Standards, Child Safe Standard 3 reads: *"Children and young people are informed about all of their rights, including to safety, information and participation."* We cannot *"develop a culture that facilitates participation and is responsive to the input of children and young people"* if the commitment is not provided in a child-friendly way.

A Statement of Commitment to Child Safety needs to be accessible and clear to interpret, especially to children. Translated Commitment Statements, the use of visuals, audio and many other media types could be used to creatively reveal this powerful message.

Child Safety and Wellbeing Policy

A Child Safety and Wellbeing Policy is what organisations create for the framework of the implementation of their Commitment to Child Safety. The benefit of having such a policy means that it is clear, regardless of your role, and regardless of the laws in the jurisdiction in which the service is operating – that the service will do everything in its power to protect children from harm.

A comprehensive Child Safety and Wellbeing Policy would clearly state that it relates to all employees, contractors, agency staff, volunteers and visitors, regardless of whether they work in direct contact with children or young people. This policy would apply across all environments.

To accommodate a children's service's existing child protection policy, as well as the Statement of Commitment, what is common nowadays is to have an all-encompassing policy such as a Child Safety and Wellbeing Policy. This is a more favourable option (many national and international services have updated their policies and altered the title and content accordingly) because emotional welfare influences how secure one feels in an environment.

You will see where we discussed regulatory authorities in Chapter 3 that Victoria has to comply with 11 new Child Safe Standards; one of these compliance indicators in Standard 2 is that services are required to have a Child Safety and Wellbeing policy implemented.

"*Under the* Education and Care Services National Regulations (2011, SI 653), *an approved provider must ensure that policies and procedures are in place with inclusion of incident, injury, trauma and illness, providing a child safe environment, a Code of Conduct for staff members, interactions with children with a sub-reference to relationships with children (regulation 168) and take reasonable steps to ensure those policies and procedures are followed (regulation 170)*" (ACECQA, 2021).

In my discussions with national bodies such as the Quality Assessment and Regulation Division and the Early Learning Association Australia, it is acceptable to combine this state requirement (for ensuring services have a Child Safety and Wellbeing Policy) and the Education and Care National

Regulations requirement (a Child Safe Environment Policy). Both these policy requirements will indicate the *environmental* conditions to promote children's safety and wellbeing. But regardless of this fact, it is preferred that the word 'environment' remains in the policy title, because that is what policy title is specifically indicated under Education and Care Regulation 168. A Child Safe Environment and Wellbeing Policy is a good example of a title that would fit the criterion.

(Note: If a service does not wish to combine national and state requirements into the one policy for child safety and wellbeing, you would keep a Child Safe Environment Policy and create a Child Safety and Wellbeing Policy. A proficient Child Safety and Wellbeing Policy will stipulate procedures to facilitate a child's good health (wellbeing) and include proactive abuse-prevention procedures and strategies. This is more than just outlining the steps that need to be taken if concerns arise.)

The Australian Human Rights Commission *Child Safety and Wellbeing Policy* (Australian Human Rights Commission, 2020) outlines the commitment to making its workplace and work safe for children. You can download a copy of its policy from its website (www.humanrights.gov.au). You can see how the Human Rights Commission implements the 10 National Principles for Child Safe Organisations into its Child Safety and Wellbeing Policy.

The headings and what you could include are outlined below:
- **Policy title** – organisation name followed by child safety and wellbeing policy
- **Policy purpose** – inform? Give guidance on Commitment to Child Safety
- **Policy scope** – who and what it applies to – should apply to everyone and all experiences in accordance with the organisation
- **Responsibilities** – this might articulate key roles, i.e. director, approved provider and the tasks they are responsible for implementing, such as recruitment and screening
- **Definitions** – of key terms in the policy, such as volunteer, child, harm
- **Statement of Commitment to Child Safety** – the organisation's statement

- **Relevant legislation and standards** – references/links to legislation relevant to the organisation, i.e. Victorian Child Safe Standards, National Principles for Child Safe Organisations
- **Related organisational policies and procedures** – Code of Conduct, Complaints Policy, Information Sharing Policy, Zero Tolerance of Racism Policy, Cultural Safety for Aboriginal Children and Families Policy, Online Environments Policy, Equity and Inclusion Policy; you might include the statements affiliated with these policies and state that the Child Safety and Wellbeing Policy needs to be read with those you outline as they are interrelated
- **Commitment to recruitment and ongoing training** – to maintain a culture of child safety; how this will be undertaken, for example, monthly check-in until three-month appraisal
- **Commitment to review the Child Safety and Wellbeing Policy and Procedures** – include stakeholder consultation inclusive of children and ensure inclusive tools are stipulated to facilitate fair and equitable processes as well as the protocols for informing community on outcomes

This is a good example to guide you in how you could set out a policy for your organisation. Remember, this sample refers to the National Principles for Child Safe Organisations, so you want to include standards you are governed by in your jurisdiction. The Child Safety Commitment, as well as the policies to support child safety, should include a commitment to positive racial identity for children and how the organisation will promote cultural safety. For example, in Victoria, Standard 1 of the new Victorian Child Safe Standards states:

"Policies and procedures, including the Child Safety and Wellbeing Policy, describe the organisation's expectations and provide detailed guidance about actions staff, volunteers and leaders must take to establish a culturally safe environment in which the diverse and unique identities and experiences of Aboriginal children are respected and valued."

For further information on this, go to the CCYP website (www.ccyp.vic.gov.au) and read through the *Guide for Creating a Child Safe Organisation*.

A Code of Conduct

To influence positive interactions with all those affiliated with an organisation, a Code of Conduct is created. Once again, just like with the Commitment to Child Safety, the Child Safety and Wellbeing Policy or Child Safe Environment and Wellbeing Policy, a Code of Conduct would clearly state that it relates to all employees, contractors, agency staff, visitors and volunteers, regardless of whether they work in direct contact with children or young people. A Code of Conduct is a governing policy that would apply across all environments – both physical, on-site or off-site (inclusive of online) because it affirms the organisation's commitment to legal and ethical principles, by making clear that all people are required to abide by this code, behaving professionally and with respect and consideration for others.

Professional boundaries are explicit in sector Codes of Ethics (i.e. ECA Code of Ethics, VIT Code of Ethics and Code Conduct) and are reiterated in the individual service codes of conduct (making explicit the service name the rules apply to).

Statements will often include: 'Adults must be conscious that their position requires them to maintain professional boundaries. Interactions with children/students can extend beyond the children's service/school environment, including outside of children's service/school hours, outside of children's service/school grounds and by any medium of technology (including social media).'

This code applies regardless of the location of where interaction occurs. Intentions for the code will often be outlined in the introduction by stating the code is intended to complement child safety legislation, the children's service/school's policies in relation to child safety and wellbeing, inclusive of mandatory reporting and reportable conduct.

Regardless of the service type, a Code of Conduct will clearly outline, in the scope, who must adhere. An example of how this could be worded is:
- This code applies to all employees, school council, direct and indirect volunteers, third-party contractors, external education providers, consultants, parents/carers and visitors.
- Adults at the organisation are expected to actively contribute to a culture of child safety and wellbeing, to observe child safe principles

(or adhere to Child Safe Standards) and expectations for appropriate behaviour towards, and in the company of, children/students as set out in this code.
- The code applies to all aspects of an adult's engagement with the children's service/school and its children/students in the school environment.

You may want to develop a separate Code of Conduct specifically for use by children and young people (child-friendly versions, previously referred to).

The Australian Childhood Foundation has a series of recordings on its website (www.childhood.org.au) under 'Safeguarding Children Foundational Knowledge': *"You need a Strong Code of Conduct to Protect Children and act in the interests of children."*

When describing the Code of Conduct, the Australian Childhood Foundation refers to it as *"more than a document that is created to prevent abuse"*. It is *one* element of the Child Protection Policy. The extensiveness of this document will determine the strength and commitment to children, so it 'speaks to the culture' of the service community.

How do you create a strong Code of Conduct?

A Code of Conduct is a continuum of behaviour that shapes staff, volunteers as well as service users by outlining your proactive commitment to quality and safety of others, particularly children. It needs to:
- Be an expression of who you want to be as a service
- Specify behaviours expected from ourselves and others
- Indicate commitment to respectful relationships with each other and service users
- Speak the language of the service so it reflects the culture (beliefs/values)
- Be clear so that staff and volunteers know what is required to uphold it
- Attend to the needs and beliefs of users so it is inclusive
- Indicate how children's rights will be respected and upheld
- Incorporate the engagement of service users, voices of children
- Reveal how open and transparent you as a service will be

A Code of Conduct should be developed by identifying the risks to children's safety that are unique to your organisation. Some risks are the same across organisations, but others will be unique to your setting.

To assess whether your Code of Conduct covers everything, ask yourself – and consult with your stakeholders – to determine if it:

- Provides adults with a clear guide on the behaviour that is expected of them, and of the behaviours that are unacceptable
- Provides guidance to support the organisation's community to recognise unacceptable or concerning behaviour
- Outlines the action your organisation will take if there is a breach of the code (clearly indicate what consequences may include)
- States that it applies to all adults working or volunteering in an organisation

It is important to highlight positive child safe behaviours, that we encourage all adults to support, as well as identify behaviours that we consider unacceptable. Engaging in unacceptable behaviour is a breach of the Code of Conduct and may result in disciplinary action, including and up to termination of employment or engagement. It should be explicit that the organisation has a zero tolerance to the breaching of its Code of Conduct.

The website of the Office of the Children's Guardian in New South Wales (www.ocg.nsw.gov.au) has a very thorough guide to developing child-safe Codes of Conduct, inclusive of a sample and a template: *Codes of Conduct: a guide to developing child safe Codes of Conduct* (2020).

When working in the forefront, it is paramount that the Statement of Commitment (sometimes the term Charter of Commitment is used), Child Safety and Wellbeing Policy and the Code of Conduct are shared among the service community prior to engagement, whatever that capacity is – volunteer, permanent, even relief agency educator or student. This information needs to be worked into both verbal and nonverbal communication *prior* to a person/family commencing at the service.

Organisations are increasingly providing a range of accessible Codes of Conduct, which describe what kinds of behaviour are expected from them. This helps children recognise what is expected and what is unacceptable behaviour for adults. Children can also participate in the creation or review of Codes of Conduct. If necessary, the creation of codes of those with accessibility needs should be considered.

This key organisational information should be clear in all means of hard and soft copies of handbooks, induction and orientation guides, and social media/websites should also entail this information, in addition to stating they should be read in accordance with any other relevant policies pertaining to the safety and wellbeing of children.

Many services will ask the stakeholder (employee, parent, carer) to sign the Child Safety and Wellbeing Policy and Code of Conduct to indicate they are not only aware of what the document is saying, but they are signing to indicate they formally agree to comply with the standard of demeanour outlined and will uphold the commitment to children's safety and acknowledge that behaviour that falls below this benchmark is not acceptable and carries serious consequences.

For an example of what a Code of Conduct Agreement could look like, see Appendix 8.

To see a list of what positive behaviours and unacceptable behaviours (misconduct) and concerning behaviours could include, and how they could be grouped according to the type of abuse, refer to Appendix 9.

Consultation should take place at all draft stages and once complete, the Statement of Commitment, Child Safety and Wellbeing Policy, complaints procedure and Code of Conduct should be communicated publicly to raise awareness, and to demonstrate your organisation's commitment to protecting children from abuse.

The Institute of Community Directors Australia has extensive information on Child Safety Policy and Code of Conduct on its website (www.communitydirectors.com.au).

Human resource practices

Inducting new staff and volunteers to requirements

Consider nominating a child-safety champion at your children's service, and create a Child Safety Team, which includes representatives from all stakeholders. Provide an induction for all child safety leadership (child safety officer/champion and/or teams), who can then assist with induction and training programmes for staff, volunteers and children. A thorough induction would cover:

- The Commitment to Child Safety with a greater focus on the cultural safety and inclusion of Aboriginal children as well as other children who could be considered marginalised
- The children's service's Child Safe (Environment) and Wellbeing Policy (or other policies that need to be read in conjunction with this policy)
- The service's Code of Conduct
- The education and care services complaints procedure/s
- The service's policy and procedures for responding to child safety concerns
- Reporting obligations internal and external
- Signs of harm and risk factors caused by peers or adults (including grooming and family violence)
- The different ways children express concerns or disclose harm
- How to build and maintain culturally safe environments
- Privacy, information sharing and record-keeping obligations
- How to help children know their rights, express their views, raise concerns and make a complaint

Wellbeing eventuates from positive interactions with the sources that surround children. A strong sense of belonging comes from feeling safe and being recognised as important, which forms stronger attachments. Chapter 1 talked about equity for people who could be vulnerable. How we endeavour to welcome prospective children and their families implies a level of acceptance. *"We need to be really mindful of what message of welcome we are providing in our indirect means of communication."*

Cultural considerations

"Culture underpins and is integral to safety and wellbeing for all cultures with a strong motivation to embrace the culture of our First Nations people, inclusive of Aboriginal and Torres Strait Islander children. Cultural consideration needs should be embedded in organisational leadership, governance and daily operations for holistic respect" (SNAICC, 2021).

Reflect on whether:
- Your physical spaces are welcoming, can accommodate and are inclusive of families and broader kinship networks
- Do you help to celebrate children's cultural identity, which is more than just being aware?
- Does the physical environment reflect Aboriginal and Torres Strait Islander culture with relevance to the local community?

Your organisation should ask children, families and the local community how they would like to see their culture reflected in the physical environment. For example, displaying an acknowledgment of Traditional Owners, having flag representation, authentic Aboriginal and Torres Strait Islander artwork, having a Reconciliation Action Plan, undertaking Acknowledgements of Country, so there is an authentic and organic representation throughout the service inclusive of provisions for the children's programmes.

Consider respectful consultation to provide feedback on policies and to inform management about how your organisation could improve in child and cultural safety. Listening to children's views to improve activities and processes is powerful in gaining an authentic understanding of your service provision. Developing avenues for children to provide advice to the board/executive level is a great strategy to consider, for example, establishment of a child council and/or inclusion of children on the board. Involving management in training is also a key aspect of building cultural awareness and enhancing safety across the entire organisation.

To assist with respectful engagement with stakeholders, refer to Appendix 1: Glossary of key terms and definitions.

Resources

There are a number of organisations that can support your respectful interactions with queer children and their families so that you can recognise and celebrate the strength, resilience and diversity of LGBTIQA+ communities. Differentiation between sex and gender is important and is explained in 'LGBTQIAP+: We help you understand 23 gender terms' (Turner, 2019).

You can access online resources such as a *LGBTQIAP+ Etiquette Guide and Glossary of Terms* as well as a range of child and family community strengthening downloadable resources for schools and childcare centres at the #StrongSafeFabulous website (www.strongsafefabulous.online).

Ensure Aboriginal and Torres Strait Islander children's rights – including cultural rights – are reflected in operational procedures across your organisation. Implement changes to policies and practices to improve cultural safety for Aboriginal and Torres Strait Islander children. Reconciliation Victoria recommends children's services undertake cultural safety assessments to determine where they are at to tailor professional development. *"We must address the underlying causes of culturally unsafe practice"* (Victorian Government, Department of Health, 2021).

There are a few accessible self-assessment tools available online to help determine your organisation's engagement and cultural safety, such as the NSW Health Service's website (www.health.nsw.gov.au), which has the *Aboriginal Cultural Engagement Self-Assessment Tool.*

Indigenous Health Northern Health's website has a document titled *CULTURAL SAFETY AND SYSTEM CHANGE: An Assessment Tool,* which is a great resource to build your capacity to understand what supports cultural safety (see www.indigenoushealthnh.ca). One of many concepts explained is 'cultural humility' being *"A life-long process of self-reflection and self-critique. It is foundational to achieving a culturally safe environment."*

You can access an Aboriginal and Torres Strait Islander cultural safety framework at the Victorian Government's website (www.health.vic.gov.au).

The Reggio Emilia Approach always saw education to be a political act: *"We can never underestimate our advocacy for children and their childhoods through the design of our daily contexts; with children, with families, and with colleagues and communities"* (2020).

It is important to use commitments evident in policies and practices and Codes of Conduct to provide clear guidance to all stakeholders about their responsibilities in upholding culturally safe and welcoming environments. This includes physical environments as well as beyond the grounds of your education and care service, inclusive of online environments to advocate for a zero tolerance for abuse, discrimination and racism. Working in the forefront needs to include both physical as well as online environments.

Physical environments

Risk management strategies focus on preventing, identifying and mitigating risks to children and young people. It is customary that prior to undertaking any outing, internal event or experience, a risk assessment is to be carried out and permission granted from parents or legal guardians. Teams need to ensure that they broaden their definition of physical injury to include the potential for abuse to take place, for example, when taking a group of children on an excursion to the local community garden. Measures would need to be taken to ensure children are kept safe when being around other members of the public, who might be present at this public location. A proactive risk-minimisation strategy could be arranging with the local swimming pool to enable private access to one of their changerooms for the duration that you take your group to the pool for swimming lessons. This preventative measure enables the safer use of toilets and changeroom facilities, to minimise risk of harm to children when un/dressing. An additional consideration (and policy practice) might be that only staff monitors changerooms, and parent helpers assist in other ways that do not involve children un/dressing.

Active supervision 'helps to protect children from hazards or harm that may arise from their play and daily routines'. We need to explicitly highlight to all educators that this statement must include 'other human beings as a possible hazard', and 'harm' can be by way of physical abuse and neglect. What we also need to articulate is the process of undertaking a risk matrix to determine the positioning of staff and children, and the opportunities that could arise that might expose children to a situation where they could be harmed.

Observing children to prevent physical harm is something educators apply to their roles in children's services, but we need to grow accustomed to what could be detrimental to their children's welfare in relation to abuse.

To minimise the chances of harm coming to children, competent supervision and rich engagement are essential. Some strategies include:
- Careful planning of rosters ought to – at the very minimal – maintain and, wherever possible, exceed adult-to-child ratios.
- Flexible supervision is needed to meet the dynamic nature of children's services, for example, individual children needing to retreat inside to eat and sleep.

- Scanning or regularly looking around the area to observe all children in the environment ensures that all children are actively supervised.
- Educators who are aware of the environment can identify appropriate positions for maximum vision of children to enable engagement with them.
- Educators should avoid standing with their backs to children and undertaking tasks that will distract them from supervising children.
- Listening carefully to children and noting any changes of tone or volume in their voice can assist in supervising children who may not be in direct vision.
- Three-way mirrors can boost visibility in blind spots, such as seeing around corners.
- Evaluating situations to determine the potential risks and benefits for children's health, safety and wellbeing is vital, as is undertaking Risk Assessments with children where possible, and embracing positive risk assessments in supporting children to challenge their own abilities.
- Observing children's play and anticipating what may occur next allows educators to assist children as difficulties arise and to intervene when there is a potential danger to children.
- Promoting peer collaboration and a culture of speaking up enables children to get the support and advocate for the wellbeing of their friends.
- Effective communication between co-educators and contacting leadership teams aids in additional support if difficulties arise.
- Ensuring IT platforms are used as an additional measure for head counting and monitoring children arriving and departing the service is important.

Let me share with you an example of being alert and the importance of active supervision in an unexpected situation. At an early-learning service in one of the outdoor areas, a drain needed to be attended to by plumbers. There were children playing outside at this time and they were accessing the adjacent bathroom area. A teacher noticed the tradespeople entering the outdoor environment. She not only moved swiftly to close the toilet door in an attempt to 'uphold the (children's) right to privacy', but additionally ensured she explained to children her reasoning for closing the door and diverting access to a nearby bathroom. These combined actions support the preventative education to children about body safety/protective behaviours (which we look at in Chapter 7).

In Tasmania, Child Protective Services hold Signs of Safety meetings – a very proactive measure designed to talk about how to make sure a child is safe. Anyone who cares about a child and their family can attend the meetings. During a meeting, four key questions are asked, and everyone is encouraged to contribute:
1. What are we worried about in relation to the child and the family?
2. What is working well in the family?
3. What needs to happen to make sure the child is safe in the future?
4. How safe is the child, from zero (very dangerous for the child) to 10 (the child is safe)?

One of the outcomes of the Signs of Safety meeting may be the development of a Safety Plan. A Safety Plan works out how to make sure a child is safe. It is also about who will be involved in the care and future safety of the child.

The insight in this chapter can be used as a catalyst for working in the forefront – making a commitment to children's safety. It is important we remember these protective measures need to be implemented into all of our environments.

Online environments

Children may be at greater risk of harassment in online spaces. Ensure your organisation implements measures to mitigate these risks, such as actively monitoring and filtering harmful content and putting in place the highest-level privacy settings. Also ensure that all stakeholders (inclusive of children) are trained in online safety. Share and discuss policies and strategies concerning physical and online environments to adhere to a terms of use for the children's service.

Organisations are increasingly establishing new methods to engage online through videoconferences, online platforms and social media forums, or over the phone.

Provided the right safeguards are put in place, technologies can be used safely and in line with the Child Safe Standards as well as National Principles for Child Safety. However, a shift to greater online- and phone-based services presents several risks to child safety that need to be managed. These include:
- Increased opportunities for unwanted or unsupervised contact with children
- Opportunities for grooming children and young people
- Potential growth in cyberbullying and abuse such as 'trolling'
- Risks of exposure to inappropriate, illicit or explicit content or imagery
- Access to content that is not age appropriate
- Possible breaches of privacy, including sharing of personal or sensitive information or personal images
- Scams targeting children and young people

There are a number of organisations that support the protection of children online in relation to inappropriate behaviour. The Australian Centre to Counter Child Exploitation is active in preventing "*the use of technology to facilitate the sexual abuse of a child, including the production or sharing of child sexual abuse material online*". Its website (www.accce.gov.au) has a section for parents and carers, which includes a range of resources such as of its latest publication, *Jack Changes the Game*. This is a children's picture book about staying safer online. In a "*first-of-its-kind for law enforcement*", the e-book was developed by the Australian Federal Police with the support of a reference group comprising some of Australia's leading experts in child protection.

There is an educator-specific section of the eSafety Commissioner website (www.esafety.gov.au/educators). The eSafety Early Years programme is designed to help early childhood educators, parents and carers improve online safety for our youngest Australians. eSafety offers a range of resources and online safety programmes for professionals free of charge as well as educational online safety videos with supporting teaching materials.

eSafety and ECA have joined forces to create a series of online professional learning modules especially for early childhood educators. There are three modules that focus on different types of digital contexts;

they identify the risks associated with them and look at how these risks can be mitigated. They are as follows:

- **We SAY and SHARE with technology** – this module examines the benefits and risks associated with using technologies as a communication tool.
- **We MAKE and DO using technology** – this one explores the uses and risks of technology as a tool for creation.
- **We WATCH and EXPLORE on technology** – this module explains the benefits and risks associated with using technologies to find out information or for entertainment.

Each module contains practical advice for building good habits as well as self-regulation skills and critical thinking around children's technology use. This is explained through each module in four key messages: be safe; be kind; ask for help; and make good choices.

Directors and managers can access a fourth module on policies and processes designed to ensure a safe online environment in early learning services. It has been created in consultation with ACECQA and aligns with the NQS and Early Years Learning Framework (EYLF) (Early Childhood Australia and the eSafety Commissioner, n.d.). You can access these modules at www.learninghub.earlychildhoodaustralia.org.au

It is important education and care services do not limit accessibility to IT if further learning and social connection can be derived from experiences, i.e. internet research.

A holistic approach

We need to commit to a holistic approach to protection – minimising harm to children as well as knowing how to best support them, who find themselves involved in the system of child protection.

The EYLF conveys the highest expectations for all children's learning – from birth to five years – and contributes to realising the Council of Australian Governments' vision that: *"All children have the best start in life to create a better future for themselves and for the nation."*

This same vision contributes to the development of *My Time, Our Place – Framework for School Age Children*, which aims to extend and enrich children's wellbeing and development in school age care settings (Australian Government, Department of Education, n.d.).

To uphold these visions, we need to work proactively and with relevance to the contextual nature of our service. Australian linkage projects have found that children who have contact with the child protection system were more likely than other children to have contact with the juvenile justice system and homelessness services, and to have lower literacy and numeracy achievement than all students. This information is reflected in the 2015, 2016, 2017 statistics for the AIHW.

Ongoing people management – means regularly checking in to see if individual staff need additional training/information to maintain a high level of understanding in relation to preventing abuse. Child safety proficiency should not wait until a team member has a three-monthly or annual review.

Child safety permanently on the team meeting agenda – will increase the ability to identify gaps in knowledge among teams. This will also create conditions that proactively respond to any complaints, concerns, disclosures, allegations or suspicions. A culture of speaking up and raising concerns is more likely when we keep child safety on the services compliance and quality improvement journey. This approach will reduce the likelihood of maltreatment to the children in your service and prompt continuous attention to remain progressive. Everyone needs to take charge in their local context – everyone, regardless of their role. This has not been the adopted approach by children's services, but it needs to be. A more explicit commitment to child safety is what everyone must adhere to.

Keeping child safety on the Quality Improvement Plan means there will always be key improvements being sought, which will prompt action, feedback and additional goals.

Victoria is required to implement an action plan, which outlines how the service will continue to work towards compliance of all Child Safe Standards, as well as having to outline how the service will build capacity in cultural safety for Aboriginal children. The table opposite shows the beginning stages of how the plan might look like in relation to the layout.

Table 6: New child safe standards action plan

Standard 1 Ensure cultural safety for Aboriginal children	How can we achieve this? Goal/intention	Tools, resources, policies, review what we currently do/utilise	Action/s and who?	When? (i.e. August team meeting check-in)	Progress notes
1.1 A child's ability to express their culture and enjoy their cultural rights is encouraged and actively supported	Establish a culturally safe environment for aboriginal children; commit to being inclusive, responsive, respectful. • Don't assume – there are no Aboriginal or Torres Strait Islander children registered • Be prepared – to be able to support and celebrate the cultural identity of a family that may arrive tomorrow • Celebrate – support children to express their culture and enjoy their cultural rights • Teach perspective • You cannot assess safety unless you are Aboriginal or Torres Strait Islander Build our pedagogy of teaching, learning, knowing, being – A Pedagogy of Place	**SNAICC: Aboriginal and Torres Strait Islander Children's Cultural Needs resource** **VAEAI (vaeai.org.au) Marrung 10-year education plan (2016–26) Koorie education to ensure Koorie Victorians achieve their learning aspirations.** Ensure broad understanding of language. ('Marrung' is the Wemba Wemba word for 'Murray Cypress Pine Tree', representing branches of education and knowledge)	**Signage** to indicate teaching a perspective to share knowledge/ways of knowing in curriculum **Cultural self-reflection** to determine where centre journey is at (Reconciliation Victoria). Identifies gaps/unsafe pockets in organisations. (After pd, re-survey to assess growth in 12 months' time.) **Indigenous plant use** City Boroondara training series on website, Nillumbik Planting in Nillumbik resource, National Environmental Science Programme Indigenous Plant Use **Four core goals of anti-bias education – identity, diversity, justice and activism.**		

If you have specific action plans, like a plan for child safety, you can make reference to them in the Quality Improvement Plan. This means instead of duplicating information, you can reveal a link to the related documents and direct the reader where to go to find the relevant information.

> *If we don't revolutionise our individual constitutions, then we as a sector are enabling – through apathy – systemic abuse in our children's services.*

To begin a commitment, to remodel with a 'proactive approach' to child protection, every service is implored to consider the likelihood of harm occurring at any moment of any day. Every possible risk must be eliminated with a way of thinking and a visual lens focused on 'what could possibly happen'. You need to remember that some of these heinous acts are not premeditated – they are spontaneous, so you need to *eradicate every opportunity* as well as remain attentive to ensure complacency does not open the avenue for a child or children to be taken advantage of.

In summary

With this chapter complete, you should now know that:
- You must scrutinise every aspect of your service provision to reduce or remove risks of abuse.
- You need to deliberate with all stakeholders regularly.
- Child safety should saturate advertising, recruitment and induction.
- A Child Safety and Wellbeing Policy should include your Commitment to Child Safety.
- There should be a strong commitment to vulnerable groups at your organisation.
- Your organisation should support and celebrate the culture of Aboriginal children.
- Your Code of Conduct should entail positive behaviours as well as unacceptable behaviours (misconduct).
- A breach of the organisation's Code of Conduct will have consequences.

Chapter 5 reflection questions

- Do you have a Commitment to Child Safety? Is this commitment explicit to your Commitment to Aboriginal Children?
- Does your philosophy statement and purpose refer to your Commitment to Child Safety?
- Are all staff and volunteers (inclusive of third-party contractors) inducted with the Commitment to Child Safety, Code of Conduct and complaints process? What about families? Visitors?
- Does your Code of Conduct make clear that there is a zero tolerance of racism and any other discriminatory behaviour?
- Have you undertaken a cultural safety assessment to detect unsafe pockets in your organisation?
- Are there places where interactions between adults and children can be obscured from sight?

- Do you have safety protocols for online environments?
- Do you consider the possibility of abuse in risk assessments for internal experiences as well as excursions? Do you consult with children about measures in place to keep them safe?
- How do we adjust policies and practices to ensure children are safe?

CHAPTER 6

Child safety – children championing their safety and wellbeing

Insight for educators/practitioners:

- How to impart preventative education into curriculums for children of all ages (a pedagogy of safety)

Chapter elements:

- Consult with children
- Informing children about their rights
- A pedagogy of safety
- Participation and co-regulation
- Empowerment for being safety literate
- Learner-centred curricula for resilience
- Preventative education pedagogies
- Tools and resources for all ages

To create an ecosystem of prevention, we need a learner-centred curriculum – teaching and learning, together, allowing for individual needs and involving children in the decision-making process regarding educational experiences. To ensure all children feel included and valued, we need to use a range of tools and strategies. Organisations need to show they value children's contributions by encouraging them to make informed choices when articulating their rights, wants and needs.

"Recognising that early childhood environments provide the ideal setting for children to begin learning about their rights and responsibilities, and to develop respect for those around them, the Australian Human Rights Commission has recently started working more closely with the early childhood education and care sector" (Australian Human Rights Commission, n.d.).

The UN Committee on the Rights of the Child endeavours to make things better for children all over the world. Detailed in the 2013 National Children's Commissioner's first report, this committee told the Australian Government what it could do to make things better and *"needs to listen to children and work harder to help them"*. It also said that Australia does a lot of good things for children, but that many of them are having a hard time:

- Some children are being treated unfairly
- Some children are being bullied and hit
- Some children are not getting the education they need
- Some children can't live with their parents
- Some children are not as happy or as healthy as they could be
- Some children do not have homes
- Some children are in trouble with the law and need help
- Some children are locked up

(Australian Human Rights Commission, n.d.)

Consult with children

As part of the selection process for the initial position of National Children's Commissioner, children (aged 9-11, from Kingsford Smith Primary School in the Australian Capital Territory) participated in the interview process. Their views were included about the criteria and characteristics required for the role.

The first National Children's Commissioner would undertake a statutory position, being responsible for protecting and promoting the rights of all children in Australia.

In 2013, the first ever National Children's Commissioner for Australia went around the country on a trip called The Big Banter, listening to more than 1,000 children in conjunction with surveys and postcards from around 1,400 more children of all ages. Children's responses were in relation to what they believed, was important to them and what would make life better. They said it was important for them to have a say and for their views to be taken seriously.

Some of the things children said made them happy include:
- Seeing my friends and family happy
- I have my family around me
- Other people are happy
- I'm playing with my friends
- I'm playing with my friends at school
- My family is happy and healthy
- I'm with my family and friends
- I'm spending time with my parents
- I'm living happily with the people I love
- I'm around friends and family and having fun
- I'm helping other people
- I'm reading, writing and laughing
- I have downtime with my family
- I'm doing art and craft
- I dance, act, sing, play piano and paint
- I'm at pre-school and have a nice teacher
- I'm playing with my little brother

Some things children said would make life better include:
- There were no bullies
- Kids were involved in political life
- Everyone had supportive parents
- Everyone could be themselves
- There was equal access to education

- There was no physical violence
- All different cultures were involved
- We have freedom to choose
- We all feel safe no matter where we are
- There was peace
- Everyone gets a voice
- All kids are treated fairly
- Everyone had a family
- Everyone was safe
- There was housing for everyone
- If we weren't stereotyped

"I want the views of our youngest citizens, who make up a quarter of our population, to be sought, heard and taken up by adults in our community. I want children's participation to become the norm," said Megan Mitchell when she commenced her role on 25 March 2013. It was certainly clear the person in this significant role had a mindset for a model of practice that values children and wanted them to champion their safety and wellbeing.

However you interpret these, it is clear that many comments refer to children being safe in their environments – and child abuse removes joy from their world.

What does the Children's Rights Report 2013 say? (Australian Human Rights Commission, 2013; there is a child-friendly version) examined the implementation of the UNCRC in Australia and included the following five emerging themes to progress the better protection of children's rights in Australia:

1. The right to be heard: We need to make sure that adults listen to children and take their views seriously.
2. Freedom from violence, abuse and neglect: We need to make sure that all children are safe.
3. The opportunity to thrive: All children need to grow up strong, healthy and happy. We need to help children who are having a really hard time right from the start, not waiting until the problems get really bad.
4. Engaged civics and citizenship: We should help children get involved in their schools and communities – to be citizens! They need to know about their rights!

5. Action and accountability: We need to know all about how children are doing in Australia, then we need to make sure that the Australian Government makes laws and rules which help all children.

It is encouraging that the National Commissioner is expected to 'consult with children'. Taking the lead and setting the standard for a no-excuses approach to responding unfailingly to children, and exhibiting an approach that denotes National Child Safety Principle number 2: 'Children and young people are informed about their rights, participate in decisions affecting them and are taken seriously'.

In 2020–21, the Victorian Commission continued to strengthen the various ways in which children and young people participated in and influenced the work of the Commission. If we are going to encourage children to express their ideas and have a voice that is attended to, then we, too, need to look at a multitude of ways to collaborate *with* children. Informing children of their rights means we must deliver information to them in a child-friendly manner and include them in important conversations as citizens who can make a difference to their world, and the future of others.

Ultimately, we want to create environments that are so well resourced that children have at their disposal provocations that teach them about their rights. We want children to know how to protect and maintain their place in the world, to advocate, but in doing so know they can truly make a difference to their own trajectory, or that of someone else. We want environments to nurture the inner child, to calm them when the chaos of the world becomes too much, until they are ready to engage again. We need to infiltrate our environments with a vibe of children as highly competent citizens and capable agents for change. Organisations need to invest in this way of thinking if they are going to be effective in creating and maintaining a culture of child safety on an ongoing basis.

Informing children about their rights

This requires more than just obtaining a child-friendly version of the UNCRC poster and placing it on the wall at a children's service. We need to breathe the information and incorporate it into our discussions with children of all ages, so the poster comes alive. The right to safety and the right to discourse, to express oneself, to be sure of being respected and heard.

> *We also need to make sure that children know we are their ally, that if they have not been respected and listened to, then we are there to support them in recovery. Posters on the wall won't do this. Books on the shelf won't do this. The occasional chat at 'group time' won't do this. To meet the fundamental needs and wishes of children, we need connection. We need rich engagement to let children know that we are truly present, truly listening and truly care about the interactions we have with them. Noticing and acknowledging the little stuff builds trust in relationships to share the big stuff.*

Registered psychologist, speaker, author and parenting educator Dr Vanessa Lapointe refers to 'neurons that fire together wire together' (Lapointe, 2020), which is neuropsychologists' term for adults being the steady, stabilising presence for children who are not able to regulate from the inside themselves, and regulating from the 'calmness they soak up' from the adult who is standing by and holding space for them.

A trusted adult, who supports children to get back to calm, enables children to practice co-regulation. The more this is experienced, the child not only builds the skill to eventually learn to self-regulate, but they also have a sense of safety and wellbeing. A trusted, responsive environment gives children the readiness to try and navigate through social and emotional interactions with peers and educators. Lifelong skills are learnt as children experience the range of emotions that day-to-day events bring. It is the daily messages children receive that helps them to know their worth, and gives them the confidence to set boundaries to protect themselves.

The NQS refers to ways we effectively communicate with children (Quality Area 5). We need to critically reflect on our use of resources, how accessible the information is, and the means for intentionally teaching and learning *with* children. We want to make sure we critically reflect on our own pedagogical practices to make sure we are not giving children the perception they are inadequate. The following explains why children and young people might be vulnerable in organisations. These points can guide you in checking in with your own attitudes:

- Adults sometimes take advantage of the power imbalance between them and young people.
- Young people may feel that adults take advantage of them.
- Young people sometimes feel that organisations prioritise the needs of adults.
- Young people are often physically smaller than adults and can't always protect themselves.
- Young people aren't always able to draw on past experiences to know what to do.

The CCYP has an Empowerment and participation guide that explains that *"children and young people who have experienced trauma may believe that they and their needs don't matter or that trauma is part of life. They may have a history of feeling powerless, particularly when decisions are made without their input. Empowerment is valuable for these children and young people because it can help to restore their confidence in themselves and others. It can assist them to take more control over their lives"* (CCYP, 2021).

Many people are not aware that cultural safety includes actively celebrating and helping to promote one's culture. *"Where organisations fail to celebrate their culture, don't act in culturally appropriate ways or fail to see their background as a strength, it can increase the risk of Aboriginal and Torres Strait Islander children and young people experiencing racism and discrimination and not feeling safe"* (CCYP, 2021).

Enabling cultural celebrations and working hard to gain knowledge from authentic sources promotes inclusion, as does recognising that there are culturally appropriate ways of involving Aboriginal and Torres Strait Islander children and young people that help them feel safer and more empowered.

Work with local communities and Elders wherever possible to understand what this looks like. Make it a priority to find out about the Traditional Owners of the land/s on which your organisation operates on the Map of Indigenous Australia, and learn about the importance of acknowledging Traditional Owners. Promoting successes of Aboriginal people values self-determination (formal recognition of identity and control over economic, cultural and social development).

Zoe Upton, Koorie education coordinator at the Department of Education, outlined that 'Womindjeka' is a word that has, in a way, been gifted to society, and means more than just welcome: 'Welcome, come with purpose'. It perhaps resonates the belief in the wisdom and capabilities of all those present.

ECA has been the voice for young children since 1938 as the *"peak early childhood advocacy organisation, acting in the interests of young children, their families and those in the early childhood field. ECA advocates to ensure quality, social justice and equity in all issues relating to the education and care of children aged birth to eight years."* ECA's vision is *"All young children thriving and learning"* and aspires its members to be clear and credible advocates in campaigning for the rights and wellbeing of young children.

ECA and the National Children's Commissioner worked collaboratively to identify key areas for action to advocate for young children's rights in Australia, formulating *Supporting young children's rights: Statement of intent (2015–2018)* (Australian Human Rights Commission, 2015).

A pedagogy of safety

A pedagogy of safety is more than just delivering content by way of instruction. It requires educators to commit to the environment in which teaching and learning take place. Children can champion their safety and welfare when they are feeling secure. Feeling safe in the environment enables the confidence to self-direct challenges through a rights-based, play-based curriculum.

Here are some resources that can be embedded into curriculums for children of all ages and added to family/service libraries to encourage co-use between educators and children, as well as self-use by children, where possible, as an avenue to build positive identity:

1. "Building Belonging *is a comprehensive toolkit of early education resources, which includes an eBook, song with actions, educator guide, posters and lesson plans. It is focused on encouraging respect for cultural diversity and tackling racial prejudice in early childhood settings*" (Australian Human Rights Commission, 2016).
2. The e-book *All My Friends and Me* tells the story of the preschool child Pax and her friends who explore their similarities and differences (Australian Human Rights Commission, 2016).
3. 'Colours of Australia' is a song that celebrates the diversity of Australia; it has an accompanying poster that contains actions to complement the song. You can listen to it at www.youtube.com/watch?v=eXW1ntCxCOk
4. Dr Red Ruby Scarlet of MultiVerse launched the song 'Like to Be Me' in December 2020. You can listen to it at www.facebook.com/watch/live/?ref=watch_permalink&v=229505895256106.
5. Katherine Locke and Anne Passchier, *What Are Your Words?* An introduction to gender-inclusive pronouns that is perfect for readers of all ages.

"*Culture is the fundamental building block of identity, and the development of a strong cultural identity is essential to children's healthy sense of who they are and where they belong*" (Commonwealth of Australia, 2010).

"*Gender-based violence exists when there is gender inequality; and rigid ideas about gender are shaped in the early years of a child's life. Therefore, early learning services play a key role in challenging these rigid stereotypes and in promoting more respectful relationships*" (Star Health, 2021).

Environments that are supportive of ongoing learning need all stakeholders to be comfortable to have considerate, yet robust conversations, to explore issues together. "*Culture is the system of shared assumptions, values and beliefs that influence the way people behave in an organisation*" (CCYP, 2021).

What this means for a child is the right to be heard

There is a need for children to:
- Be recognised as successful, competent and capable learners
- Be supported to access the information needed to be safely connected to and contribute to their world and the decisions affecting them
- Know that their family is recognised and respected as having the key responsibility for their upbringing
- Have privacy
- Be consulted in decisions about what is best for them
- Be encouraged to express their views and opinions and know that these will be listened to and valued

For professionals working with young children

There is a need to:
- Recognise children's agency and their individual and evolving capacity to participate in day-to-day considerations relating to their lives; an example might be allowing children to choose if they do or do not want to undress down to underwear for sleep
- Identify and promote the use of appropriate resources and tools to promote children's voices and to support their participation in decision-making. Consider the creation of variations to governance documents
- Build capacity, skills and knowledge of children's rights to enable professionals to implement these in their day-to-day practice, including in inductions, children's rights documents and reinforcing the need to support children to be heard
- Ethically contribute young children's voices to the public debate on issues of relevance to young children; with children being active participants in NAPCAN Child Protection Week events and experiences
- Facilitate learning environments that foster opportunities for all children to express themselves, large and small group experiences, both planned and spontaneous

- Listen to and value children's views and opinions and show that their views have been heard and acted upon, and also celebrate children's ideas and initiatives in community, i.e. newsletters and displays at the service
- Include children in governance meetings

(Adapted from 'The right to be heard table' from Supporting Young Children's Rights – Statement of intent 2015–18, *Australian Human Rights Commission, 2015)*

Through elaborating on what is needed to provide a pedagogy of safety, I believe it may not be possible without first and foremost having a pedagogy of *professional love*. In an article on The Spoke, ECA's blog, Sarah Louise Gandolfo dispels common myths relating to this academic concept and reasons that it is more than attachment. "*At its core, it* [professional love] *requires early childhood professionals to prioritise the needs and interests of children above their own, and to ensure that all children's emotional needs are met*" (Gandolfo, 2021).

The following quote from *The Boy Who was Raised as a Dog* is the discourse we need for participation and co-regulation: "*The more healthy relationships a child has, the more likely he will be to recover from trauma and thrive. Relationships are the agents of change and the most powerful therapy is human love*" (Perry, 2007).

Participation and co-regulation

"*Professional love builds on this and includes the behaviours of reciprocity and authenticity*" (Gandolfo, 2021).

The everyday is our platform for teaching and learning to recognise our feelings and emotions and help children who have deregulated get back to a calm state.

Recognising that many organisations want to engage more effectively with children and young people, *Empowerment and participation: A guide for organisations working with children and young people* was developed in 2021 by NSW Government Office of the Children's Guardian, the CCYP, the University of South Australia and Australian Centre for Child Protection.

"Organisations have an obligation to empower children and young people, and to uphold their human right to participate in decision-making that affects them" (CCYP, 2021).

Drawing heavily on the views and experiences of children and young people themselves, the guide is filled with achievable and practical strategies to empower children to take an active role in making organisations more child-centred and safe. Empowerment recognises and builds on the strengths of children and young people. It is a process of allowing them to become stronger and more confident. It gives them greater say in and control of their lives, and helps them understand their rights so that they can act on them if they need to.

Empowerment for being safety literate

By investing in children and young people, child safe organisations aim to help them become more resistant to change and adversity. Child safe organisations need to work closely with children to help them to identify risks, know what to do if they are unsafe and know how to seek support if they need it.

Claire Warden, a colleague in Scotland, said that she is now troubled with the term 'empower' because that means adults have the power first and then give the opportunity to children. So, what if we give children equal power, or radically consider giving them the platform first and later conversing with adults when it comes to notions of safety?

"Children and young people bring unique capabilities, experiences and views that can assist organisations to be child safe" (CCYP, 2021).

To guide you in determining whether you have an empowering culture, visit the CCYP website (www.ccyp.vic.gov.au) and access the *Empowerment and participation* guide. On page 16 you will find a 'Developing empowering cultures checklist', and on page 17 an 'Empowering relationships checklist'. To help determine whether relationships in your organisation are empowering, consultation with children is required to determine their opinions. Leadership needs to foster a collaborative approach to dialogue and speaking up among all stakeholders – inclusive of children.

Positive peer relationships are a strong focus in the Victorian Child Safe Standards and the benefits are expanded upon in the *Empowerment and participation* guide. The fact is that *"most often, young people will tell their friends about abuse before they tell adults... Young people benefit from having strong friendships and feeling part of a team. They may see their friends as their primary source of support, information and advice, and go to them when they need help"* (CCYP, 2021).

Strategies for supporting positive peer relationships

- Look at the layout of your spaces – ensure there are areas that are clearly set up for children to work side by side, be opposite, in small groups and even in teams, for example, during a game or a project.
- Consult with children about the resources available and allow them to move furniture and access materials to meet the demands of their play.
- Ensure there are opportunities for children to build their sense of agency – especially through routines and transitions.

Peer relationships

Peer relationships can sometimes need targeted intervention. Child-on-child abuse is often not spoken about. It may involve children from different families, as well as sibling abuse.

Children with problem sexual behaviours and their families was created in 2012 (funded by the Victorian Government) as a human services specialist practice resource using a best interests case practice model. The resource states: *"For some children, these problem sexual behaviours are highly coercive and involve force; acts that would be described as 'abusive' were it not for the child's age."*

There is a table on page 8 of this resource that is useful for guidance when intervention might be necessary and prompts the need to notice the frequency and persistence of particular behaviours. The examples listed are categorised according to 'age-appropriate sexual behaviours', 'concerning sexual behaviours' and 'very concerning sexual behaviours' to guide whether behaviours are within the normal or age-appropriate range for children aged 0-4, 5-7 and 8-12, or whether therapeutic involvement should be sought. It is important to seek assistance because problem sexual behaviours may turn into a long-term pattern if they are not addressed. Professionals need to support parents and carers in responding to both children's needs (the victim and the child with problem sexual behaviours) to engage each of them in specific treatment programmes (Victorian Government, Department of Human Services, 2012). Berry Street has a comprehensive outline of problematic sexualised behaviour on its website, broken down into the categories and age brackets mentioned above.

Early childhood professionals should be mindful of the triggers that are likely to precede a child acting out problem sexual behaviours. All educators in a team environment need to be well informed about circumstances where a child could become dysregulated. A clear plan, created with educators, specialist guidance and the child's family, should be created and understood. Clear communication will empower significant adults to intervene with pre-planned strategies to support the child so that the sexualised behaviours are prevented from being enacted.

Learner-centred curricula for resilience

Routines and transitions can be rigid and are often influenced by the clock as well as the bias of adults. Consider slowing down these key times and allowing flexibility – children eating for longer periods, chatting even if not eating, progressive snacks and the choice about whether (or not) to come together for singing, eating or storytelling. All these predicaments provide children with the opportunity to practice decision-making for themselves, and this can be very morale-boosting. Sure, some guidance about hunger and thirst might be offered at the time, and in some cases some discussion later. If things don't quite go to plan and children end up anxious, sad, disappointed, afraid or frustrated, some positive solution-focused reflection together is invaluable for building trusted relationships so children can take chances in a safe and secure environment, with support from a trusted person. Some brainstorming for future alternatives builds autonomy, and by children having a say about things that affect them in their day, it makes a big impact on self-assurance and resilience.

"Resilience helps them understand that these uncomfortable emotions usually don't last forever. They can experience these emotions and know they'll be OK before too long" and revert to a practised wellbeing plan to reregulate (Raising Children Network, 2021).

The Zone of Proximal Development is a term psychologist Lev Vygotsky founded to describe *"good learning is that which is advance of development, the next developmental space"* (McLeod, 2019).

It takes repeated opportunities (practice) to be able to challenge yourself, to know yourself and to make better choices. Having the space to do that in early learning environments is helpful – after all, it is a lifelong skill to recognise what is best for us. Responsive educators, who can hold space for children when they are dysregulated, help them back to calm and contentment. It's these relationships that are memorable and these people who are considered significant in children's lives.

If you are wondering why this chapter didn't hone straight into body safety and setting boundaries, it's because what we have talked about thus far supports children's sense of wellbeing – so the environment is attuned in all facets to being nurturing and respectful for self and others. These foundations provide a strong underpinning for being able to champion safety for oneself and others.

Children cannot champion safety on their own – it requires a safe environment that is safe to be themselves. Children navigating their emotions requires, as we have explored, a number of resources – primarily the connectedness with key adults that care about them. Educators who have built and maintained a culture of caring see children challenge their thinking, and therefore move them beyond what they already know, into the waters of the unknown. That can be a scary place, so it needs a strong foundation to enable this to happen.

A pedagogical model

A pedagogical model of consideration could also be used to describe a core component of the Victorian Curriculum from foundation to Year 12 primary prevention initiative, *Respectful Relationships* (Victorian Government, Department of Education, 2019). It is all about embedding a culture of respect and equality across the entire school community – not about teaching radical gender theory. It is a primary prevention initiative to reduce family violence by helping to positively influence attitudes and behaviours. This school-aged programme helps students learn how to build healthy relationships and prepares them to face challenges by developing problem-solving skills and building resilience and confidence.

This is the case for any child, but with greatened need for stability when working with children who have already been affected by trauma. Trauma-informed care and education includes supporting children to work through feelings and emotions, plus being sensitive to triggers and unease, to build relationships.

Children in the child protection system

Providing an environment that enables children to feel safe, heard and confident counteracts what children involved in the child protection system feel:

- **Fearful** – of the abuse continuing, of talking about it, of being blamed, of losing their family, of losing control, of being unloved
- **Unheard** – being disbelieved, being talked at or 'down to', being silenced, becoming 'invisible'
- **Uncertain** – doubting what is right, doubting feelings, doubting experiences, losing trust and hope

These feelings have been recorded by international, national and local researchers (for example, Cashmore, Dolby, Brennan and Muskett, etc) and used in child abuse prevention campaigns (for example, NAPCAN, Australian Childhood Foundation, ECPAT). Children and young people currently or previously in care have also voiced these sentiments loud and clear through projects such as *I'm not a jigsaw puzzle* – a Tasmanian project sponsored through the CREATE Foundation. Find out more about it on the AIFS website (www.aifs.gov.au).

Children involved in the care and protection system say they want:
- To feel like they 'belong'
- To participate in decisions made about their own lives

- To have meaningful relationships
- To be respected as individuals
- To feel supported

It is too easy for adult needs, views and voices to obscure those of the children who are at the centre of a child protection process. Professionals engaged to act in the best interests of children and young people will better support children if they are competent in having the following:

- **Understanding** – of child development and ways to promote resilience
- **Awareness** – of the impact of trauma on child development so educators can design curriculums that support trauma-informed practices
- **Humility** – in seeking out other known and trusted adults or friends of the child to help build bridges of communication
- **Sensitivity** – in creating a context where a child may feel safe when talking to a strange adult
- **Patience** – in allowing time for a relationship to build
- **Flexibility** – in fitting in times to talk to the child which least disrupts their routine
- **Clarity** – in describing what our respective roles are in ways that are most appropriate for the child
- **Honesty** and **authenticity** – children and young people are rarely fooled!

(I'm not a jigsaw puzzle, AIFS)

When people don't feel heard, they can get louder. Behaviour is communication, so we have to listen to the underlying need, and this is echoed in research by Beyond Blue. To build resilience:

- Build good relationships with others including adults and peers
- Build their independence
- Learn to identify, express and manage their emotions
- Build their confidence by taking on personal challenges

(Beyond Blue, 2022)

Holistic family psychologist Ashleigh Warner says, *"Beneath every behaviour there is a feeling. And beneath each feeling is a need. And when we meet that need rather than focus on the behaviour, we begin to deal with the cause, not the symptom."*

Emotions and sensations

When educating children about emotions, we need to refer also to sensations, as these link to feelings when the body begins alerting us to danger. It is important not to confuse sensations with emotions. A sensation is a physical feeling in the body. For example, fear is an emotion but can come with different sensations, i.e. feeling cold and tension throughout the body. The language of sensation allows you to describe the physical feelings using words based on the five senses: sight, taste, touch, smell and sound. *"By learning the language of sensation, you can connect with and express what you are experiencing in your body"* (@annatheanxietycoach, 2022).

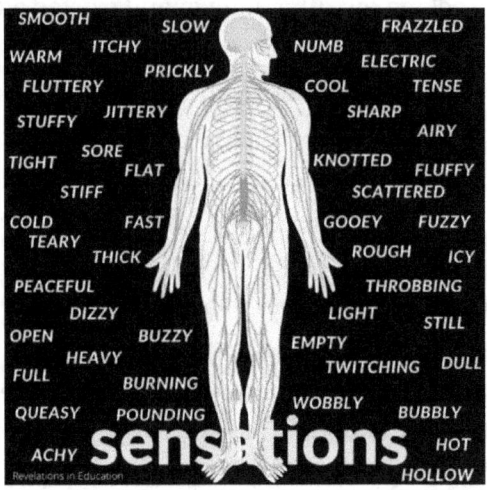

When you become in tune with your body sensations, you gain the confidence to articulate your feelings and emotions. Building sensations into the vocabulary that you use with children helps them to develop their correlation between emotions and feelings and therefore helps build awareness when they might be starting to feel unsafe based on the recognised sensation such as tingling, feeling hot or cold, or having a heavy stomach.

This skill of emotional literacy aids interacting with others – knowing what feels OK for you, what's acceptable and what behaviours or actions are not OK. Language (nonverbal cues and verbal communication) helps gauge how others might be feeling so you can read social cues of others. Overwhelming traumatic events can push physiological energy down into the body, and trapped energy such as this can present itself as headaches, pain, digestive issues, dissociation, fatigue, emotional flashbacks, food cravings, non-epileptic seizures and other symptoms.

Fostering an ethical paradigm to care about what others want requires communication. Naming your feelings with specific words – emotional granulation – helps with emotional regulation because while trying to describe the feelings, the sympathetic nervous system calms down.

Co-regulation is effective for helping children get back to calm. Sometimes it is tricky to re-regulate on your own, so when educators hold space for children, it allows them the time to find the way through the thoughts and feelings in a supportive place. The goal of regulation is not to stay calm, it is to recognise the transient nature of emotions and know that you can – and will – move through a range of them each and every day, and return to calm. This positive relational experience and repeated exposure to a reliable, trusted adult means children will develop the ability to assert their right to feel safe and know who they can talk to if they don't feel safe.

Working models

If we are utilising a trauma-informed lens, we want all children to be able to access 'working models' – access things that help to positively influence thoughts and feelings, for example, a heat bag, water play or alone time in a tent with textured pillows.

Helping children reshape their representations takes time. Repeated exposure to positive messages about themselves counteracts negative messages that have given them a traumatic representation of sense of self. Educational environments that are rich in care enable healing, allowing children to know that they may come out of the window of tolerance, but they will soon return to feeling safe. This responsive environment helps condition children to build their own internal platform for responding to change – even negative experiences.

To raise problem-solvers and children who believe they know how to articulate and promote their safety, we can refer to them as being safety literate. By not including body safety in the curriculum, and by not consulting children about the means to keep them safe, you are not sheltering children from the awareness of abuse, nor will you *prevent* it from happening!

Preventative education pedagogies

This new knowledge – new because educators are still not imparting body safety into their curriculum for children of all ages – is staying at adult level: a) because of the belief children are too young to know about this stuff, which is ironic because abuse is happening to them; and b) because of the backlash they may get from families.

Let's clear up this misconception. Respectful, developmentally appropriate resources are used to teach and are used for children to learn. When families are well informed about your plan, they will understand you are not teaching their children about sex.

Protective behaviours

Educators are often reluctant to communicate body safety strategies to parents and carers at their children's service. Essentially, preventative education is helping children to navigate relationships in a developmentally appropriate way. As many experts will tell you, the perception of parental pushback is worse than actual pushback. Be transparent and provide opportunities to ask questions. I believe that people only get their back up if they are not well informed and feel like they don't have a say.

Deanne Carson, founder and CEO of Body Safety Australia, is renowned for advocacy for protecting children against sexual abuse. Body Safety Australia education programmes help children navigate uncomfortable feelings and help them learn to communicate their right to bodily autonomy. Ten learning objectives are conveyed to early learning and primary schoolchildren through songs, activities, stories, games and group conversations. Online and technology safety are embedded in all 10 objectives:

1. Identify and clearly communicate emotions in themselves and others
2. Learn their body's 'early-warning signs' that tell them something doesn't feel safe
3. Understand that humans have different fear responses: fight, flight and freeze
4. Assertively communicate their right to bodily autonomy
5. Identify their safe adults using felt finger puppets

6. Know that their body belongs to them, and nobody has the right to touch it without permission
7. Accurately name their genitals using words that healthcare professionals would use
8. Understand that sometimes adults make decisions about a child's body for health, hygiene and safety reasons
9. Understand the difference between a surprise and a secret
10. Identifying that sometimes adults and older children's behaviour can be 'tricky'

These intentions are utilised to inform whole communities of strategies to prevent abuse happening, making them safer for children.

Jayneen Sanders, an internationally recognised author in this space, wrote a piece for Hey Sigmund, an internationally popular online resource, with particular emphasis on strengthening the mental wellness of children and adolescents. This insight, directed towards families, refers to 10 empowering body safety skills for keeping children safe from sexual abuse. She suggests the following to assist children to grow into assertive and confident teenagers and adults:

1. **Name the body parts correctly** – inclusive of genitals, which reduces miscommunication if a child is trying to state inappropriate touching
2. **Private zones** – these parts go under a swimsuit (penis, vagina, vulva, bottom, breasts and nipples). (Note: A child's mouth is also a private zone.)
3. **Invite children to choose their own safety network** – this should be three to five trusted adults (teaching children that no one has a right to touch their private parts, and if someone does, they tell a trusted adult straight away – and keep telling until believed. According to statistics, children will need to tell three people before they are believed (Sanders, 2022).
4. **If other people ask to look at or touch a child's private parts**, show their private parts to the child or show them images of private parts, this is wrong and the child must tell a trusted adult immediately. Again, reinforce telling until believed.

5. **Encourage children to talk about feelings in daily activities** – for example, sad, angry, excited and happy. It can help them to develop the language to verbalise if they are touched inappropriately.
6. **Talk about safe and unsafe** – and times when again during a normal day when they might feel safe, for example, scared and unsafe on a rollercoaster with a feeling of a sick tummy, and in comparison, happy sitting with their dog on the couch watching TV, with a warm, cosy feeling inside.
7. **Discuss early-warning signs** – for when they start to feel unsafe, i.e. feeling sick in the tummy, feeling like crying, having sweaty hands, having a burning sensation under the arms, feeling like they need to wee. Encourage children to communicate if any of their early-warning signs have happened in a situation. Reinforce believing them.
8. **Secrets** – discourage secrets and differentiate between a secret and a happy surprise, like a party being kept quiet. Someone touching private parts is an unsafe secret.
9. **No! Stop!** – discuss when it might be necessary for someone to touch their private parts, for example, a doctor, but only if someone on their safety network is in the room with them. No! Stop! can be used if someone touches their private parts without the safety network person there.
10. **The invisible bubble** – children need to know their body is their body and they are the boss of it. Reinforce the idea that everyone has an invisible bubble around them (personal space), and they do not have to hug or kiss anyone they don't want to.

I remember a friend of mine once said to one of my children: "It's OK, I can see you are saying hello with your eyes", which was such a versatile statement we used ongoingly to be proactive in a greeting situation that felt uncomfortable. We need to support children in their body autonomy and change the dichotomy that refusing to speak, hug or kiss people hello (or goodbye) is being rude. You can be respectful and polite without forced contact.

I have shared with you similar undertones in body safety experts' suggestions because I think it's important to be well informed, so you can present useful content to *everyone* in your communities. Creating safe spaces to be heard, to disclose and promote whole-community prevention education is best practice. In addition to experts, children's services educators are also allies for this preventative work, to help children know how to protect themselves, and be safe. Adopt a multidisciplinary approach to safety and wellbeing.

The aim of protective behaviours education is for children to build their capacity to predict, assess a situation and act accordingly, so they can build skills to champion for their own wellbeing and safety. This requires continuous empowerment, communication, self-esteem, resilience and social skills.

"Our brains continually form maps of the world – maps of what is safe and what is dangerous" (van der Kolk, 2020).

You want to ensure your preventative education is a constellation of many necessary things in a curriculum. You do not want those mind maps to be imprinted with gender assumptions, promoting an ableist framework for heteronormative ways of thinking, which can be counterproductive, for example, 'boys are mean to girls they really like'. Co-teaching with experts is a strategy that many services adopt to ensure the teaching is contextually autonomous, but in line with the new nuance way to teach.

Empowering children

Founder and managing director of Safe4Kids Holly-ann Martin has been teaching and advocating for children for more than 30 years with protective education in schools, helping prevent sexual abuse by empowering children and giving them a vocabulary to protect themselves. Holly-ann recommends starting protective education by age three and that conversations about pornography need to happen by age six at the latest.

"I don't call it pornography with six-year-olds, I call them private pictures and private movies, but there is so much pornography on YouTube and even YouTube for Kids isn't 100% safe, so we talk about private pictures and private movies and what to do if you see those sorts of things," she says.

Teaching children about the right to protect themselves and ways to do that does not have to be a fear-provoking experience, nor does it need to give them information that will mature them prematurely from talking about sex (a phrase I have heard on many occasions). Holly-ann advises teaching children about consent and she's not talking about consent and sex, but instead talking about consent and body autonomy. She also advises setting up a safety team of trusted adults including family, teachers and people from the community to help empower children to speak up should the worst happen.

I have followed Holly-ann's work for some time. I think this statement of hers from a podcast is of cognisance: "*Our early-warning signs are our bodies' way of telling us that we feel unsafe. So, it's our fight, flight, freeze or faint response and humans are the only ones that don't always listen to their bodies.*"

I think it's instrumental for families to hear the realisation that "*because of the grooming process, because kids want to protect their families – there's lots of reasons why children don't always come forward and tell their parent, but they might tell their teacher or somebody a bit further removed than somebody in their family,*" according to Holly-ann.

Tools and resources for all ages

The power of song

Holly-ann has worked in more than 70 remote communities, and Safe4Kids created a video clip as part of the Protective Education Programme. In collaboration with the MusoMagic Outback Tracks, Safe4Kids created 'Consent' with the students and community of Imanpa in the Northern Territory. This catchy and powerful song includes lyrics that every child needs to become acquainted with:

- My choice is my own
- My body is my home
- My body is my body from my head to my toes
- Respect my words
- Yes means yes
- No means no
- It's my body and I say what goes

(*Safe4Kids, 2019*)

The power of stories

Children can use stories to prompt conversations to take place in a safe setting. They are a great tool for imparting to children ways to set boundaries. They build understanding of respecting others and personal space. Stories enable children to read over and over and retell stories, which builds confidence in body safety.

We are fortunate to have access to many preventative education books and resources being used to empower children all over the world. Find a wide range of resources from the following places:
- Body Safety Australia (www.bodysafetyaustralia.com.au/store)
- Educate2Empower Publishing (www.e2epublishing.info)
- Safe4Kids (www.safe4kids.com.au)

Teaching and learning tools

Use intentionality with teaching and learning tools to ensure children's programmes:
- Expand body sensations vocabulary – I often see emotions barometers being used in curriculums for children of all ages. The Resilience Project has assisted many children's services, inclusive of schools, to implement zones of regulation – it's important to ensure the aim is not to stay in the green zone – it is to move through the zones and know you will get back to a calm state, through co- and/or self-regulation
- Supports children to recognise, name, trust and express feelings when children do not feel safe
- Offer understanding and acceptance of children expressing a range of feelings, for example, when displaying unhappy or sad feelings, ask, "*How would you like to feel? What could you do so that you feel happy/safe?*"
- Are implemented by educators who are good role models through explaining body responses and owning feelings using the "*I feel... when...*" format
- Create inclusive learning environments and adopt flexible and informed practices, including making reasonable adjustments to optimise access, participation and engagement in learning (ACECQA, 2022)

Open-ended resources

You can also use open-ended resources such as:
- Dramatic and imaginary play provisions
- Clipboard and paper
- Texts
- Music
- Puzzles
- Mirrors, which help children see their facial expressions and for reinforcing positive body image/individual identity

Think about the available tools in your setting to practice feelings. Think about tools in your communities that allow children to safely show up. Do your provisions support children to freely develop their understanding of gender? What about cultural responsiveness? Can children feel social and cultural freedom and joy in your environments?

Body signal curriculum experiences

These can include the following:
- Board games are a good tool for exploring emotions – dialogue about anticipation, disappointment, anger, joy and excitement
- What's the time, Mr Wolf – this game injects dealing with the unpredictable
- Risky play – involves balance
- Swinging high – this is being in control of one's body
- Jumping from a platform – taking safe risks even if they're scary

One-step-removed problem-solving

Dramatic play can allow children to act out worries and concerns through roleplay using objects such as:
- Dolls house figurines
- Home corner/house area
- Puppets

You can also offer scenarios to prompt conversation and talk through managing feelings and situations. Some examples could include:
- Dog barking
- Lost in a shopping centre
- Stranger offers to drive you to the park

Just as there are child-friendly versions of the annual *Children's Rights Report* by the National Children's Commissioner, there are many other publications by the Australian Human Rights Commission intended to be used by and with children. One example is *A Guide for Children and Young People: The National Strategy to Prevent and Respond to Child Sexual Abuse (2021-2030)* – this aims to help children and young people understand child sexual abuse, as well as how and where to get help. It also outlines the National Strategy to improve Australia's response to child sexual abuse (aimed for children aged nine years and above). There is a simplified version that makes the information easy for children to follow (Australian Human Rights Commission, 2021).

Encouraging children to speak up

"*Having the* right *to speak up means you are allowed to and must be listened to*" is the advice for children and young people by the National Office for Child Safety. The National Office engaged the Commissioner for Children and Young People Western Australia to develop resources to help children and young people understand their right to speak up when they feel unsafe, unhappy or unfairly treated.

This may feel scary or hard to do, so breaking the complaints process down into three steps can help children action their worries:
1. **Find support** – ask someone you trust to help you.
2. **Talk** – tell your support person or people about your problem.
3. **Make your complaint** – you don't have to do this by yourself; your support person can be there to help you.

Speak up and make a complaint resources are available on the National Office for Child Safety website and are available in 10 additional languages.

The Department of Education in Victoria also has information on child-focused, culturally safe complaints that make them accessible to everyone. Children attending OSHC services and holiday programmes should be:
- Given age-appropriate material, using simplified language and visual aids, such as flowcharts
- Empowered to give their views
- Consulted on complaints procedures and offered an opportunity to provide feedback on their experience

(ACECQA, 2022)

We must be driven to impart astuteness to children, to help them protect their bodies. It is the responsibility of us all to equip children with understanding as well as communication tools to be as safe as possible to minimise the chance of harm. We need to be advocating children's rights in our curriculums. To live up to the dominant discourses around the rights of the child, we need to make sure children know how to be responsive to deal with encounters in their environments. To support all children's inclusion, educators recognise and respond to barriers that some children face, including attitudinal and practical barriers. Such barriers can be related to disability, family diversity, cultural and linguistic diversity, neurodiversity, and children and families living through trauma and adversity. Children are not equal or the same, so to uphold equity, some children may need greater access to resources and support to participate in early childhood settings (EYLF, 2022).

I know that Holly-ann Martin has taught a group of children in remote Australia that phoning 000 will get them help. She arranged with the school principal for children to have access to the office phone and to ensure that all teaching staff are immediately responsive if a child tells them they need to make an important phone call. Let's give children's voices a position of prominence in our curriculums and critically reflect on how well we do this, in our planning and reflections.

In summary

With this chapter complete, you should now know that:
- Children have a right to know how to protect their bodies.
- Professional love and commitment facilitate safe environments.
- A range of experiences are needed to become safety literate.
- Preventative education is everyone's responsibility so that children can champion for their own safety.

Chapter 6 reflection questions

- How are we listening to children?
- Do we encourage children's participation in decision-making to show that we value their opinions?
- Do you adopt children's ideas so they can see their contributions are truly valuable and worthy?
- Do children know how to raise a concern or complaint at your service?
- Do children of all ages have access to body autonomy resources at your service?
- Do you support families with tools for preventative education?
- Are protective behaviour strategies currently included in teaching and learning practices?
- Would you know how to highlight body autonomy to children who are under two years of age? What about for five-year-old children?
- Have you accessed body safety professionals to guide you in preventative education in your curriculum?
- Do children know how to set boundaries to protect their personal space?
- Are children considerate of respecting the boundaries of others?
- Do educators engage in active supervision?
- Do children engage in risk assessment to learn to self-assess and manage risk benefits as well as hazards?

CHAPTER 7

Child safety – auditing your space

Insight for educators/practitioners:

- How to assess risk in your own settings
- Safeguarding strategies to minimise harm
- How to build capacity to be child safe

Chapter elements:

- Your standpoint
- An absence framework
- Adjusting policies
- Risk management
- Where do you start assessing risk?
- Transitions, routines and excursions
- Scanning the setting
- Online safety auditing

You might have refreshed your child protection training this year, but is children's safety and wellbeing at the centre of your thoughts, values and actions every other day?

We, as early childhood professionals, have an innate desire to want to protect children. While I know most people share this sentiment, what I find fascinating is that it doesn't drive educators to be proactive in preventing harm. We need to see the protection of children in a new light, by bringing our own instinctive caution to the public realm. We don't have time to sit with the notion of tapping into child safety on a yearly basis, because it will mean children blend into the landscape at all other times of the year. If we lean into the culture of child safety and build ongoing momentum, we have a much greater chance of identifying anything out of the norm. To do this we need a new wave of security to saturate daily rituals, as well as the special activities that are comprised in your entire service provision.

Your standpoint

We must work with the attitude that everyone can be a potential suspect. Our systems need to be so tight that they deter predators, so it would be too hard for them to execute grave acts. To do this, we must determine what people could do if they had the chance. Advocating children's rights means proactively safeguarding children by providing a stronger defence. We must tighten our security to the point where we deter anyone who considers breaching a child's right to safety. It is time for early childhood professionals to step into a new paradigm of protection.

Why have we spent so many years only focusing on reporting abuse when we should have also been taking a greater leap forward to be working from a position of what could be possible and not just what has transpired?

To ensure *"children are protected from harm and hazard, adequate supervision and reasonable precautions"* are necessary, according to Children's Services Regulations. Preventing physical injury is the fundamental focus for educators, but we need to stretch our gaze to include the possibility of abuse. This is a concept that educators may not have considered when undertaking risk assessments within their environments and before going on outings.

Assessing your own domain is something we have got to lean into with confidence – not shame. Embrace the comfort from knowing you are making ongoing, regular attempts to alleviate situations where harm could come to children within the capacity of your service provision. Risk assessing, the possibility of abuse occurring within a service, is a concept that educators find confronting. Guilt is felt for not realising there were potential dangers present while undertaking daily rituals. There is, however, great relief through eliminating these risks, which is doing more to protect children in care and education settings.

To build a culture of child safety, attitudes need to be built into everyday thinking and practice within an organisation. A Child Safety and Wellbeing Policy, Statement of Commitment and Code of Conduct validate strategies to reduce risk, but regardless of your declaration, it's your routines and transitions that need to be regularly reviewed and revised to adapt dynamic safety measures. You also need to ensure your complaints process is communicated in user-friendly ways to ensure it is understood by all stakeholders.

The creation of this book has come about as a practical tool to give clarification about the reporting of abuse, as well as the confidence to create a culture of child safety at your service. A lot of these strategies can, however, be adopted to help safeguard children in all environments, not just in a children's services setting, for example, the swimming pool, the library, shopping centres and even at sporting events. Scrutiny, supervision and communication are the fundamentals for safety environments to protect children from abuse.

By working with services over the years and undertaking extensive research, I have educated my eye and built up my skill and confidence in knowing what works when it comes to safeguarding children during the times a children's service is operational.

"With the right amount of interest, patience and passion, this is something anyone can do" – these are the words of Charlotte Coote of Timeless Interiors, describing her relationship with textiles. You see, this tapestry of success can easily relate to any profession, because it requires what she is really describing: *commitment*. So, let's contextualise this devotion to that of the early childhood profession. Let's focus our attention on building capacity to gain confidence to know how to act proactively towards children enrolled in our children's services.

An absence framework

A significant number of children's services, inclusive of schools, fail to account for what could go wrong while children are in attendance. In response to this, an absence framework can be used to focus on what is not present in safety, rather than just what is. The absence framework allows stakeholders, inclusive of children, to shift how they critically think from things that are present to what is absent. An example of an absence framework in practice is a teacher asking a group of children what makes them feel 'unsafe' when at their children's service. By focusing on these cracks, teachers and children can brainstorm ways to ensure children can feel more secure.

"Children and young people are experts in their own lives, and their insights are critical for understanding how we can better support their safety and wellbeing" (Australian Human Rights Commission, 2021).

To reveal to you just how effective this approach is, a startling response came from a four-year-old child to her teacher when asked: *"What makes you feel unsafe when you are here?"* The child responded: *"I feel unsafe when Hannah [the music specialist] arrives and you turn your back to go and get my friends outside."* This revelation uncovered a significant gap in the transition from play to music. The child felt vulnerable and unsafe, due to the body language of her teacher and the position she found herself in, waiting for the group to commence the music lesson. This dialogue enabled the group to change the way they come together at music time. The child's feedback also raised awareness regarding supervision and rectified staff positioning, so as not to count specialists in ratio. The teacher now remains in the presence of the children and the visiting music teacher, and children alert their peers, who may be outside.

The outcome in this instance prompted a change in practices (and required an adjustment to policy) surrounding visitors to the service, whether they be regular or a single occurrence. Now, one educator must always remain with the group, but in addition to this, it was decided, as a result of another child's suggestion during consultation with children, that visitors now wait outside until the group is ready. Be proactive when it comes to visitors coming into your space. You and the children decide the best time and location for the guest to position themselves. It is also the teacher's responsibility to liaise with visitors, to determine the most suitable location (dependent on best visibility for ample supervision) for an experience to be undertaken.

For educators to be competent in implementing an absence framework, they need to be skilled at auditing in the moment (dynamic supervision) as well as for planned times. To be proficient, staff and volunteers need to understand their responsibilities for child safe practices and use this to inform their actions.

Organisations should:
- Child safe policies are integrated into everyday work practices, and everyone understands what they need to do.
- Check to see that Child Safe Standards (if any are applicable to the service) and otherwise the National Principles for Child Safe Organisations are included in policies.
- It is clear who the people are and how to access them to discuss issues, raise concerns and/or make a complaint.
- Policies and procedures refer to additional information, support and contacts.
- Responsibilities of all staff and volunteers are reflected in position descriptions.
- All staff take responsibility for their actions to ensure child safe practices.

(Australian Human Rights Commission, 2018)

Adjusting policies

Do services meet their policy obligations because there is weight in the fear of not being up to scratch if inspected or assessed by a regulatory organisation? No doubt there is this fact, but isn't it also the moral culpability for better protecting the children in our care? Rightful obligations certainly motivate leadership teams to review policies, but this is considered an arduous task, especially if a service undertakes regular critical reflection and self-assessment to measure quality. How do you recall all the changes in practices over the course of a year?

Are we predominantly using policies and writing procedures that are so ambiguous they tick boxes (because of key phrases and terminology) and that can easily 'correlate' to our current existence, even if practices change? On the flipside, do we 'add things' to the service operations manual because of a legislative change or because we think we should? And do we do this without re-educating all our key stakeholders?

This account of policy (re)development I'm describing here actually raises alarm bells. If we are not methodical in our policies, and we are not specific enough to outline our exact practices, then how can we possibly assume these directives will effectively support people orientating into the space? More alarming, children are not going to be shielded if there is a lapse in detail (policy and/or practice).

Appraising policies and practices needs to be continual throughout the year to keep them 'live', so we practice what we preach – and we preach what we practice. I suggest child safety is added to every team meeting agenda, in both small and whole team meetings. This activates whole-service discussions around things that have been noticed, and/or changes that have already occurred (or need to), to better protect children. Let me give you a prime example of systemic change happening from child safety being on a team meeting agenda. A staff member recalled a prospective family tour that included the nappy-changing and toileting facilities. Amenities are important for families to view, however, the team agreed that protocols needed to change so that bathrooms are not accessed until they are vacant. All team members needed to become aware of this change in policy and practice. Meeting minutes, a policy update email and verbal clarification were the key actions to support this sharing of information. The policy alteration 'suggestion' included stipulating 'tours are not to be undertaken over the lunchtime period when children are accessing bathrooms more regularly, prior to sleep and rest'.

Once we generate ideas for new protocols, we need to be in the practice of making them clear to all stakeholders. It is necessary to extend information sharing to children, too, so they are actively involved in the auditing of spaces and scenarios. Children need to know the measures in place to keep them safe – but also to know how to help ensure the safety and wellbeing of their peers, too.

In this example, Quality Improvement Planning included further consultation with families and the local community to determine whether 'tours by appointment' would be the preferred option for this service. It is important to consider that communities include local organisations, groups and First Nations people.

If we are going to review accurately, extensive consultation with all stakeholders needs to take place, so everyone ruminates ideas and helps to make informed decisions from multiple perspectives. Consider how safety, wellbeing, communication and participation might differ for people from diverse backgrounds. It is vital to foster a collaborative approach towards everyone being agents for social change, inclusive of children themselves. Staff and volunteers in the organisation need to:

- Listen to what children say, including times when determining how to minimise risks.
- Understand that children may communicate their views nonverbally, for example, through changes in behaviour or participation.
- Consider and reflect children's views to improve their activities and processes, for example, through discussion in team or management meetings.
- Provide age-appropriate platforms for children and young people to communicate and participate, for example, through games, creative activities and group discussion.

Critically reflecting and reviewing service provision regularly will strengthen your child safety culture.

Follow-up is significant; document in Quality Improvement Plans the following questions:

- Who is responsible?
- What actions/tools are required?
- How will we communicate outcomes/change to *all* others? (Inclusive of child-friendly options.) And when will we check in to update and review strategies and actions?

Giving feedback on final outcomes is also vital so that everyone in the community knows the new expectations from the audit and can adjust behaviour/actions/expectations accordingly. In actual fact, the example used of an audit process of accessing children's bathrooms equated to evidence for all three Exceeding themes in the NQS: 1) embedded in service provision; 2) critical reflection; and 3) consultation with families and community (predominantly Quality Area 2: Children's Health and Safety, and Quality Area 7: Governance and Leadership).

Many municipalities are committed to creating and maintaining a child safe organisation. The City of Casey Council has implemented a range of policies, procedures and initiatives to keep children safe and prevent abuse and reflect the council's intention to be aspirational – not just compliant – in meeting the requirements of the Victorian Child Safe Standards. One of the ways it has been endeavouring is by creating an 'easy English version' of its child safe policy. It is a summary of the Child Safety Policy that only includes the key points. The policy has been written in an easy-to-read way and uses pictures to explain some ideas (City of Casey, n.d.).

Just as the City of Casey has done, the following can be included in a simplified version of your child safe 'environment' and wellbeing policy, so it is suitable for someone who would prefer simplified language, inclusive of children:

- What is this policy about?
- Why do we need this policy?
- What the policy is/means
- The laws that apply
- Glossary of terms

Children can also read alongside a trusted adult such as a teacher, educator, family member or friend.

Language

Multiple tools to project safety messages in different communication forms should saturate the organisation. Audio versions of languages relevant to your community is a good strategy to action. I was delighted when I once received three separate audio messages from the director of an education and care service – one in Cantonese, another in Mandarin and the third in Hindi, clearly outlining the same message: *"If you need any help, or if you are feeling unsafe, please come and talk to me. I can speak your language."* If a service does not have the advantage of having team members who speak children's first language, a family member could possibly record for you.

Grooming is damaging and the impact is not well understood. Specificity matters in policies and procedures, so use the offence name. For instance, it is harmful to use the word 'relationship' when referring to any abuse.

Risk management

We need to audit our settings – both physical and online – so that we diminish the chances of abuse happening through our programmes and events. We need to be trying to identify all the possible circumstances where children might be in a position where they could be taken advantage of when they are in the care of the children's service.

A child safety risk management strategy should:
- Identify, assess and take steps to minimise the opportunity for children to be harmed
- Focus on preventing child harm, including peer-to-peer harm
- Consider increased risk with specific roles and activities, and children with heightened vulnerability, for example, children with a disability
- Be outlined in policies and procedures and included in training of staff and volunteers

We need to embrace a sociocultural approach towards protecting children, just like we do when we are communicating children's learning with families, so we can better support individual children within a group. We need to utilise the framework of consultation and collaboration with others to facilitate a holistic understanding of the best ways to prevent harm – a public undertaking towards child safety.

Working with all stakeholders, inclusive of children themselves, is how we can audit the most thoroughly, obtain the best feedback and take action to enhance practices. Quality Improvement Planning needs regular attention to determine if strategies are effective or whether they need tweaking to achieve desired outcomes. Creating a child safety culture with the child in mind goes beyond legal compliance and child protection training.

"To effectively address sexual violence against children it is necessary to recognise that it is not only a social problem perpetuated by the adults abusing/exploiting the children, but by non-abusing adults through complicity, silence, denial and failure to take appropriate action" (Governance Institute of Australia, 2019).

Respectful partnerships are needed to ensure transparency. The National Principles for Child Safe Organisations are designed to address the needs of diverse communities when creating organisational cultures and practices that promote child safety and wellbeing. During consultations on the National Principles, stakeholders highlighted the need for additional culturally appropriate support for implementing the National Principles in Aboriginal and Torres Strait Islander communities and organisations.

The Australian Human Rights Commission's Child Safe Organisations National Principles include an *Introductory self-assessment tool for organisations*. It aids organisations when considering child safety; it can be used to help them:

- Identify priority areas for improvement in their child safety policies, procedures and practices
- Learn about the National Principles for Child Safe Organisations
- Commit to future action
- Monitor improvement

(Australian Human Rights Commission, 2018)

It is recommended that more than one person completes an initial assessment of how safe their organisation is. You want to have multiple perspectives to ensure you get an accurate prediction. You cannot guarantee safety for a culture you have not been born into, so wherever possible, collaborate with individuals and community groups. You complete the assessment questionnaire (which gives indicators for what best practice might look like) and then you go back and fill out the next steps section, with particular focus on the statements for the responses that were not favourable. In any effective plan of action it is necessary to indicate who is going to be responsible for the actions required and when the goal is ideally going to be completed. I always suggest the additional check-in because this prompts regular accountability, feedback opportunities and strategy review within your timeline.

If you work across multiple sites, you may wish to complete this assessment for each site, or clearly define which site you are completing the assessment for. Services are encouraged to use the National Principles, their key action areas and indicators to help consider future actions.

Where do you start assessing risk?

The most thorough way to audit your setting is to think hard about what could go wrong and what you can do to reduce or remove these risks. This means being proactive by having an ongoing commitment to:
1. Review/audit
2. Forward plan
3. Action

Routines and transitions

Every educator should review the routines and transitions that take place for every different day of the week, as the dynamic of children and staff may vary. Think about the schedule of the day, from the minute the service commences operation until it closes. This includes family grouping, setting up and packing away times, both indoor and outdoor. It also includes opening and closing housekeeping, for example, accessing external rubbish bins. Ask yourself:
- Are there places where interactions between adults and children can be obscured from sight?
- Are there circumstances or activities that expose children to risk?

Outings and in-service events

Consider supervision on regular outings and during in-service events. Ask yourself:
- What could go wrong and what you can do to reduce or remove these risks?
- Engage children and young people in the process of identifying and managing risks

- Communicate with children and young people about the measures you are putting in place to keep them safe.

While a service may be focused on observable threats, it may not be well informed by incorporating children's perceptions and past experiences. Many services have implemented Children's Council Meetings as an official forum in addition to spontaneous dialogue at education and care services. This strategy adds to the options for information gaining to mitigate risk. It is valuable because no one knows more about whether they feel safe than the children themselves. Evaluation by adults alone could be counterintuitive, and therefore erroneous.

Regular review

People and experiences continuously change in the education and care sector. Regular review is paramount to sustain and improve the culture of child safety, so it develops according to the unique context of the service. Consider the following:
- Do you have exit interviews with team members and families before they move on?
- Do you include child safety prevention measures, to prevent abuse, in both written and verbal orientation for staff and families?
- Do you have printed information translated into the languages of the families who are enrolled at your service?
- Do you have a child-friendly handbook that supports transition into your service? Does it highlight children's rights to safety and protection, and how these needs will be supported at your service?

To do this respectfully and accurately, you need to consider appropriate places and times, the type of support that family, parents and carers need, and the most appropriate, evidence-based practices for engaging with children. Children have the right to give consent. At the Early Childhood Australia Research Symposium 2023, an assent form was shown that used graphics to help children to understand and give informed consent to partaking in research with the University of Southern Queensland. This child-friendly way gave children a user-friendly tool to support dialogue so they could give their approval for being observed, asked questions, photographed, recorded and, of course, also gave the right to stop and withdraw their involvement at any time.

SNAICC's resource *Keeping Our Kids Safe: Cultural Safety and the National Principles for Child Safe Organisations* quotes the Victorian Aboriginal Child Care Agency: *"If you don't get to know kids, build trust and understand their family and culture, kids are unlikely to talk with you about the tough stuff."*

SNAICC goes on to say that operational staff ought to:
- Use culturally appropriate language, photographs and artwork for Aboriginal and Torres Strait Islander children and links to cultural safety and child safe information
- Help children identify trusted adults or friends they can talk to
- Listen to what children say, consider and reflect on children's views to improve their activities and processes, for example, through discussions in team and/or management meetings
- Use culturally appropriate ways of asking Aboriginal and Torres Strait Islander children if they feel safe, such as during story time, yarning, cultural activities or through art surveys
- Understand that children may communicate their views nonverbally, such as through changes in behaviour or participation
- Build children's capacity and confidence to speak up by regularly providing them with opportunities to voice their opinions, as well as by encouraging and listening to them
- Be attuned to signs of harm and facilitate child-friendly and culturally safe ways for children to raise their concerns
(SNAICC, 2021)

There are many organisations that can support you to audit your space in relation to cultural safety. This means respectful practice is ensured. The Koori Curriculum is an Aboriginal early childhood consultancy operated by Jessica Staines, a Wiradjuri woman, who drives the importance of *"products, services, advice and content [being] reflective of the diversity of First Nations peoples in our Country"* (Koori Curriculum, n.d.).

AJ Williams of Aboriginal-owned consultancy Girraway Ganyi aims to *"inspire individuals, communities, businesses and organisations to work more effectively within the Indigenous space, and to increase cultural safety and mental health literacy for all."*

Transitions, routines and excursions

Using Child Safe Standards to guide you

Services need to give precedence to compliance with state/territory requirements and subsequently utilise the National Principles to make the probability of child abuse low. All policies, events and activity planning need to consider threats to children's wellbeing and safety, and instil practices/ actions to take the risk away. This includes times you are inside as well as outside the grounds of service (inclusive of online environments).

As yourself:
- Does your service complete and document a risk minimisation plan before going on an outing or before internal events in relation to the likelihood of child abuse occurring?
- Do you consult with families and the community about the measures in place to mitigate abuse?

Here are some questions to help you rethink what happens in your service, to provoke ideas for improving safety measures against abuse:
- If you have a multi-level building, do you have surveillance cameras in lifts and stairwells? Do educators use these conduits alone with children?
- Are there security cameras in your carpark? What about in playgrounds?
- Do you rely on digital platforms for recording children's attendance?
- Do you headcount before and after transitions to rooftop playgrounds?
- If there are two staff on the late shift, would one be left with children alone at any time?
- Do you sign in children at family groupings before they transition to rooms?

Scanning the setting

Challenge your physical and online environments – the resources, as well as the people interacting in them – to determine whether you create a culture that says no to violence and promotes inclusion, respect and equity.

All educators should self-reflect regularly and check-in with their own biases to determine how 'affective' their pedagogy is. For example, if a group of children was playing forcefully with dinosaurs, would you challenge the aggressive behaviour in the play? If you were taking resources out of the shed with children, would you offer the basket of footballs to a male-identifying child before/if ever offering to a child who identifies as female?

The Anti-Bias Approach in Early Education (4th edition) edited by Dr Red Ruby Scarlet is a text all educators should have. "*Places where children spend large parts of their day also contribute significantly to the development of attitudes and bias. We need to make sure provisions do not ignore, stereotype or diminish certain groups of people*" (Scarlet, 2020). LGBTIQA+ issues in early childhood are explored – cisgender, transgender in addition to caring for children with intersex variation, which gives insight on sharpening our lens to be truly inclusive.

This guiding resource challenges educators to recognise bias they may unintentionally foster and is a tool to provoke respectful, robust dialogue among teams to analyse the powerful messages being portrayed about which societal groups are considered worthy by the children's service, and those which are not. The role of adults, in combination with the resources and materials, is what influences children's "*evaluative frames of reference of groups in their world*" (Scarlet, 2020), which is why we need to offer a fair curriculum.

Here are some self-reflection prompts:
- Do you encourage children to participate in all activities regardless of their gender?
- Do you encourage children to explore gendered activities in different ways (dress-up, trucks, make-up station, etc) using intentional teaching practices to model use of appropriate language?

- Do you talk about and brainstorm ideas for exploring complex issues about body diversity, bodily autonomy, self-determination, biological diversity, sex, gender and sexuality?
- Do you challenge incorrect assumptions that all children are either girls or boys and that everyone's body looks clearly male or female?
- Do you foster relationships among boys that nurture kindness, compassion and respect?
- Do you respond to staff and children who use discriminatory language, and have a classroom discussion about inclusion (for example, *"that's so gay"*, *"throwing like a girl"* or transphobic jokes)?

(#StrongSafeFabulous, Rainbow families, 2021)

Gender stereotypes

Research shows that breaking down traditional gender stereotypes can reduce the level of violence in the community (#StrongSafeFabulous, n.d.). As gender is learnt at an early age, children's services are key places to support the development of a diverse understanding of gender. We need to *"deprogram our contexts because there are narratives in our cultures and sometimes those scripts are going to cut children off from being part of something; we can act and connect gender in a more human way"* says Nathanael Flynn, MA, co-author of *Supporting Gender Diversity in Early Childhood Classrooms*.

The team from #StrongSafeFabulous has endorsed the use of the tip sheet *Preventing domestic and family violence in LGBTIQA+ families*. Access it at www.strongsafefabulous.online/wp-content/uploads/2021/09/early-childhood-tipsheet_final.pdf (Rainbow Families, n.d.).

Star Health's Being Equal programme involved a two-year, whole-of-service approach to ensuring children experienced more respectful relationships and less rigid gender stereotypes through their experiences attending early learning services. The Being Equal pilot programme promoted and embedded gender equity into five early learning services across Port Phillip and Stonnington municipalities in Melbourne, Victoria (Star Health, 2021).

Critical dialogue saw change *"very early on in our journey, an educator had carefully sorted out the clothing in lost property into 'girls' and 'boys' baskets. After drawing awareness to this and having a discussion, we created a single 'lost property' basket and presented it to families in a gender-neutral manner"* (Star Health, 2021). The strength of whole-of-service approaches in creating sustainable change was certainly revealed.

Language is important when we are advocating for equality in our children's services. Words like 'pretty', 'cute', 'handsome' and 'strong' to describe children are sometimes incited by gendered provocations. Use a 'gender lens' to review the messages being projected in your space through the resources available (Star Health, 2021). If you go to the Star Health website (starhealth.org.au), you can access a link to the Being Equal Booklist 2021 – this resource was developed by the early learning services participating in the Being Equal programme.

I encourage you to undertake this assessment process with children, so they too can recognise potential bias in their own setting and be motivated to fix 'systemic failures'. We have a long way to go to redefine in society what strong is. As a co-educator once said to me, *"use everything as a learning tool"*. I've taken this notion with me right through my career, and with my own children. I never remove or avoid things without saying anything – I use them as an education tool, to reveal to children that there *are* unjust things in our world. Calling out biases respectfully means you can role model to children that speaking up is important, because it is acknowledging that some contexts could be/are offensive.

Access Health & Community has a book selection guide within its *Free to be Me* programme. It helps to determine whether your existing books challenge gender stereotypes and can be used to assess suitability for new books. Access the book selection checklist at www.accesshc.org.au/app/uploads/AHC109_Book-Selection-Checklist_170607.pdf

These checklists can also help select books for your children's service or borrowing library that embrace diversity beyond gender. These can include race, culture and ethnicity, sexual orientation and ability.

As a general guide, an appropriate book will include characters that challenge or break traditional ideas about gender roles and femininity/masculinity. Characters will be positively portrayed and celebrated for their uniqueness. Look at the storyline, the characters and the illustrations when you analyse a book to help gauge whether it is appropriate. Where fitting, you could undertake this book review process with children.

Stories are such a universal tool – educators and families can utilise texts to help have conversations with children in a non-confronting way. Books like *Someone Should Have Told Me* (Martin, 2018) can help address sensitive topics such as children seeing adult photos (pornography); face-to-face and online grooming by predators; sexting; and children exposing other children to adult photos. Stories can provide information to support adults in their explanations of the potential dangers and what to do if a child has seen pornography, as well as what to do if a child discloses that they have been abused.

Sensory and nervous system practices

Sensory and nervous system practices are important for wellbeing. Do you offer opportunities in your environments for children to calm and de-escalate their emotions and nervous systems? Do you relate to, connect and hold space for children through the process of co-regulation?

To support children with ways to calm their bodies back to a comfortable state, readily available multisensory experiences can be useful. Traditionally, Snoezelen rooms were set up and used for therapy to support children with additional needs. The word 'Snoezelen' itself originates from two Dutch terms: *snuffelen* (to snuffle) and *doezelen* (to doze). These rooms enabled children to absorb and relax from the multisensory opportunities in the environment. We have adopted this pedagogical approach and incorporated multisensory experiences into our programmes for all children, as they are extremely effective for relaxing someone who has become heightened in their sense of self, momentarily dysregulated and needing support to get back to 'the green zone' of calm.

Some examples of multisensory resources that can be utilised in children's programmes include:
- Snow domes
- Textured wheat packs
- Cold packs/cubes

- Watching lava lamps
- Cause-and-effect push-button toys (sound, light)
- Fish tank gravel and scoopers
- Feeling textured stones
- Torches
- Textured cushions
- Soft toys
- Slinkys
- Small wrist/ankle weights
- Cocoon swings
- Therapy balls

Dr Barbara Sorrels advises that the path of healing is through play:
- Active play
- Dramatic play
- Manipulative play
- Sensory play
- Rhythmic play – rocking equipment, weighted blankets and circle games to experience moving in sync with others
- Rough and tumble play (crash mats, pillow area)
- Construction and block organisation – making order out of chaos
- Cause and effect – manipulating variables

Have you readily available opportunities where children can access and enjoy using multiple senses?

Having these resources available means children learn what calms them best in given situations. It is important that educators connect to know children and look for opportunities to *co-regulate*, as Dr Lori Desautels refers to as touch points, which could be facial expression, tone, noticings and deep listening as we follow children's agenda. When ready, remind them of what might work to feel better. This repertoire of 'wellbeing' allows children to build upon their capacity to self-regulate. Breathing with an educator, or by oneself, is another strategy that can be implemented into curriculums for children of all ages. It can be something as simple as breathing in and out as you touch each finger and thumb (five-star breathing) or blowing candles.

Online safety auditing

The office of the eSafety Commissioner is the national leader in promoting online safety. It provides a complaints service, research and audience-specific content. eSafety's *Best Practice Framework for Online Safety Education* "*establishes a consistent national approach that supports education systems across Australia to deliver high-quality programmes, with clearly defined elements and effective practices.*" Find out more at www.safety.gov.au

The eSafety Toolkit has been created for schools. It has been designed with flexibility in mind, enabling schools to tailor how they use it, based on each community's needs. It is certainly relevant for all children's services to use in self-assessing their online safety environment. It was developed in response to the Royal Commission into Institutional Responses to Child Sexual Abuse and the Education Council's work programme to address bullying and cyberbullying. The resources are categorised into four elements: Prepare, Engage, Educate and Respond. Whether the resources from each element are used on their own or collectively, each contributes to creating safer online environments for school communities.

The online safety self-assessment tool (part of the eSafety Toolkit) prompts questions and suggestions to improve practice (essentially, it's an online safety audit). It asks:

- Is the school (or other type of children's service) leadership committed to creating and maintaining a safe online environment?
- Is the school (or other type of children's service) actively implementing the National Principles for Child Safe Organisations?
- Does the school (or other type of children's service) have staff members with responsibility for online safety?
- Does the school (or other type of children's service) have policies and procedures in place to safeguard against, and respond to, online safety incidents?

The eSafety checklist for developing effective online safety policies and procedures aims to help schools develop and implement online safety policies and procedures, tailored to the needs of their communities. (Note: Policies and procedures should be consistent with and informed by the education department in addition to specific sector policies and procedures.)

The eSafety checklist for effective online safety policies in schools and other types of children's services includes:
- Detail the school's commitment to online safety.
- Clarify the expected behaviours, rights, responsibilities and roles for each member of the school community.
- Provide guiding principles and procedures that seek to mitigate online safety risks.
- Inform school actions when responding to online safety incidents.
- Support school community awareness of how the school is meeting its obligations to support a safe online environment.

The subheadings influence schools (or other type of children's service) to 'Engage staff, students and parents/carers' to regularly determine if current policies and procedures address key and emerging online safety issues. To ensure a diverse range of voices is heard so that responses are inclusive to all groups, consider the needs of all children and young people, including those with a disability, Aboriginal and Torres Strait Islander students, LGBTIQA+ students, those from diverse linguistic and cultural backgrounds, students experiencing family breakdown or in out-of-home care and others who may be more vulnerable and susceptible to online harm.

Checklists used to help assess risk allow organisations to take appropriate action to mitigate potential harm before using certain IT platforms. Staged implementation may help to avoid unintended or unexpected consequences of student use. Usage should be used as per the note above.

It is important to always *proceed with caution and continue to monitor for risks*. For further information and guidance, refer to eSafety's *Online safety self-assessment tool* for schools and *eSafety checklist for early learning services* links in the References section.

Safety online

Early learning services have a responsibility to ensure children and educators are protected from harm when they engage with digital technologies. Managers and directors should aim to be creating a safe online environment at their service.

Early learning services that have a safe online environment:
- **Understand the risks** associated with being online for children, families, educators and the service more broadly
- **Provide experiences for children** that help them learn and remember key strategies for being safe online
- **Support staff** through the development of policies and practices
- **Support and communicate with families** about safe online practices at home and in the community

eSafety has created a checklist for early learning services with these safe online environment aims in mind. You can download resources inclusive of the checklist at www.esafety.gov.au (Early Childhood Australia Learning Hub, n.d.). The checklist has been developed in consultation with ACECQA and is referenced to the NQS and EYLF. You are able to use it as evidence in assessment and rating. ACECQA advises you to share and discuss this type of checklist with educators to ensure it is understood by your whole team.

Research by the Australian Government's eSafety Commissioner has recognised that some individuals and communities are more at risk of being targeted online and at risk of serious harm due to a range of intersectional factors. These factors include race, religion, cultural background, gender, sexual orientation, disability and mental health conditions. The risk can also increase because of situational vulnerabilities, such as being impacted by domestic and family violence.

"Creating an Online Safety Agreement in collaboration with children is a great way to develop their critical thinking and self-regulation skills, encouraging them to build good habits with digital technology" (eSafety.gov.au).

There are also online learning modules to help educators implement online safety strategies into their curriculums, as well as posters, songs and picture books (all downloadable on the eSafety Government website). The message behind these child-friendly tools is to encourage children to ask for help when they are using digital devices, to keep them safer online.

The Queensland Organised Crime Commission established the *Out of the Dark* programme in 2015 to address internet-related child sexual abuse. *"The Byrne Report acknowledged that the proliferation of new and emerging information and communication technologies has increasingly exposed children and young people to risks and harms in the online environment."*

Plan-do-check-act cycle

Best practice requires you to continually audit your culture of child safety in all environments because if you do, it is more difficult for abuse to occur – and if you don't, it can remain hidden. Are there any weaknesses, gaps or improvements needed at your service, both online and in your physical spaces?

This organisation process can be portrayed as a 'quality circle' or 'plan-do-check-act' cycle, as shown in the following illustration:

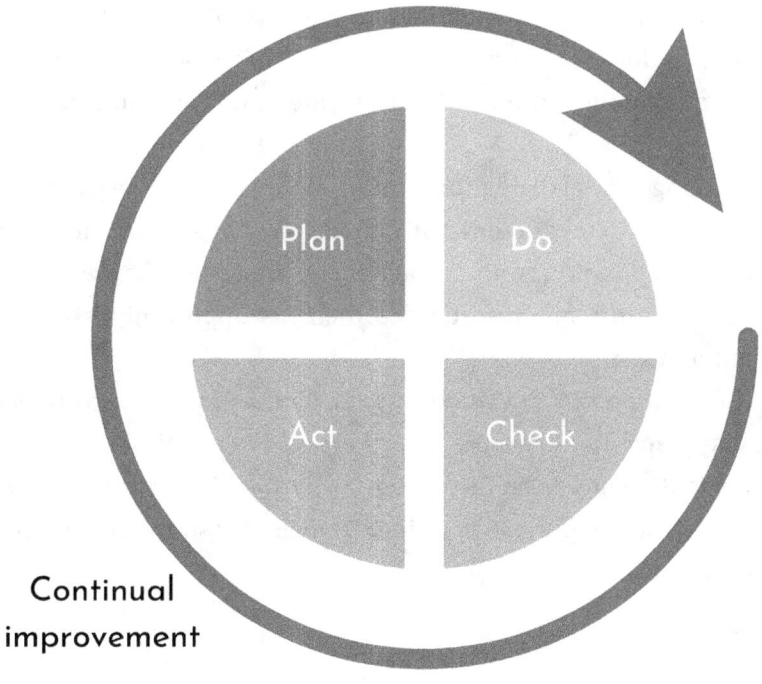

(Milton, 2019)

A culture of child safety requires actions to be carried out on an ongoing basis because you are working in the defence, preventatively. We are doing more than just adhering to a system of response when we suspect a child has been/is likely to be harmed. We need to utilise the framework of consultation and collaboration with others to facilitate a holistic understanding of the best ways to prevent harm. Be obliged to have your safety procedures meticulously planned, executed, regularly reviewed and improved if you are going to be attentive to your service provision in its entirety.

Advocating children's rights means *proactively* safeguarding children, by providing a *stronger resistance*. We must sharpen our clarity and tighten our security to the point where we deter anyone who considers breaching a child's right to safety. It is time early childhood professionals step into a new paradigm of child protection, one that endorses child safety prevention, as well as detection.

Child protection training and body safety resources are praiseworthy, but as we have explored, not without a strong commitment to address child autonomy, safety and wellbeing in the context of your own children's education and care service. An environment needs to be audited, analysed and regularly reviewed in terms of the lived experience of participants. Implied safety structures are needed to create and maintain a culture of child safety.

By promoting critical dialogue around children's safety, we can uncover issues together and create ideas with all stakeholders to provide a safer environment. Responding to the cataclysm of abuse, it takes fearlessness to accept all systemic failures and see them as opportunities to evolve our environments.

Shift the momentum to agitate as dedicated advocates for protecting children. As Grace Tame would say, "*Keep making noise*" because our "*work in prevention has never been more important*". Inspire others in your workplace to act and apply safeguarding strategies for short- and long-term systemic change.

In summary

With this chapter complete, you should now know that:
- You must be mindful of what could go wrong in your settings.
- Ongoing review is paramount to maintaining a strong safety culture.
- Every service type and individual context is different.
- Policies must mimic current practices.
- Consultation is needed with all stakeholders for suitability.
- Anti-bias and gender-equity curriculums are necessary every single day.
- Children have a right to learn body autonomy from birth.

Chapter 7 reflection questions

- Do you consider the possibility of abuse in risk assessments for internal special events as well as excursions?
- Do you consider the possibility of abuse in risk assessments for regular outings?
- Do you hold Children's Council Meetings, so they have an official forum for consultation?
- Do you assess existing resources to ensure they are inclusive and represent equity and diversity in society?
- Does your curriculum educate and embrace all gender expressions?
- Do you commit to knowledge building to promote wellbeing and inclusion for Aboriginal and Torres Strait Islander children?
- If you had a child at your service that identifies as non-binary and uses 'they/them' pronouns, would you know how to respectfully communicate with this gender-diverse person?
- How do you continue to make sure every child is seen in your curriculum to promote equity, inclusion and high expectations?

CHAPTER 8

Child safety – governance and leadership

Insight for educators/practitioners:
- Embracing solidarity, aligning your vision with universal education and care sector aims, while also being effective in local contexts for progressive change

Chapter elements:
- Being a dedicated advocate
- Global governance models
- Australia in context
- Advancing your service's child safety
- Stakeholder consultation
- Declaring your Child Safety Commitment
- Micro-level changes and long-term systemic change

Tailoring systems and processes to meet the diverse needs of children and their families creates social cohesion within an organisation. This happiness filters satisfaction into the community and is the key to a proficient reputation and the foundation for high-quality education and care.

We do, however, want community gratification for its education and care services, and to be inclusive of its vigilance towards abuse prevention and response. "*Child abuse in organisations is a prevalent and evolving issue, and we cannot afford to think of it as something from the past*" (CCYP, 2022). The previous chapters of this book have provided insight into the legal and ethical responsibilities of an early childhood professional. The staying power for high-quality service provision will depend on continuous momentum. We have attested that this comes down to the degree of children's wellbeing and safety.

A commitment to review is often what is lacking. Policies, procedures and record-keeping need ongoing maintenance to improve delivery of child-safe services. Recognising and facilitating the participation and involvement of staff, volunteers, children and young people, families and community mentors in these reviews will strengthen the organisation's child-safeguarding capacities.

Organisational change is often necessary to ensure services are effective at preventing harm to children. A paradigmatic shift in early childhood is what is needed if we are going to be leaders in this aspect of education and care.

Despite significant differences in early childhood systems between countries, similar issues have emerged, and early childhood education has become a global 'situation for concern'. If we see the "*crucial role of early childhood education as a common good and public service, essential for the functioning of societies*" (Urban, 2022), then we cannot argue with epistemologies that suggest a new paradigm is needed.

Mathias Urban (2022) argues the "*necessity and possibility of fundamental reconceptualisation of the practices and policies that have shaped early childhood systems*". If we do this, organisations will be identifying and assessing "*vulnerability, propensity, the situational and institutional risks*" in every individual activity (CCYP, 2022), making the entire service safer for children.

We need shared, situated knowledge creation in response to profound configurations of a new paradigm. Grant yourself permission to be an activist in this space. Let your service be a platform to drive this agenda. It is time to forge ahead fiercely, and make good of what is likely to have been inconsequential child safety arrangements.

Being a dedicated advocate

To achieve integrity in your work, *you need to know how* to be responsive in your contextual environment. *You* need to gain insight into the rigorous system designed to protect children in your state or territory, but there is usefulness in gaining insight from other areas, to know more than just the information to which you are bound. If you keep child safety at the forefront of your thinking, then you will remain *au fait* when it comes to being pre-emptive and responsive.

There are many things that we can all do every day, in all the different aspects of our lives – in our jobs, in our families, in our neighbourhoods, in our clubs or organisations and in our social groups. NAPCAN's Play your Part Strategy looks closely at what we can do in our roles in society, because "*Protecting children is everyone's business.*"

Incremental change is no longer sufficient; what are the challenges – and possibilities – of a radical step towards a new paradigm?

Global governance models

In the international discourse, quality has assumed a hegemonic position. It has become unquestionable, and we have seen a pervasive construct of early childhood education and care and its acronym ECEC. It composes the realisation of children's right to education.

"*Participation in high-quality early childhood education and care, with highly skilled staff and adequate child-to-staff ratios, produces positive results for all children and has highest benefits for the most disadvantaged*" (Urban, 2022).

However, this rights-based framework is constantly being whitewashed by motivations reflective of a competitive economy, with neglect towards social responsibilities. At the 18th Annual Social Justice in Early Childhood Conference (July, 2022), Professor Ann Merete Otterstad of Norway's Oslo Metropolitan University stressed the problem with individualism, consumerism being the norm and children being in the middle of privatisation. "*Neoliberalism turned solidarity into competitions.*" This attitude shifts the view of families and children to being seen as customers.

As a sector (not an industry!), we must resist discourses evolving strong takeover regimes, where early childhood is seen as an investment. ECEC is an inseparable concept and is now widely accepted, although in the reality of service provision, the institutional and conceptual split persists in many countries. We see greater value in the conceptualisation of services for young children as education settings that offer professional care; a comprehensive integration of services incorporating nutrition, health, wellbeing, education, care, social cohesion and equality, but continue to exclude crucial aspects of holistic development from the picture, i.e. children's rights and wellbeing. Children's rights and wellbeing drive a culture of child safety and the reality is, by these aspects not taking precedence, early childhood has reached a critical juncture.

Articulated by Peter Moss (2001) and others, "*We cannot continue as we are.*" Early childhood education, Moss alerts us, must reinvent itself as "*education for survival. This may sound alarmist to those still positioned within the dominant paradigm of universality (of development), measurability (of predetermined outcomes), and governability and manageability (of quality). For indigenous scholars, however, 'education for survival' has been the foundation communities' engagement with young children all along.*"

Approved providers of early childhood services have proven to reveal stark differences in quality, not only between, but within countries. Governments have embarked on addressing these discrepancies through more integrated and multi-sectoral early childhood policies, bringing together early childhood development, education and health services. "*The problems facing early childhood education are no longer limited to individual settings – the point of delivery; they are endemic in the entire ecosystem, the 'critical ecology*" (Urban, 2022).

In Urban's research article 'Scholarship in Times of Crises: towards a transdiscipline of early childhood', he gives rise to *"fields of tension that currently characterise the state early childhood education globally... that surround, enable, and govern the daily practices of educating young children. It encapsulates a frame of thinking, a possible epistemology, that enables us to fundamentally question"* new discourses being introduced to the field.

We absolutely could abandon the dominant paradigm of early childhood education – the paradigm of the universal, individual child and its development of decontextualised knowledge and its creation of simplistic evaluation and comparison. If we do this, policies and practices cannot be seen as tools for *solving* distinct social problems. We can use this international thinking to our advantage. If we take on this suggestion of a new paradigm to conceptualise present experiences and future direction with a holistic, uniquely multifaceted approach to education and care, we reposition children front and centre.

Australia in context

The Australian Government is working collaboratively with state and territory governments to address and implement the Royal Commission's recommendations. All state and territory governments committed to provide separate annual reports on their progress in implementing the recommendations of the Royal Commission from December 2018 until December 2022. The reports articulate ways that institutions that engage in child-related work, such as education services, were making progress towards better promoting children's safety and wellbeing.

In 2018–22 inclusive, the National Office for Child Safety worked with 122 institutions to facilitate their public reporting and submit a progress report. From accessing these reports it is apparent that schools and colleges were part of the groups representing education, but early childhood education and care services *were not included*. Omission of the early education and care services is erroneous, seeing as we engage with Australia's youngest citizens. The organisations were invited to report the sharing of examples that reflected a positive approach to child safe culture and practices, so could it be that we haven't yet put ourselves on the map as standout institutions regarding child safety governance, leadership and culture?

Data collection is certainly needed by the National Office for Child Safety, but that is not the method we want to rely on to provide our evidence that reflects a *positive approach* to child safe culture and practices. This is a conceivable likelihood, as there has been a strong drawing towards IT platforms for documentation in Australia, but this ubiquity is revealing itself in the early childhood sector across the world.

"*As a strategy for demonstrating accountability and performance, digital platforms shape the learning that is seen by early childhood educators: tag-ability, trackability, completeness and co-constitution*" (White et al, 2020). Children's services streamlining processes to remain accountable. The risk here is that when Child Safe Standards and National Principles for Child Safe Organisations are loaded into these systems, the attentiveness to meticulous thinking is at risk. We need to prioritise brainpower over tech power.

Until 31 December 2022, the Quality Assessment and Regulation Division (QARD) worked with the CCYP to regulate the new standards. From 1 January 2023, the Commission will only regulate some organisations that have to comply with the standards. Laws have been passed that will allocate types of organisation to six different regulators, including the Commission.

The six regulators and their sectors are:
- **Early childhood education and care:** The Department of Education, through its Quality Assessment and Regulation Division, is the regulator for early childhood services. This includes long day care, family day care, outside school hours care and vacation care services, as well as limited hours and occasional care services.
- **Schools:** Victorian Registration and Qualifications Authority (VRQA) is the Victorian regulator for registered schools, school boarding premises, school-sector providers of courses to overseas students, student exchange organisations, non-school senior secondary providers and registered training organisations that are registered with VRQA.
- **Social services:** Department of Families, Fairness and Housing is the Victorian regulator for providers of out-of-home care, housing services, family violence and sexual assault services, and support services for parents and families.

- **Health services:** Department of Health is the Victorian regulator for hospitals, community health services, mental health services, drug and alcohol treatment services, and maternal and child health services.
- **Employers of children:** Wage Inspectorate Victoria is the Victorian regulator for organisations that employ children and hold a permit under the Child Employment Act 2003 (Victoria).
- **Other Victorian organisations:** The CCYP is the regulator for the standards for organisations where there is no specified co-regulator.

Keep in mind that some organisations will have more than one regulator if they provide more than one type of service or facility to children (for example, an early learning centre and a registered school).

Visit the CCYP website (www.ccyp.vic.gov.au) for a complete list of sectors and their regulators from January 2023.

In addition to advocating for brainpower over tech power, for child safety there is the additional point that organisations need to have explicit online child safety protocols we discussed in Chapter 7. What's more, I'm also problematising the barrier, the tech devices place, between educators and children in their environments. I'm putting forward the contention that child safety cannot be thorough if *"early childhood educators 'see' through digitally cast eyes"* (White et al, 2020).

The *Keeping kids safe and well: your voices* report *"conveys the views of children, young people and families, collected by the National Children's Commissioner, in face-to-face and online consultations and surveys between May and July 2021. The report presents key issues, identifies priorities and makes recommendations for action, to inform the Government's five-year action plans under the* Safe & Supported: The National Framework for Protecting Australia's Children 2021-2031 *(the National Framework)"* (Australian Human Rights Commission, 2021).

We do need a sharper view towards groups that are at greater risk of abuse and neglect. *"People who are LGBTIQA+ can face unique challenges and disparities in quality of care when accessing services"* (Farrugia, 2022).

Safe & Supported: The National Framework for Protecting Australia's Children 2021-2031 is for all Australian children, young people and families, with a targeted focus on groups that are experiencing disadvantage or are vulnerable to abuse and neglect. As it says, "*Protecting children is everyone's business*". The best interests of the child are at the centre of the National Framework and the subsequent Action Plans.

A national approach

To improve outcomes for priority groups, there needs to be a national approach, meaning every single service needs to make clear its commitment to prevention, early detection/intervention and information sharing.

The National Framework states: "*Children and young people in Australia have the right to grow up safe, connected and supported in their family, community and culture. They have the right to grow up in an environment that enables them to reach their full potential.*"

The National Framework aligns and interacts with other national initiatives to support systemic change for children, young people and families. Most importantly, it has close linkages with the next National Plan to End Violence against Women and Children, recognising that the two issues are closely intertwined at all levels.

The National Framework aligns with the National Strategy to Prevent and Respond to Child Sexual Abuse 2021-2030 and the National Aboriginal and Torres Strait Islander Early Childhood Strategy.

Australia has a duty to make sure that all children in the country enjoy the rights set out in the agreement, which is why the National Principles for Child Safe Organisations are:
- Underpinned by a child rights, strengths-based approach
- Designed to allow for flexibility in implementation across all sectors engaging with children and young people, and in organisations of various sizes
- Aligned with existing child safe approaches at the state and territory level

And the guiding principles in the United Nations Convention on the Rights of the Child are:
- The best interests of the child as a primary consideration
- The right of children to survival and development

- The right of children to express their views freely on all matters affecting them
- The right of all children to enjoy all the rights of the CRC without discrimination

Australia's Children's Commissioner, Anne Hollonds, declares the need for Australians to be responsible for what happens to children during this crucial time in their lives: "*Childhood is quite rightly described as critically important for people's social, health and economic outcomes, but the value of childhood is not only about the future adult that a child may become,*" she says. "*Children must be respected for who they are in the 'here and now', which is why Australia needs a human rights framework that values childhood, respects children, and supports the wellbeing of children and their families.*"

Our country's message of how perpetrators of abuse are punished is not unanimous. Justice for children should not look different in different places. The Harmony Campaign has been established by The Grace Tame Foundation and is "*aimed at getting consistent laws around the country that pertain to sexual assault. Currently, there are eight definitions for sexual intercourse, the age of consent to sex, consent and grooming between the eight state and territory jurisdictions, as well as eight different sets of punishments for these inconsistently worded offences.*" Find more information at www.thegracetamefoundation.org.au

National leaders do need to be part of our nation's future, and therefore need to invest and successfully contest for children's rights to safety. We need more than a role-modelling effect to shift norms. We need to continue to shift the parameters of debate in our nation to keep strengthening legislation and mobilise more resources.

"*Australia needs a contemporary and unifying approach that harnesses our children's strengths and potential, to protect them effectively... Now more than ever, we need strong leadership that moves forward – not back... Our thinking needs to look ahead, to build upon proven strategies*" (Tsorbaris, 2022).

While campaigns such as this push for greater consistency, we need to make sure we clearly articulate our zero tolerance for child abuse. We need to be very specific about what culture we create, maintain, expect and therefore promote within the context of our own services. We also need to make it very clear what behaviour *will not* be tolerated.

Tasmania believes that its children and young people will have the best chance of growing up as healthy, happy adults if they are cared for by adults they know well and trust – this gives them security, stability and continuity, connection, care and protection. The outlook is that the rest of the community helps families by supporting them in the demanding job of bringing up their children to be healthy and happy adults. The Government cannot provide continuity, connection, care and protection for children alone – this state accepts that supporting families and protecting children is *everyone's* responsibility.

Advancing your service's child safety

Ask yourself: are we as an organisation making our arrangements clear to everyone about the ways we prevent abuse and how it is managed? Is your ethos about this subject matter prevalent to your local community? Are you making a stance in the education and care sector beyond the boundary of your service?

Recognising that the safety of children is *everyone's* responsibility means the organisational leadership model at a service needs to reinforce attitudes and behaviours that value children and young people. It is vital to foster a collaborative approach towards everyone being agents for social change, inclusive of children themselves.

It is time to think about the way you represent yourself as a service, both on the premises and when operating programmes externally. Your signage, advertisements, open days, interviews and orientations should indicate your commitment to child safety. Every single visitor and member of the community should be able to see this allegiance from the multiple means of information on show, in addition to what is provided (i.e. Commitments, Code of Conduct and Child Safety and Wellbeing Policy).

This public portrayal, where your service is concerned, needs a deep commitment to child safety. To be praiseworthy, everyone must have a vested interest in children's rights, safety and wellbeing. Knowing how to frame this invitation to work in partnership will have some bearing on your community's desire (and ability) to be involved. Inviting representation from all stakeholder groups, inclusive of children, to be part of Child Safety Committees as Child Safety Champions will positively drive activeness and permeate awareness through all user groups at the education and care service.

Choosing safe staff and volunteers

Developing appropriate selection criteria for the position and emphasising child safety and wellbeing are the first steps in reducing the risk of employing someone who poses a child safety risk. Provide induction, supervision, support and monitoring of staff and volunteers so that they understand their responsibilities to children, including record-keeping, information sharing and reporting obligations, how to keep children safe. Supporting employees to prevent and minimise harm so they can act confidently is important, but first invest the time in recruiting. The Commitment to Child Safety, the Child Safe Environment and Wellbeing Policy, Code of Conduct, complaints process and related policies and procedures are the framework to guide professional high-quality practice.

Organisations need to consider the necessary steps that are suitable for them. As examples, the following measures are what courts have previously considered to be *reasonable precautions* in the context of organisational child abuse:

- Employment screening and reference checking
- Supervision and training
- Implementing systems to provide early warning of possible offences
- Random and unannounced inspections to deter misconduct
- Encouraging children and adults to notify authorities or parents about any signs of aberrant or unusual behaviour

HR practices

Ensure recruitment processes reflect the commitments of your organisation to child safety and wellbeing, with a specific focus on cultural safety for Aboriginal and Torres Strait Islander children. Remember, your ethos needs to be evident in advertising, interviewing, induction and in the continuation of the affiliation with your service. Emphasise your organisation's standpoint towards inclusion and equity to building cultural understanding, including self-determination and social justice, as part of child safety and wellbeing. Consider the following:

- Include commitments to child safety and cultural competency in job advertisements.
- Include specific questions in the interview process that relate to a potential staff member's understanding of Aboriginal and Torres Strait Islander history and current issues, or a willingness to learn about these issues.
- Explain in pre-interview screening questionning your Code of Conduct, including the organisation's commitment to cultural safety and intolerance of racism and cultural abuse.
- Ensure staff and volunteers agree to commit to ongoing training, workshops and supervision regarding cultural awareness and safety (include this in position descriptions and contracts).
- Train staff and volunteers in any statutory obligations relating to Aboriginal and Torres Strait Islander children.
- Ensure staff and volunteers understand and advocate the specific human and cultural rights of Aboriginal and Torres Strait Islander children.
- When advertising, encourage Aboriginal and Torres Strait Islander people to apply for positions.
- Draft duty statements to reflect the principles of child safety and cultural safety.
- Professional development training should be referred to as a continuing process (more training, simplified or translated materials, audio versions to ensure information is well understood).

For individuals or teams, note that you cannot offer cultural advice or teach culture, and can only offer a perspective (if you are not an Aboriginal and/or Torres Strait Islander person).

Screening and due diligence

- When screening potential staff or volunteers, your organisation should include questions about child safety, discrimination and cultural responsiveness as part of their referee checks.
- Ensure that local Aboriginal and Torres Strait Islander community members are heavily involved in the design and implementation of recruitment and staff development policies – this helps to develop respectful relationships and enhances culturally safe processes.

Reflect and review

- Establish and sustain awareness and knowledge of the needs of diverse communities, and proactively ensure that your organisation is accessible and responsive to these needs.
- Develop, implement and maintain – or adapt existing – reporting, monitoring and evaluation frameworks for incidents of racism, discrimination and abuse, and your organisation's response.
- Engage in consultation and provide feedback on policies and practices so your organisation can improve in child and cultural safety.
- Individual growth plans enable individuals to steer their professional development for growth and to incorporate and seek relevant mentoring/training.

Training

Provide ongoing training to staff and volunteers regarding:
- Identifying and responding to signs of child abuse and harm
- Supporting someone making a disclosure about harm to a child
- Assessing and managing risks of child abuse and harm
- Empowerment and participation of children
- Child safe reporting and response obligations
- Cultural safety and inclusive practices for equity
- Record-keeping and information sharing

(CCYP, 2022)

Statement of philosophy

When you are committed to children's wellbeing, it is important that you have readily available the current and underlying ethos of your service provision. As Quality Area 7 of the NQS states: *"All services are required to have a current statement of philosophy in place, which is reviewed on a regular basis... The rights and best interests of the child underpin all practice. Their safety, health and wellbeing are paramount"* (ACECQA, 2018).

The statement of philosophy reflects the beliefs and values of those who are associated with a service. Together with the approved learning framework, it assists educators in considering the service's approach to learning, development and wellbeing. It should also underpin policies and procedures and guide all aspects of a service's operations and practices.

Make the most of the power and potential of your philosophy by keeping it current and documenting how it is constantly evolving. Prospective families are likely to research your service before they make a time or just turn up on your doorstep, so your website needs to include this written statement of intent that outlines the purpose and principles under which the service operates. The initial point of contact should reveal an Acknowledgment of Country with specific relevance to the location and the peoples the service resides on. Separate to the Acknowledgement of Country should be any other commitments, such as supportive reference to LGBTIQA+, to people of all abilities.

When looking at principles/outcomes for your statement of philosophy, you may wish to consider the following through consultation with all stakeholders, inclusive of children:

- The rights and best interests of the child underpin all practice. Their safety, health and wellbeing are paramount. Each is respected without discrimination or bias and has a voice.
- Children are viewed as successful, competent and capable learners, who are given opportunities to construct their own understandings, contribute to the learning of others and participate in decisions that affect them.

- Equity, inclusion and diversity are embedded in practice. Children are given every opportunity to succeed, and their diverse circumstances, cultural background and abilities are respected and valued.

Refer to Appendix 10: Reflection and discussion prompts for reviewing your service philosophy.

Children's voices

Principle 1.2 of the National Principles for Child Safe Organisations states that *"A child safe culture is championed and modelled at all levels of the organisation from the top down and the bottom up"* (Australian Human Rights Commission 2018), which includes children, as they are considered key stakeholders.

An organisation can underestimate the powerful impact children's voices and vision can provide in an array of areas including safety and wellbeing. The UNCRC provides that children have a right to be heard and involved in all decisions that affect them. Parents and caregivers, by virtue of their relationship to their children, can see things differently when it comes to safety concerns, which may not be apparent to the organisation.

As Liana Buchanan, principal commissioner, in the annual report 2020-21, says: *"Every day, I remain in awe of the insights that children and young people bring to complex and seemingly intractable problems."*

To build capacity, to be child safe in your individual context, Professor Stephen Smallbone stated in a submission to the Royal Commission: *"Staff [and volunteer adults]... should have a culture of 'extended guardianship' or shared personal responsibility, where preventing abuse is seen as the ordinary responsibility of all adults,"* and suggests that: *"If child safety governance is not lived at a leadership level, then the culture of child safety will not permeate throughout the organisation, which puts children at risk of harm and abuse"* (Milton, 2019).

The journey to a culture of child safety

Essential steps in the journey to a culture of child safety are to ensure everyone in your children's education and care organisation:
- Understands the guiding principles of the UNCRC, because this is the main international agreement on children's rights
- Becomes familiar with the National Principles for Child Safe Organisations
- Considers how your organisation currently addresses child safety and wellbeing (measure against state/territory Child Safe Standards and the National Principles for Child Safe Organisations)

As we have mentioned previously, you can utilise the Child Safe Organisations' *Introductory self-assessment tool for organisations* on the Australian Human Rights Commission website. This will help determine what key actions you currently do as well as what you need to implement into your Quality Improvement Plan. Your goals/intentions will be in line with the indicators the principle is upheld.

One of the key things to remember is that children cannot be denied access to experiences that help them to develop. It is up to organisations to work out ways that children can benefit from opportunities while remaining safe.

For example, number 8 of the National Principles for Child Safe Organisations refers to physical and online environments: "*Children have the right to get information that is important to their wellbeing from radio, newspapers, books, computers and other sources. Adults should make sure that the information children get is not harmful and helps them find and understand the information they need.*"

For example, one key action: Staff and volunteers identify and mitigate risks in the online and physical environments without compromising a child's right to privacy, access to information, social connections and learning opportunities.

For example, one indicator that this principle is upheld: Children and their families are informed, in culturally appropriate ways, about the use of the organisation's technology and safety tools. Read more at childsafe.humanrights.gov.au

A child safety culture is not a set-and-forget approach. It must be constantly reviewed through surveys, interviews, consultation and even complaints. We need to *consistently review*, with the outlook to improve. Refer back to the 'plan-do-check-act' cycle we referred to in Chapter 7. Reflect, plan, do and learn is another sequence referred to when talking about the process of empowering all stakeholders to facilitate positive change. What can we learn from other organisations? What strategies have other early childhood education and care services used to measure how safe (physically and emotionally) children feel? What hurdles were overcome? Networking beyond the silo of your own children's service is invaluable.

For more information about organisational empowerment, there are three tools you can access on CCYP's website (www.ccyp.vic.gov.au), such as pages 35–47 of the *Empowerment and participation* guide. These tools provide a clear template for supporting your organisation with what to do before developing an empowerment strategy, while developing one and how to assess your empowerment strategy after its implementation.

Child safety on the agenda

Child safety permanently on the team agenda will increase the ability to identify gaps and share new knowledge among teams. I strongly advocate for this strategy to be adopted by all education and care services, which is why it has been mentioned previously. Ongoing people management means regularly checking in to see if individual staff need additional training/information to maintain a high level of understanding in relation to preventing and responding to abuse. Child safety proficiency should not wait until a team member has their 'three-monthly' or 'annual' review.

Child safety permanently on the team agenda not only creates conditions that proactively respond to any concerns, disclosures, allegations or suspicions, it also enables opportunities to see if targeted support needs to be provided to a single person or an entire team.

Raising concerns

Everyone needs to take charge in their local context, from the top down, from the bottom up – everyone, regardless of their role. This has not been the adopted approach by children's services, but it needs to be.

To live up to the saying 'from the top down, from the bottom up', a child safety culture must be led and championed by the top tier of leadership within the hierarchy of any organisation. The National Principles for Child Safe Organisations states: *"Child safety and wellbeing is embedded in organisational leadership, governance and culture."*

The organisation has an accessible, child-focused complaint-handling policy, which clearly outlines the roles and responsibilities of leadership, staff and volunteers, approaches to dealing with different types of complaints, breaches of relevant policies or the Code of Conduct and obligations to act promptly and report with consideration to reporting, privacy and employment law. Consider how publicly reporting on a review may impact on parties involved in any incidents referenced – especially consider the need to warn any victim-survivors that the report will be published.

The Child Safe Organisations' Introductory self-assessment tool for organisations says: *"Leaders in the organisation model attitudes and behaviours that show they are committed to child safety and wellbeing."* This might look like leaders do the following:
- Informing themselves about child safety and wellbeing
- Making a public commitment to child safety and wellbeing
- Always putting the best interests of children first
- Encouraging all staff and volunteers of the organisation to value and ensure child safety and wellbeing
- Supporting anyone to safely disclose their concerns and are responsive
- Being open to suggestions and complaints
- Improving practice from feedback and complaints

(Australian Human Rights Commission, 2018)

This means, if you are asking educators to undertake child safety training, then the board of management would undertake that training, too. A child safety culture cannot be activated and maintained with an attitude of viewing child safety as something that only people working directly with children need to be familiar with. It must be 'a priority for all of us and we will do everything we can to make sure the whole organisation understands this, and our practice will reflect this.'

Handling criticism

Sometimes people affiliated with your organisation do want to raise a concern or feel they need to make a complaint. Effective complaint-handling processes are those that are easy to understand by children and young people, families, staff and volunteers, and are culturally safe. Children should know who they can go to if they want to raise a concern or make a complaint. Children may be more comfortable talking to an educator other than those who are designated to their room/group. I see many children who have trusting relationships with cooks in centres, with a director of an early learning centre, with educators who relieve breaks and those in aftercare. Children decide who their safe people are, and child-friendly complaints processes should be evident in all education and care services (i.e. visual displays, audio of complaints process).

A common cause for criticism is due to people feeling they have not been involved or informed about happenings at your organisation. Communication and respectful partnerships are integral to lessen the likelihood of stakeholders feeling unhappy. So, make sure your communication channels are open and you are well versed with systems throughout your children's service, as well as updates in the sector, that impact your service provision – for example, state reforms such as Information Sharing Schemes.

If you live in Victoria and are wondering if your organisation should be implementing any or all of the reforms, you will firstly need to determine whether your organisation is supposed to be sharing information to protect children. Consider the following points:

1. Confirm you are an Information Sharing Entity.
2. Familiarise yourself with the ministerial guidelines.
3. Check your organisation is ready.
4. Inform your stakeholders about the schemes.
5. Request information.

6. Share information.
7. Use the schemes together.
8. Understand record-keeping.
9. Understand the complaints process.

We need to reflect on our organisational leadership model and gauge how well it reinforces attitudes and behaviours that truly value children, families and community.

Stakeholder consultation

Your organisation should publicly commit to child safety and wellbeing. After all, Nelson Mandela enunciated: *"There can be no keener revelation of a society's soul than in the way it treats it's children."*

To maintain a high level of quality service provision, you need to consistently consult with *all* stakeholders to review and make changes to your policies and practices, as well as reinform centre communities of modifications to these guiding principles. Community consultation with stakeholders, inclusive of children, allows you to get an accurate portrayal of people's level of understanding, viewpoints and their ideas.

"When the voices of the families and communities we work with are involved, solutions and strategies are much more likely to be effective" (SNAICC, 2021).

Do you invite local residents to join you for discussions as part of your community research before creating or redeveloping documents that govern your service provision?

"Being safe and feeling safe are not the same." An environment needs to be reviewed in terms of the lived experience of participants and implied safety structures. While an institution may be focused on observable threats, it may not be informed by valuable children's perceptions and experience" (Milton, 2019).

Cultural considerations

"Lead your organisation towards an organisation-wide ethos of accountability for cultural safety for Aboriginal and Torres Strait Islander children and families" (SNAICC, 2021).

A cultural lens

"*Everyone, regardless of cultural background, makes decisions through a cultural lens, which shapes a person's view of what is 'normal'. As all decisions – no matter how simple or complex – are made through this lens, everyone needs to recognise and remember that if you are not [from a particular culture], your cultural lens is different*" – and remember you cannot measure cultural safety for that specific culture (SNAICC, 2021).

Looking at cultural diversity

"*While there are some common elements to Aboriginal and Torres Strait Islander cultures across Australia, each community has its own unique cultural context. Organisations should engage with their local communities to clearly understand what culture means to their communities*" (SNAICC, 2021). Rather than rely on Aboriginal Elders to come to you, attend Aboriginal and Torres Strait Islander events to build rapport with the local community.

"*[This is] an important first step before applying a cultural lens to your organisational policies and procedures, and to understanding what cultural safety will look like for your organisation*" (SNAICC, 2021).

"*Create, implement, and maintain an Aboriginal and Torres Strait Islander employment strategy*" (SNAICC, 2021). An Aboriginal Inclusion Policy would support human and cultural rights protections for Aboriginal peoples. We have policies for all non-negotiables, so why wouldn't we ensure our organisation has this?

In the community

To build commitment, members of your organisation can attend forums and promote the broader social purpose of enhancing Aboriginal and Torres Strait Islander child rights to your stakeholders. Influence Government policy through engagement in strategic forums and build relationships with senior public servants and ministers as appropriate. Also build alliances with education institutions, which can develop and deliver training. And, where practicable, encourage community events at your organisation, so community groups can use the facilities for community gatherings – acting as a welcoming and safe community hub (for example, Elders councils).

Your organisation should provide a variety of opportunities, both formally and informally, for families and communities to be involved in conversations around child safety. This might be through social media and online events, community events, barbecues, open days, newsletters, family focus groups or, in some instances, targeted consultations might be the safest, most comfortable and effective option for a family.

Some consultation topics are sensitive and have the potential to bring up past trauma and trigger negative emotional responses. Therefore, appropriate supports should be put in place for the community. Is it clear what support networks are available to support your community?

Cultural safety

Undertake a cultural assessment to determine where your service is currently at with cultural safety. This is vital because gaps in knowledge and understanding are considered danger zones. Organisations in your state, such as Reconciliation Victoria (if you live in Victoria), can assist with this process, and determine training that is needed specific to your children's service. Other organisations, such as Girraway Ganyi Consultancy, is an Aboriginal-owned consultancy 'aiming to inspire individuals, communities, businesses and organisations to work more effectively within the Indigenous space, and to increase cultural safety and mental health literacy for all'.

Increased vulnerability

To support Aboriginal and Torres Strait Islander children who identify as LGBTIQA+, staff and volunteers should be familiar with gender expression in Aboriginal and Torres Strait Islander communities. Find out about the impact of domestic and family violence on LGBTIQA+ families and the practical things that you and your education setting can do to help build safe communities for LGBTIQA+ people and families and the wider community.

Meaningful engagement with children, young people, parents, carers and communities in local contexts and abroad is what is required to achieve better outcomes for children against child abuse and neglect. Positive life experiences come from feeling a sense of connection and belonging to your community, due to reciprocal relationships.

Take the time to invest in accessing a glossary of terms to help everyone to better understand the terminology and to use inclusive language in service provision. Be mindful that social and cultural understandings vary from country to country, and different acronyms and terms are used across developed and developing countries. Note the following:

1. There is no single LGBTIQA+ community, rather a plurality of identities and experiences.
2. Other variations of this acronym exist. Acronym choice can vary depending on the groups or issues being discussed and the available evidence. The acronyms used in this resource reflect the research conducted.

(AIFS, 2013)

Approaches to best protect children at your service need to be well understood and therefore supported by the immediate and surrounding communities. Clear, strong messages about child safety and wellbeing within and projected into the community are needed, otherwise, if we are not saying anything or *"trivialise and confuse the issue"*, then there is a chance of being *"exploited by perpetrators"* (Revell, 2022).

Quality Improvement Plan

Quality Improvement Planning should always include the goal of analysing and identifying how practices can be improved to prevent, identify, respond to and report abuse, which measures to strengthen equity and inclusion. There are more and more tools becoming available to inform educators about how to promote wellbeing and safeguard children from racism, discrimination and abuse, so it makes sense to always keep child safety on the plan and if you have a comprehensive child safety plan, you can cross-reference to it with a link in the Quality Improvement Plan.

Children's services are established to support the health, wellbeing and education needs of children and young people but *"when they lose sight of this mission or fail to make the safety of the children in their care their number one priority, the impacts are devastating"* (as we've become aware of through the work of Royal Commissions) (Australian Childhood Foundation, 2020).

Annual policy review

Annual policy review and development should be a non-negotiable for governance and leadership undertakings, to uphold the commitment to the continuous improvement of your child safety strategy. Regular reviews within the time frame of a year are suggested for overall effectiveness and to ensure compliance with all child safe related laws, regulations and standards.

"Far too many children have been abused by staff and volunteers in organisations that parents entrust with the care and safety of their children" (Australian Childhood Foundation, 2020).

Make sure your policies are unequivocal and the consequences for breaching your guiding principles for maintaining children's wellbeing and safety are comprehensible.

"Softened wording doesn't reflect the gravity of the crime"; it doesn't reveal your strong standpoint against such acts, and it also *"feeds into victim-blaming attitudes, [and] eases the conscience of perpetrators"* (Revell, 2022).

This list, derived from ACECQA (June, 2021), prompts dialogue when reviewing and redeveloping policies:
- Does the title provide a clear and concise statement identifying the intent of the policy?
- Is it clear why this policy exists?
- Have you referenced the relevant regulations and are these reflected in the policy?
- Have you checked the policy requirements and referenced related legislation that applies to your service type?
- Does your policy statement provide a framework for decision-making and ensure consistent practice?
- Does your policy statement reflect your service philosophy?

I would add in another dot point:
- Is the policy accessible in multiple ways to meet diverse community needs, including those considered marginalised?

If we utilise the message we are hearing here, we need to be specific. Your governance documentation should be explicit in its wording. *"The amendment to the Crimes Act, passed on 3 August [2022]... changes the language in the offence of a 'Sexual relationship with child or young person under special care'. The crime is now referred to as 'Persistent sexual abuse of child or young person under special care'. The problem with the former is that a 'relationship' does not capture the true nature of the crime and implies the cooperation of the victim in the act"* (Revell, 2022).

Grace Tame, Australian of the Year 2021, is an activist and advocate for survivors of sexual assault – particularly those who were abused in institutional settings. She pushes for legal reform and raises public awareness about sexual violence and its impacts on its victims, and she supports vulnerable groups in society. Grace's pursuit in lobbying for change in her pursuit for social justice is prompting national conversations. If we are going to disturb prevalence of abuse, then policy and decision-makers need to support survivors. Systemic change is needed in every organisation to not only strengthen our resolve, but also advocacy goals.

Primary prevention

To reduce the incidence of child abuse and neglect, there is profound research to recognise that the protection of children is closely linked to the concept of strengthening families.

The Center for the Study of Social Policy (CSSP) in the US explored through research what makes families thrive and what characteristics were associated with a lower risk of child abuse and neglect (Pika, 2019). This research was the catalyst for a new approach that would transform the way that early care and education providers worked with and supported families, with a focus on parents' strengths. This strengthening families movement was the spirit for a framework of five critical protective factors. Find out more on the CSSP website (www.CSSP.org).

"Protective factors are described as 'conditions or attributes of individuals, families, communities, or the larger society that mitigate or eliminate risk.' Promotive factors are described as 'conditions or attributes of individuals, families, communities or the larger society that actively enhance wellbeing'" (Pika, 2019).

We often talk about risk factors, but a reframe to encourage promotive factors opens the way for strengths-based conversations with families, which in turn embraces wellbeing.

"Strengthening families is an approach, *not a model"*; *"viewing parents as partners in achieving positive outcomes for their children"* (Pika, 2019).

This angle of engagement with families not only marries with the notion we support here in Australia, of families as the first educator, it also aligns with developmental science. Identifying early childhood is an impressionable period of development, so it is wise to greatly support the relationships that are most critical to development in the early years.

There is always more work to be done to support families to be strong in both protective and promotive factors, and in communities that support families to build those factors (Pika, 2019).

Throughout this book, we have explored primary prevention strategies targeted at whole-community awareness, with the aim of stopping abuse before it starts (advertising, education, communication and participation).

Secondary prevention

In previous chapters – and by no means excluding this one – we have addressed secondary prevention strategies to target specific sections of the population considered to be more at risk of abuse and in greater need of support. We have stressed that, by acknowledging complex family environments and supporting diverse families, it is possible to formulate strategies for prevention for families who are considered marginalised and vulnerable. A large part of that is recognising that not everyone is equal – some people are in a more vulnerable position due to their life circumstances.

The context of our community is very important to consider in your management. *"Even though the contexts of leadership vary, the universal essence of leadership... appears to be collaborative, participative, inclusive, learning focused as well as developing capacity by building on existing knowledge"* (Strehmel et al, 2019).

Bringing together multiple standpoints facilitates stronger leadership. A fusion of knowledge and a fluidness of ideas is more likely to occur when there is transparency. Offering a 'hybrid model of connection' will allow your community to decide when and how they would feel most comfortable to meet. Depending on the circumstances, regardless of whether you are communicating online, face to face, via email or phone, a flexible approach will best meet the needs of your community. Listen to what all stakeholders are saying, even in informal conversations with others, and feed this to conversations with management.

Governance arrangements should be transparent and include:
- A Commitment to Child Safety (inclusive of, or in addition to, a Commitment to the Cultural Safety of Aboriginal Children and a zero tolerance for racism)
- A Child Safe Environment and Wellbeing Policy (see below for more on this)
- A Code of Conduct and practice guidance that entails what a breach of conduct could include and consequences
- A risk management framework inclusive of a strong complaints process

Governance arrangements vary depending on the type, nature and size of an organisation. Organisational leadership provides an authorising environment for the sharing of information about risks to children and young people.

Remaining well informed of your obligations under the Education and Care Services National Law, and Education and Care Services National Regulations, as well as other applicable state and territory requirements in your jurisdiction, is vital, for example, child protection laws and child safe standard requirements. Your policies and procedures should address these requirements, as well as quality practices relating to providing a child-safe environment that aligns with the NQS.

For example, under the Education and Care Services National Regulations, *"An approved provider must ensure that policies and procedures are in place for providing a child safe environment"* (regulation 168), *"and take reasonable steps to ensure those policies and procedures are followed"* (regulation 170). Access *Providing a child safe environment, 2021* at www.acecqa.gov.au

The CCYP clearly outlines in Victoria's new Child Safe Standards that *"Governance arrangements facilitate implementation of the child safety and wellbeing policy at all levels."*

If services do not wish to blend policies to accommodate both national and state requirements, it is essential that services have separate policies that address these separate requisites.

This sharing of updated information should saturate the service communication and marketing platforms (all modes of communication, verbal, soft and hard copy).

Consider the following when looking at your commitment to child safety:
- Do you have visible (and user-friendly) messages about child safety around your organisation? Is it obvious how to raise a concern?
- Is your commitment to child safety part of your dialogue at open days and on centre tours for prospective families and orientation days?
- Do you have a reputation in the community for high-quality service provision? Would this include accolades for your stance on abuse and your efforts to prevent it?
- Is there opportunity for ongoing consultation to reflect, review and adjust policies with all stakeholders, inclusive of children? Do you consult peak bodies for dependable information?

Declaring your Child Safety Commitment

Tell the world how you care about children, as this will help to inspire your community and ward off perpetrators who are trying to infiltrate your organisation. Community awareness requires advertising your Commitment to Child Safety and making your policies and procedures accessible to all via your website, through your marketing material and, of course, when on the premise. Even if a visitor just came to your front door, could they see an explicit commitment to the protection for children against abuse? And the cultural safety of Aboriginal children?

In what ways does your organisation publicly commit to child safety? What have you done to proactively practice activism in your setting? What is already in place? Consider the following:

- Are posters of your Statement of Commitment to Child Safety displayed on noticeboards?
- Is your Statement of Commitment to Child Safety stated clearly to prospective families before they enrol at your service?
- If your service held an open day, would information that communicates your service support for child safety be visible to the community, inclusive of children?
- Is your Statement of Commitment included in orientation for all community members, staff and families, inclusive of children?
- Is your Statement of Commitment included in relief and volunteer induction? Is it verbal and written?
- Do you declare a zero tolerance for racism?
- Do you commit to capacity building to enhance cultural as well as social safety (accepting of all societal groups)?

If we are publicly caring about children's safety and wellbeing, then a diverse and truly inclusive environment should be the goal. Your philosophy to the community should be recognised beyond the service itself. Being renowned for a positive way of thinking and behaving will attract people whether they are interested in connecting as a service user, or for employment prospects. Children, team members and community members need to feel safe, welcome and know they can reach their full potential from affiliation with your service, whatever their gender, age, ethnicity, faith, ability or sexual orientation.

Here are some ways you could you portray your service better in your local community:

- Attend local events and communicate with others.
- Partner with local children's services and create a reciprocal relationship.
- Advertise your service in the local e-news or hard-copy newspaper.
- Ensure your website clearly states you are an organisation with a zero tolerance for abuse.

- Have a link on your website taking viewers to your Commitment, to Child Safety as well as your Child Safety and Wellbeing Policy and Code of Conduct and options for raising concerns and/or making a complaint.

Another way is to take part in initiatives of large organisations that advocate for children's safety and wellbeing, for example, NAPCAN. Did you know that NAPCAN is 'Australia's first secular for-purpose organisation to focus entirely on the prevention of child abuse and neglect before it starts?' Determined to change the trajectory of abuse and neglect of children being a taboo topic in Australian society, since 1987, NAPCAN has "*remained dedicated to bringing the eradication of child abuse and neglect to the forefront of Australian society*" to create safer communities for children.

What we think about abuse, and how we act in response to this prevalent issue in society, matters. Child abuse emits feelings, thoughts, fears and apprehensions in people. Janise Mitchell, deputy CEO of the Australian Childhood Foundation, talks about the extensive work the foundation has done on community attitude tracking towards child abuse (see the video *Taking Care of Yourself* at www.vimeo.com/433811459).

This research has proven that "*In the general community there is a desire not to want to think about it, to turn away, to believe other adults couldn't possibly engage in these acts with children and it's confronting and distressing*" (NAPCAN).

Research shows that many adults have had experiences of abuse, so it can trigger. With incidents of family violence prevalent, there is a great impact on community members' thoughts and feelings influencing their behaviour, actions or *inaction*. It is complex, challenging and distressing knowing what to do and who to get support from – our own informal and recognised support systems protect us and the children we are concerned about.

The language used makes a difference to clearly articulate your public narrative. You want the perception and attitude encircling your service to be one that dissuades abuse. You may need to reconstruct your communication, to make it both respectful and powerful, but you have the power and the potential to make the changes needed.

Micro-level changes and long-term systemic change

There are many things that we can all do every day in all the different aspects of our lives – in our jobs, families, neighbourhoods, clubs or organisations and social groups. NAPCAN's Play your Part strategy looks closely at what we can do in our roles in society because: *"Protecting children is everyone's business"*. NAPCAN's strategy is to support and encourage changes in individual and community behaviour, and its strategies as service providers and advocates for children's safety can be adopted into our everyday practice by:

- Promoting quality research – helping people understand the causes and impact of child abuse and effective ways to prevent it
- Ensuring child safe polices and strategies are revised to best meet the wellbeing of children and young people
- Aligning your support by involvement in community-led prevention programmes

How could you communicate research and impart strategies to your service community? Perhaps via:

- Information session with a guest speaker
- Accessible resources that are visible at your service
- Open invitation to online training/information sessions
- Newsletter/blogs
- Service library (for educators and families)
- Secure social media/IT platforms
- Curriculum resources and documentation, for example, children's artwork in response to their rights to being safe

By taking part in events, you can foster allyship to protect children, together with your community. There is a wealth of opportunities in all states and territories – private and not-for-profit organisations, and funded programmes.

Comrades in solidarity are likely to undertake workshops and webinars to build capability, which could include seeking out sessions on respectful relationships, child abuse and neglect prevention, safer communities, child wellbeing and parenting, to name just a few. Abuse will continue to permeate all structures in society, so we need to pull together collectively. Networking is heartening because being an ally can be tough, too. Ill treatment is often directed towards those who are standing up for the rights of others and it can be the closest of contacts who taunt.

To find out what's crucial to your surrounding community, you must challenge blind spots and your own privileges. Dr Colette Murray of Technological University Dublin and keynote speaker at SJIEC, 2022, said: *"Belonging is complex. We, in early childhood education and care, have to find ways of reconceptualising belonging in the pursuit of justice."*

The governance in our individual service provision needs to support critical race theory (Murray, 2022), which acknowledges that we all have a part to play to address racism being endemic in society.

How do you practice active anti-racism?

In a culturally safe environment, people from different cultural backgrounds define what is comfortable and safe. The service providers should seek guidance from Aboriginal and Torres Strait Islander children and families on how to provide service, and should consider how service provision will impact Aboriginal and Torres Strait Islander children's culture.

It is more than just the absence of racism or discrimination and more than 'cultural awareness' and 'cultural sensitivity' – it empowers people and enables them to contribute and feel safe to be themselves. Cultural safety is the positive recognition as well as the celebration of cultures. We all have a responsibility to improve our cultural responsiveness so we can better support others to experience joy and celebrate their culture.

Celebrating unique identities

"Experiences of stigma or discrimination when accessing non-LGBTIQA+ specialist services can affect service engagement and potentially impact individuals' health and wellbeing outcomes for segments of LGBTIQA+ communities" (Farrugia, 2022).

Negative outcomes do not stem from being LGBTIQA+, but are driven by the fear of, or actual, discrimination via institutions that are important in the lives of young people, including schools, health services and welfare services (Australian Human Rights Commission, 2015).

Competent use of LGBTIQA+ relevant language and an affirmative approach to inclusive communication (documentation, for example, enrolment forms) can help support LGBTIQA+ people to feel welcome and able to disclose who they are when seeking help (Farrugia, 2022).

Organisational practices that promote inclusion means everyone understanding and using the language/terminology associated with LGBTIQA+ and other sexually or gender-diverse people because it helps to ensure that services and organisations are inclusive and respectful to anyone who becomes affiliated with the service. Can someone record their pronouns on your enrolment forms? And is it easy to alter sensitive information?

Community connections

When you build community connections, you bring stakeholders together and provide them with support, which strengthens the community vision and facilitates practical actions to drive progressive and sustainable change. Local solutions contribute to keeping children safe and well. Practical actions may include developing resources and some training tools, families reaching out to other families or services for support to improving relationships and inform best practice.

Be the instigator to facilitate local plans of action, bringing together existing resources and networks within communities. Partner with a range of agencies, groups and individuals such as national, state and local government agencies, community leaders, community sector organisations and groups, corporate and small business, health and education institutions, child protection services and children, parents and families.

Here are some examples of local services and organisations that your children's service can connect with to create or strengthen an existing relationship:

- Kindergartens
- Education and care services
- Maternal and child health services
- Playgroups

- School/s
- Counsellors or psychologists
- GPs
- Local MPs
- Municipal office departments (i.e. children's services teams, social workers, Koori officers)
- Police stations
- Sporting clubs

In Queensland, Child Protection Week is coordinated by the Child Protection Week Committee under the auspicing body of Act for Kids, while NAPCAN coordinates National Child Protection Week every year in other states. A callout for submissions (2022) hoped to see artworks based on meaningful conversations with children and young people (in their children's services and other influential settings) to show what they think about their neighbourhoods. These individual and collaborative visual representations will influence *"campaigning to help show that protecting children is about working together as a community"* (NAPCAN).

If we are aiming for true assimilation for families, then children's responses may provoke some insight and direction for further inquiry into the neighbourhood. The suggested talking points by NAPCAN below certainly prompt dialogue, but they also give educators an opportunity to promote social justice and anti-bias content into their curriculums:

- We want to learn more about what things *you* think are most important in making the place where you live great for your family.
- What are the things that help you feel like you belong in your neighbourhood?
- What things in the neighbourhood are important for your parents or other members of your family?
- It's up to the whole community to make sure that every family has the things they need.
- So, what things make life easier for grownups and children, for example, if they have jobs and enough money, if they don't have to drive a long way to school or work, if there are fun free things to do like

going to the park, if they have education and care services, if they have shops with healthy food and if they have friendly neighbours.
- Do you think that all neighbourhoods have all the things that families need? Do you think that's fair?

There are other services you can connect with to crusade alongside, obtain resources (posters/videos) or access training from for your community. You can even change the virtual background of your virtual meetings to show your support and share this strategy with contacts and colleagues.

The safety and wellbeing of children and young people is at the forefront of commitment to many organisations and local communities, and many have their mantra along the lines of 'protecting children is everybody's business'. Here are some examples:

Bravehearts aims to forge a 'movement for change' in how child sexual assault is dealt with by the criminal justice sector, Government and the community at large and to provide survivors with a voice.

The Daniel Morcombe Foundation is committed to keeping kids safe with two main aims: to educate children on how to stay safe in a physical or online environment, and to support young victims of crime.

Aboriginal community-controlled organisations work closely with children and families in culturally safe environments to provide support and give families a voice in decision-making about their children. They reach out to SNAICC, Reconciliation Australia, organisations in your state/territory or your local Koorie education support officer for guidance and best practice. Committing to a Reconciliation Action Plan and investing in your own knowledge gaining are priorities to corroborate authentic alliances.

The Pride Foundation Australia provides funding for projects that address the systemic disadvantage of LGBTIQA+ communities and individuals in Australia. This funding is possible through year-round fundraising, sponsorship and philanthropic partnerships.

Showing value

Building respectful relationships with children tells them that you respect and value them and their families. Building respectful relationships with organisations tells children you value citizens in society. Even those who may not be directly associated with you.

What else can you do to tell your immediate and broader community that you value them? One thing could be to check that your signage is well kept. For example, are posters in a good condition? Torn posters falling off the wall indicates a lack of care for what is being presented. Other things could be:

- Encourage help-seeking behaviour by discussing the role of community services and how to access them (directory local services).
- Have discussions about difficult topics such as bullying.
- Promote co-regulation between children and educators in your settings.
- Offer calming experiences to re-regulate emotions/nervous systems.
- Have reader-friendly information available (recognising the diverse needs such as ability, language, identity, cultural variations and making sure the content is relevant and inclusive).
- Encourage children and young people to participate in their 'community celebrates children's place as citizens in our society'.
- Help and support parents in continuous improvement of their parenting skills.
- Congratulate families and children for good things happening.
- Involve children in planning and evaluating experiences.

Risk assessment

As an educator and/or leader of a service, you can use your potential to drive a child-centred, safe, rights-based approach. Talking about safety with children, and what being unsafe might look and feel like in their community or online, is critical. Exploring options together and planning through consultation with all key stakeholders, including children, is important to determine uncomfortable and unsafe pockets in your organisation.

You can download risk assessment templates for use with children (aged under five and over five) on the ACECQA website (www.acecqa.gov.au).

Wherever possible, risk-assess community outings with children. When mentoring, I encourage services to create risk assessments with children using photos of the local surrounds and creating child-friendly versions (simplified language and symbols, for example, X, *, ☑). See below for an example of an entry on a child-friendly risk assessment before an outing to outline strategies that will be utilised to ensure adequate supervision in a public toilet block, to minimise the likelihood of abuse.

A photo of a toilet block and the toilet cubicles indicating with a tick (☑) the furthest toilet that would preferably be used if a child wanted to keep the door open – this strategy being used to promote privacy. An asterisk (*) being used to indicate where the educator would position themselves for ample supervision and to stop members of the public passing that point in the bathroom.

Refer to Appendix 11 for risk assessment and management templates for excursions (it includes a risk matrix to assess likelihood of harm).

Your governance and leadership

Let's recap to assess whether you truly advocate children's rights, safety and wellbeing in your governance and leadership. Does your organisation:

1. Have a process to regularly review, evaluate and improve child safe practices, including cultural safety?
2. Consult with all stakeholders to action feedback from reviews?
3. Consult with all stakeholders child safety policies utilising child, family, staff, volunteer and community feedback?
4. Use complaints and system failures to develop a continuous Quality Improvement Plan?
5. Ensure record-keeping and information-sharing practices are understood in relation to cultural considerations?
6. Keep Aboriginal and Torres Strait Islander children safe and receive feedback on cultural safety?

The strategies and links to resources in this book aim to build the capacity of individual educators and teams to prevent, as well as respond to, abuse and neglect. To optimise wellbeing outcomes for children, we need to ensure we are committed to creating and maintaining environments where children can truly thrive. To successfully do that, our children's services need to be so inclusive that they become a shining example of what a safe space looks and feels like.

So, let's speculate about what could happen and let *now* be the pivotal turning point for you and your children's service to reduce inequality and better safeguard *all* children. Let's create a balance of power so that, together, we change this discourse. Let us, in our diverse roles, lean in to respectful and robust debate about what can and should be done to protect children from abuse. Let children be fellow protagonists in the journey of child safety. Choose an agenda that will create a solid culture of child safety.

"*When will leaders lead?*" summated an article (Vijeyarasa, 2022) on Women's Agenda, an online hub, to inspire the current cohort of female leaders to do more and to do better for fellow women, but I want to ask you the same question but in relation to children: When will leaders lead? To do more and to do better? Make no mistake, we are all leaders!

The citation that Urban (2022) uses to amplify his argument "*for a transdiscipline of early childhood*" kept resonating with me as I brought this book to a close. "*We have simply no idea what is around the next corner, something most of us have learned to forget*" (McCann, 2007).

We cannot close our eyes to what confronts us. Please don't turn your back – we owe it to children to be present and take notice. Pay close attention to *everything*, make everything perceptible. With grit and resilience, it's time to proclaim your culture of child safety. A child will thank you for it. Your community will thank you for it. The early childhood sector will thank you for it.

In summary

With this chapter complete, you should now know that:
- Governance and leadership regarding child safety is always in progress.
- Community involvement is vital from within, and beyond, the children's service itself.
- Networking elevates high-quality practice in abuse prevention.
- There are global patterns of discrimination, and we need to campaign for social justice together as an education and care sector.
- The outcomes in the EYLF and the anti-bias goals are compatible, which means anti-bias education and care is in our legislation – it is non-negotiable.
- A prerequisite for a strong culture of child safety is children being heard and truly consulted about matters that affect them.

Chapter 8 reflection questions

- Do you know the shared value you have with each family at your children's service?
- Do you celebrate Aboriginal culture and LGBTIQA+ events, history and people?
- Is there information about maintaining a child-safe culture on the website of the service you work at?
- Are there resources for culturally diverse families?
- Do your events promote contemporary families or traditional stereotypes?

CONCLUSION

So, here we are at the conclusion of this book but, as cliché as it is going to sound, this is not the end. If you have carefully considered the information provided to you through reading this book, you will have a clear understanding that prioritising child safety is a forever commitment.

When I am undertaking face-to-face training or delivering webinars online, I am often asked if I have a checklist for *what to do* to be a child-safe organisation. My answer is a firm no, and the reason for this is that I want to deter the mindset of ticking boxes and feeling accomplished and completed in this space.

Some of this book is heavy to divulge, but *do not stop here*. Children will thank you if you can keep the momentum of talking, thinking, speaking up and creating change. Child safety is an ongoing journey of consultation with everyone within your silo and abroad. Collaboration is key if you are going to continue to improve your environments for children in relation to how strong your culture of child safety is, can be and remains.

In conclusion, there are two parts to identifying abuse and/or neglect and responding accurately as an educator/staff member:

1. To act in a manner that considers all children 'at risk' and introduce preventative measures to minimise the potential harm. These measures must be considerate of children participating in the programmes being run on-site, online, as well as externally in the public domain.
2. To respond swiftly to suspicions or allegations of abuse that have occurred both internally as well as outside the realm of the service, i.e. when the child is 'at home'.

We need to consider this doom if we are going to shield children from harm, which would no doubt negatively impact their wellbeing and their ongoing learning. Children need safe and secure environments to thrive in life and learning. Our education and care services need to embrace preventative strategies and nurture those children who have slipped through the protective blanket of society. Trauma-informed practice is something we, too, need to be aware of, as early childhood practitioners.

No doubt you would have noticed throughout this book that there has been a consciousness towards providing fairer and more just treatment for those whose life circumstances tend to exclude them from mainstream opportunities and provisions. If we are going to authentically mitigate harm to children, then we need a social justice approach to frame our thinking. This impartiality needs to inspire us in our efforts to observe and act for and with children we have the privilege to engage with.

We can reconstruct public confidence in the systems that welcome children into our care. To do this we need to ensure reports of abuse are transmitted to authorities without delay, but just as importantly is the need for a reform of our mindsets so we continuously think preventatively instead of working in damage control. If we don't revolutionise our individual constitutions, then we as a sector are enabling, through apathy, systemic abuse in our children's services.

To begin a commitment, to remodel with a 'proactive approach' to child protection, every service is implored to consider the likelihood of harm occurring at any moment of any day. Assess every interaction that takes place with children and adults. Every possible risk must be eliminated with a way of thinking and a visual lens focused on 'what could possibly happen'. You need to remember that some of these heinous acts are not premeditated, they are spontaneous, so you need to eradicate every opportunity as well as remain attentive to ensure complacency does not open the avenue for a child or children to be taken advantage of.

You have knowledge of ways to mitigate harm coming to children – you will have this at the forefront of your thinking and your responsiveness will be enhanced.

Our roles and responsibilities are excessive as early childhood professionals, regardless of what capacity we are working in. There is the moral obligation that we feel towards children and their families, but there is also a judicial system to influence decision-making. Standards and regulations do change, but regardless of these broad systemic amendments, it is so important that we continuously monitor and review policies and practices in our own contextual environment. Only then will we thoroughly make the modifications needed for our protocols based on the new information we derive.

Let's be serious when we say we are going to change the trajectory and live up to the dominant discourses around the rights of the child. We need to make sure children are truly aware of their right to feel safe and be protected, as well as be involved in the decision-making that affects them.

Early childhood professionals have worked tirelessly and, now more than ever, we need to advocate for ourselves as agents for the change we want to see. Early childhood will have a greater chance to truly *thrive* if every one of us is empowered to advocate for the safety of children.

As a passionate child-safety advocate, I have written this book to canvas child protection from the position of capacity building. The content in each of the chapters is not exclusive, nor does it define the entire arena of child safety. This book immerses traditional and contemporary models of child protection so it can be used as a working document for individuals within teams to target gaps in understanding. This book can be used repeatedly in the journey of community knowledge building. What has been provided here is information that constitutes key elements for prevention and responsiveness to abuse and neglect. Children's services can utilise this tool to gauge service competency by recognising gaps in service provision and making plans for quality improvement to rectify any current and future systemic failures.

Please speak of this book – to at least one other – so that there can be a domino effect in the upstanding for children's safety and wellbeing not only in education and care environments, but in society in its entirety.

We have to believe we can make a difference – and we absolutely can make a difference in this sector. I'm hoping this book has inspired you [and will provoke many other educators] to commit to strengthening the culture of child safety in your professional environments and to scream out loud what you are doing with children in your curriculums.

APPENDICES

Appendix 1: Glossary of key terms and definitions

Key term	Definition
Aboriginal and Torres Strait Islander child/children	A person under the age of 18 who identifies as Aboriginal and/or Torres Strait Islander.
Abuse	An act or acts that endangers a child's health, wellbeing and/or development. Abuse can happen once or multiple times and include: • Physical abuse • Sexual abuse • Emotional abuse • Cumulative harm • Family violence • Neglect • Grooming • Multi-dimensional harm
Child/children	Any person up to the age of 18 years.
Child safety	A range of timely and appropriate measures to protect a child from abuse.

Child safety officer	Dedicated council officer responsible for receiving and processing child safety concerns and reports received from the organisation.
Child safe organisation	In the context of the Child Safe Standards, a child safe organisation is one that takes deliberate steps to protect children from abuse and is embedded in an organisation's culture and policies.
Children from culturally and/or linguistically diverse backgrounds	A child or young person who identifies as having cultural or linguistic affiliations by virtue of their place of birth, ancestry or ethnic origin, religion, preferred language or language spoken at home or because of their parents' identification on a similar basis.
Code of Conduct	A statement of the way organisational staff will conduct engagement with all stakeholders. It establishes a common understanding of the values and guiding behaviours to be applied in everyday work activities, and it states what behaviours are not acceptable as well as consequences for breach of conduct.
LGBTQIAP+	Acronym for lesbian, gay, bisexual, transgender, queer, questioning, intersex, asexual/aromantic, pansexual communities. The plus sign represents other queer identities not included in the acronym.
Sex and gender	**Sex** refers to one's biological sex they are born with relating to their chromosomes, hormones, genitalia and reproductive system, etc. This generally falls into 'male', 'female' or 'intersex'. **Gender** refers to the identity a person chooses regardless of their sex, which relates to their societal and cultural portrayal of sexuality and gender. It is a broad spectrum that differs from one person to the next. *Remember that it's safest to not assume and best practice to ask respectfully and believe people if they share about who they are. Please also remember that in most circumstances people are not required to share with you how they identify, and folks have a right to keep their sex, sexuality and gender identities to themselves if they choose to.*
LGBTQIAP+	Acronym for lesbian, gay, bisexual, transgender, queer, questioning, intersex, asexual/aromantic, pansexual communities. The plus sign represents other queer identities not included in the acronym.

Appendix 2: Examples and indicators of abuse and neglect

Abuse types	Indicators
Emotional abuse happens when a child is treated in a way that negatively impacts their social, emotional or intellectual development	• Constant belittling, shaming and humiliating • Name calling, teasing, bullying, criticising, making negative comparisons to others • Telling a child they're 'no good', 'worthless', 'stupid', 'bad' or 'a mistake' • Frequent yelling, threatening or bullying • Ignoring or rejecting a child as punishment, giving them the silent treatment • Isolating or locking a child up for extended periods • Limiting physical contact with a child – no hugs, kisses or other signs of affection • Exposing a child to violence against others, whether it is against the other parent, a sibling or even a pet
What emotional abuse evidence could look like:	• Not playful, or play dominated by concerning themes (for example, violence) • Extreme separation anxiety • Regression in toileting behaviours (for example, soiling self, bedwetting) • Hypervigilance • Aggressive/violent behaviour • Emotional dysregulations • Dissociation/freeze response • Poor attention • Risk-taking behaviour • Avoiding home (particularly if the abuser is in the family home) • Extreme behaviour ranging from being overly aggressive to submissive • Delayed emotional development • Compulsive lying or stealing • High levels of anxiety • Frequent crying • Overcompliance • Lack of trust in adults • Regressive behaviour, such as baby talk or thumb sucking • Having feelings of worthlessness about life and themselves • Overeating or hardly eating at all • Running away • Fear of the dark, not wanting to go to bed or nightmares • Poor self-image/self-esteem, poor academic performance, poor peer relationships • Secretive, demanding or disruptive behaviour • Self-harming/suicidal

Physical abuse happens when a child has been hurt or injured, and it is not an accident; physical abuse does not always leave visible marks or injuries	• Slaps, shoves, hits, punches, pushes • Shaking • Choking • Smothering • Being thrown (downstairs or across the room) • Kicking • Twisting of arms • Being burnt • Stabbing • Biting • Poisoning • Using physical restraints
What physical abuse evidence could look like:	• Bruises in unlikely places (face, back, ears, hands, buttocks, upper thighs and soft parts of the body) • Inconsistent or absent explanation of bruises • Any bruising on a baby • Pressure marks from fingers on the face, chest or back • Swelling, bump, ligature or bite marks • Skull fracture, subdural bleeding, multiple fractures of different ages • Suspicious burns • Poisoning or significant over-medicating • Frequent injuries or unexplained bruises, welts or cuts • Injuries may appear to have a pattern such as marks from a hand or belt • Being always watchful and alert, as if waiting for something bad to happen • Avoiding physical contact • Shying away from touch, flinching at sudden movements or seeming afraid to go home • Wearing inappropriate clothing in warm weather (to hide bruises, cuts or marks) • Broken bones or unexplained bruising or burns in different stages of healing • Being unable to explain an injury or giving inconsistent, vague or unlikely explanations for an injury • Having unusual or unexplained internal injuries • History of family violence • Delay between injury and seeking medical assistance • Repeated visits to the doctor with injuries, poisoning or minor complaints • Being unusually frightened of a parent or carer • Becoming scared when other children cry or shout • Being excessively friendly to strangers • Starting fires or being fascinated with fire • Destroying property • Hurting animals

Child neglect happens when a child's basic needs are not met, affecting their health and development	Basic needs include: • Food • Housing and clean-living conditions • Healthcare • Adequate clothing • Personal hygiene • Adequate supervision
What child neglect evidence could look like:	• Starving, begging, stealing or hoarding food • Abnormally high appetite • Consistently poor hygiene (unbathed, matted and unwashed hair, dirty skin and noticeable body odour) • Frequent infections or sores • Untreated illness and physical injuries • Sallow or sickly appearance • Talking about no one being at home to provide care • Being frequently unsupervised or allowed to play in unsafe situations • Frequently late or absent from education service • Wearing ill-fitting, filthy or inappropriate clothing for the weather • Alcohol or drug abuse at home • Delayed physical, emotional or intellectual development
Child sexual abuse happens when an adult, teenager or child uses their power or authority to involve another child in sexual activity; sexual abuse can be physical, verbal or emotional	• Kissing, holding or fondling a child in a sexual way • Exposing genitals to a child • Talking in a sexual way that's not appropriate for the child's age • Making obscene phone calls, text messages or remarks • Persistently intruding on a child's privacy • Penetrating a child's vagina or anus by penis, finger or another object • Having sex with a child under 16 years of age • Showing pornographic films, magazines or photographs to a child • Having a child pose or behave in a sexual way • Forcing a child or young person to watch a sexual act • Forcing a child or young person to have sex with another child • Oral sex • Rape • Incest • Child prostitution

What sexual abuse evidence could look like:	• Having trouble walking or sitting • Persistent soiling or bedwetting • Sleep disturbance • Promiscuous affection-seeking behaviour • Obsessive and compulsive washing • Wary of physical contact with others • Unusually fearful of having their nappy changed • Know more about sexual activities than other children their age • Playing in a sexual way • Masturbating more than what's normal for their stage of development • Not wanting to change clothes in front of others and often wearing layers of clothing • Not wanting to participate in physical activities • Having bite marks, bruising, bleeding, swelling, tears or cuts on their genitals or anus • Having unusual vaginal odour or discharge • Having itching or pain in the genital area, difficulty going to the toilet • Having a sexually transmitted disease, especially in a young child • Having torn, stained or bloody clothing, especially underwear • Being afraid of being alone with a particular person • Being frequently depressed, feeling suicidal or attempting suicide • Creating stories, poems or artwork about abuse • Making strong efforts to avoid a specific person, without an obvious reason • Trying to run away from home
Sexual exploitation is when someone does any of the following things in front of you without your consent and without a valid medical or caregiving purpose	• Sexual contact as defined by law • The abuser knows (or should have known) these acts would cause shame, humiliation or other harm to someone's personal dignity
What sexual exploitation evidence could look like:	• Showing a child their genitals • Exposing a child to sexual acts • Exposing a child's sexual organs

Cyberstalking is a term that refers to the misuse of the internet or other technology to stalk and harass someone	• A stalker may contact a child by email, social media sites, a messaging app or through other online spaces/websites
What cyberstalking evidence could look like:	• Messages posted about a child • A child's personal information or pictures posted online • Some stalkers may use technology to find/track a child's location and to monitor what the child does online (or offline)
Domestic/family violence can include physical, sexual, emotional and psychological abuse. Family violence is when children are victims of family violence in their own right by law in Victoria, even if they do not directly experience or witness violent and abusive behaviours. (Australian Childhood Foundation, 2013)	• Slapping • Hitting • Rape • Verbal threats • Harassment • Stalking • Withholding money • Deliberately isolating someone from their friends and family
What the impact of complex trauma could look like in children	• An arousal state (includes hypervigilance and an increased startle reaction) • Avoidance state (numb or seemingly daydreaming)
Spiritual and cultural violence	• Denying the victim access to cultural land, sites or family • Denying the victim access to cultural or spiritual ceremonies or rites • Preventing religious observances or practices • Forcing religious ways and practices against the victim's own beliefs • Undermining the person's cultural background, particularly for people from culturally and linguistically diverse backgrounds • Threatening deportation, or to withdraw support for applications made through the Department of Immigration and Multicultural Affairs

Appendix 3: Child protection legislation across state and territory jurisdictions in Australia

Find out about the child legislation in your state and territory jurisdiction here:

Australian Capital Territory	www.legislation.act.gov.au
New South Wales	www.legislation.nsw.gov.au
Northern Territory	www.legislation.nt.gov.au
Queensland	www.legislation.qld.gov.au
South Australia	www.legislation.sa.gov.au/legislation
Tasmania	www.legislation.tas.gov.au
Victoria	www.legislation.vic.gov.au
Western Australia	www.legislation.wa.gov.au/legislation/statutes.nsf/default.html

Appendix 4: Legislation and Applications Acts in states/territories

State or territory	Indicators	Application Act
Victoria	Education and Care Services National Law Act 2010 (www.legislation.vic.gov.au/in-force/acts/education-and-care-services-national-law-act-2010/013)	Children (Education and Care Services National Law Application) Act 2010 (www.legislation.nsw.gov.au/view/html/inforce/current/act-2010-104)
Australian Capital Territory		Education and Care Services National Law (Act) Act 2011 (www.legislation.act.gov.au/a/2011-42/default.asp)
Northern Territory		Education and Care Services (National Uniform Legislation) Act 2011 (www.legislation.nt.gov.au/Legislation/EDUCATION-AND-CARE-SERVICES-NATIONAL-UNIFORM-LEGISLATION-ACT-2011)
South Australia	Education and Care Services National Law Act 2010 (www.legislation.vic.gov.au/in-force/acts/education-and-care-services-national-law-act-2010/013)	Education and Early Childhood Services (Registration and Standards) Act 2011 (www.legislation.sa.gov.au/lz?path=%2FC%2FA%2FEDUCATION%20AND%20EARLY%20CHILDHOOD%20SERVICES%20(REGISTRATION%20AND%20STANDARDS)%20ACT%202011)
Tasmania		Education and Care Services National Law (Application) Act 2011 (www.legislation.tas.gov.au/view/html/inforce/current/act-2011-048)
Queensland		Education and Care Services National Law (Queensland) Act 2011 (www.legislation.qld.gov.au/view/html/inforce/current/act-2011-038)
Western Australia	Education and Care Services National Law (WA) Act 2012 (www.legislation.wa.gov.au/legislation/statutes.nsf/law_a146885.html)	

Appendix 5: Children receiving child protection services

Child protection component	NSW (a)	Vic	Qld	WA	SA	Tas (b)(c)	ACT	NT (d)
	No.	No.	No.	No.	No.	No.	No.	No.
Children who were the subject of an investigation of a notification	42,056	30,026	23,583	11,777	4,959	755	1,738	5,880
Children on care and protection orders	23,133	19,172	14,260	6,894	5,354	1,634	1,029	1,267
Children in out-of-home care	18,392	12,809	11,716	5,683	4,937	1,262	830	1,242
Children receiving child protection services in 2020	**58,473**	**45,552**	**36,060**	**17,691**	**9,347**	**2,247**	**2,595**	**6,848**

(Source: AIHW Child Protection Collection 2020-21; Table P1)

To aid interpretation of this data:
- One in 32 children received child protection services in response to notifications for abuse and/or neglect
- 103,400 of the 178,000 children were subject to notification only (this is just over half, at 58%)
- 42,000 children were the subject of protection orders and placements for out of home (24%)
- 116,600 children were already known to child protection (65%)
- 58,000 children who received child protection services were Aboriginal and Torres Strait Islanders

Appendix 6:   What to include in a child protection report

Information

When reasonable suspicion of child abuse or neglect exists and you need to make a report, you need to be able to tell the child abuse report line as much information as you have of the child's name, age, date of birth and address. Other information to consider includes:

- Whether the child is Indigenous – Aboriginal, Torres Strait Islander or both
- The cultural background of the child, language(s) spoken, religion and other cultural factors (Clan group of the child, if known)
- A description of injury, abuse and/or neglect (current and previous)
- The child's current situation
- The location of the child, parent or caregiver and alleged perpetrator
- When and how you found out about the abuse

The report line staff will ask more detailed questions similar to below.

Child identification details and context

You will need to provide enough detail to identify the child or young person and give context to your report, including the child's full name as well as their:

- Date of birth or age
- Current address
- Contact number
- School/kindergarten/childcare centre
- Ethnicity (i.e. Aboriginal, Torres Strait Islander, kinship group, non-English speaking)
- Disability, if they have one – nature/type, severity, impact on functioning
- Incident details (date, type of risk, person's causing or contributing to harm)
- Network of support around the young person
- Current whereabouts

The report also needs to include:
- Whether the child/young person is subject of an Apprehended Violence Order
- Whether the child/young person is under the care of the Minister or residing in out-of-home care
- The impact of the incident on the child or young person
- Who the parents are – do they all live in the same house, and are there siblings in the house?
- The alleged perpetrator's name, age, address, relationships to the child/children and their current whereabouts
- Details of when the next expected contact with the alleged perpetrator will occur

Your details

You will be asked to provide details about yourself, including:
- Your full name
- Your organisation/service name, address, phone and email details
- Your position
- Your reason for reporting
- Your relationship to the child/children of concern
- The type of contact you have with the family and the frequency and last time you saw the child/children
- Whether you are working with the child or the family, and if so, in what capacity

What not to report as child abuse or neglect

While criminal activity is important to report to police, it may not be a reportable child abuse matter. The following are examples of scenarios where contacting the child abuse report line is **not** necessary:
- Criminal behaviour – parents' recreational behaviour not involving children, for example, drug use
- Family issues – siblings fighting, a child has a bruise

(Informed by www.communities.tas.gov.au/children)

Appendix 7: Statement of Commitment to Child Safety and Wellbeing sample

Service name COMMITMENT TO CHILD SAFETY AND WELLBEING

ial*Service name* is committed to creating a child safe organisation where all children and young people are safe and feel safe. *Service name* supports and respects all children, as well as our staff and volunteers.

We have a greater focus on supporting the wellbeing and safety for those children and young people who are vulnerable and considered more at risk to abuse and neglect.

Service name* aims to actively celebrate Aboriginal and Torres Strait Islander children's culture and develop the capacity to provide a culturally safe environment for Aboriginal and Torres Strait Islander children and their families.

Service name* supports children from culturally and/or linguistically diverse backgrounds, those who are unable to live at home, children living in under-resourced households, children with a disability and/or children from sex and gender-diverse groups (LGBTIQA+).

Service name* has a commitment to managing both physical and online environments to keep children and young people safe through governance, systems and processes.

Service name* has a zero tolerance towards discrimination, abuse, racism and bullying.

Every person involved in **service name*** has a responsibility to understand the important and specific role they play individually and collectively to ensure that the wellbeing and safety of all children and young people is at the forefront of all they do and every decision they make.

This statement provides the framework for the organisational approach to complying with best practice by aligning with Child Safe Standards in conjunction with the guiding National Principles for Child Safe Organisations, National Quality Frameworks, Service philosophy and UN Convention on the Rights of the Child.

Appendix 8: Code of Conduct Agreement sample

Organisation name [Name of organisation]

Commitment to child safety [Outline the organisation's commitment to child safety]

[Define the various forms of child abuse]

[Outline positive staff behaviours that are consistent with the organisation's culture and values]

I will:
- [List the types of behaviours your organisation encourages to keep children safe]

[Outline unprofessional staff behaviours that the organisation considers concerning or unacceptable]

Unacceptable behaviours

Concerning behaviours

I will not:
- [List the types of behaviours your organisation considers unacceptable]

I understand these types of behaviours may be of concern:
- [List the types of behaviours your organisation considers may be of concern]

[Outline internal and external reporting obligations including whistle-blower protection]

[Specify the penalties for staff and volunteers who breach the Code of Conduct]

[Outline criminal offences for not acting to protect children or reporting abuse]

[Specify the penalties for staff and volunteers who breach the Code of Conduct]

I have read this Code of Conduct and agree to abide by it and its terms.

Signature _____

Name: Date:

Last reviewed: Next review date:

Responsible officer:

(www.ocg.nsw.gov.au/sites/default/files/2021-12/ChildSafeCodeofConduct_1_3.pdf)

Appendix 9: Positive behaviours and unacceptable behaviours (misconduct) and concerning behaviours

Codes of Conduct do not have to list all these types of behaviours (as they relate to the different forms of child abuse). They may be grouped into different categories or referred to generally based on your risk analysis. The list below will help you identify which behaviours your Code of Conduct should focus on to prevent abuse in your organisation's unique operating environment.

Examples of positive behaviours
- Treat all children and young people with respect.
- Listen to and value children and young people's ideas and opinions.
- Welcome all children and their families and carers by being inclusive.
- Actively promote cultural safety and inclusion.
- Listen to children and respond to them appropriately.
- Welcome parents and carers to participate in decisions about their child's education and care, and any other matters about their safety.
- Report any conflicts of interest (such as an outside relationship with a child).
- Adhere to all relevant Australian and state/territory legislation and child safe policies and procedures.
- Work within a team to ensure that the needs of the child (and their family) remain the paramount focus.
- Participate in all compulsory training.
- Raise concerns with management if risks to child safety are identified, including cultural, environmental and operational risks.
- Report and act on any concerns or observed breaches of this Code of Conduct.
- Take all reasonable steps to protect children from abuse.
- Respect the privacy of children and their families by keeping all information about child protection concerns confidential.
- Inform parents and carers if there are situations that need to be safely managed but are outside the boundaries of this Code of Conduct.
- Take a child seriously if they disclose harm or abuse
- Ensure breaches of this code are reported immediately.
- Uphold the rights of the child and always prioritise their needs.

Examples of unacceptable behaviours

General
- Condoning or participating in behaviour with a child that is illegal, unsafe or abusive
- Ignoring or disregarding any concerns, suspicions or disclosures of child abuse
- Exaggerating or trivialising child abuse issues
- Using hurtful, discriminatory or offensive behaviour or language with a child
- Failing to report information to police if they know, believe or reasonably ought to know that a child has been abused
- Trivialising the subject of child abuse, such as telling jokes that make light of children being hurt
- Using unacceptable language or telling unacceptable stories or jokes in front of children

Physical abuse
- Hitting, striking, punching, kicking or slapping a child
- Engaging in rough physical games
- Throwing items or using items to hurt a child
- Dragging or pushing a child
- Threatening to hurt a child through words or gestures, regardless of whether the person intends to apply force
- Using hostile force towards a child and/or a pattern of hostile or unreasonable and seriously inappropriate physical conduct

Sexual abuse
- Sexual touching of a child
- Sexual contact with a child
- Masturbating in front of a child or exposing genitals
- Possessing or creating child abuse material
- Sharing sexually explicit photos of a child
- Exposing a child to pornography or other indecent material
- Giving a child gifts, food, money, attention or affection in exchange for sexual activities or images

- Not respecting the privacy of a child when they are using the bathroom or changing
- Communicating (including online) with a child about romantic, intimate or sexual feelings for a child
- Using a camera to record a child while they are dressing, bathing or using the bathroom
- Making comments that express a desire to act in a sexual manner with a child
- Using sexual language or gestures in the presence of children
- Sexual comments, conversations or communications with a child

Emotional abuse
- Teasing a child
- Yelling at a child
- Bullying a child
- Persistent criticism and discrediting of a child
- Persistent rejection of or hostility towards a child
- Refusing to acknowledge a child's worth and the legitimacy of their needs
- Deliberately preventing a child from forming friendships
- Depriving a child of essential stimulation and responsiveness
- Encouraging a child to engage in destructive, antisocial behaviour
- Exposing a child to family violence
- Making a child feel worthless, unloved, alone or frightened

Neglect
- Depriving a child of necessities such as food and drink, clothing, critical medical care or treatment, or shelter
- Failing to protect a child from abuse (such as failing to report abuse when a child discloses it or when a staff member observes it)
- Exposing a child to a harmful environment (such as an environment where there is illicit drug use or illicit drug manufacturing)
- Failing to adequately supervise a child, resulting in injury or harm

Ill treatment
- Making excessive and/or degrading demands of a child
- Disciplining or correcting a child in an unreasonable and seriously inappropriate or improper manner
- Seriously inappropriate and/or degrading comments or behaviour towards a child
- Repeated hostility towards a child
- Seclusion and other types of restrictive practices
- Locking up a child in a room
- Pushing a child to train or perform when they are injured

Grooming
- Engaging in unauthorised contact with a child online for the purpose of developing a sexual relationship
- Using a computer, mobile phone, camera or other device to exploit or harass a child
- Unacceptable personal communication that explores sexual feelings or intimate personal feelings with a child
- Sharing details with a child of one's own sexual experiences
- Inappropriately extending a relationship with a child outside of work
- Giving a child special attention or isolating them from peers with the intention of making it easier to access the child for sexual activity
- Offering a child gifts, food, cigarettes, money, attention or affection with the intention of making it easier to access the child for sexual activity
- Making close physical contact, like inappropriate tickling and 'play' wrestling

Failure to prevent/report abuse
- An obvious or very clearly unreasonable failure to respond to information strongly indicating that another adult working at the organisation poses a serious risk of abusing a child
- Knowing or believing that a child has been abused and not reporting it to police (or not reporting in circumstances where the person ought reasonably to have known)

The following types of behaviour may be of concern

- Being alone with a child when there is no professional reason for doing so
- Showing favour to one child over others
- Babysitting, mentoring and/or tutoring a child out of work hours (without managerial approval for this kind of secondary employment)

(*www.ocg.nsw.gov.au/sites/default/files/2021-12/ChildSafeCodeofConduct_1_3.pdf*)

Appendix 10: Reflection and discussion prompts

This table could help when reviewing your service philosophy:

Why? Philosophy	How? Practice	What? Principles
Why do you do what you do? How do you view teaching and learning? Who is it benefitting? Why is it important? What is unique about your service?	How does your philosophy shape and guide the operation of the service? What practices are embedded in the service that promote the service's values and beliefs? How do you involve stakeholders in the process of reviewing the philosophy, inclusive of children?	What is achieved? What are the outcomes for children, families, educators and the community? Is the right to safety and wellbeing clear? Would this philosophy be inclusive to all citizens?

Adapted from ACECQA, 2018, Quality Area 7 – Reviewing your service philosophy (*acecqa.gov.au/sites/default/files/2018-10/QA7_ReviewingYourServicePhilosophy.pdf*)

Appendix 11: Risk assessment and management template for excursions – (risk matrix to assess includes likelihood of harm)

Proposed route and extra spotlight

You can include an image of the route sourced online and indicate where child safety (against abuse) will have an extra spotlight (strong consideration), for example, at a public toilet or a bus stop.

Agreeance signing

Has every adult involved in the excursion read and signed their agreeance to uphold our Commitment to Child Safety, Code of Conduct, Child Safety and Wellbeing Policy, and any other relevant policy?

Adequate supervision

What strategies will be utilised to ensure adequate supervision in regard to abuse? For example, only room staff monitors public toilets, remains outside cubicle doors when in public toilets, arranges for exclusive use of changing room for group at sports complex.

Child involvement

Have children been consulted about safety measures and contributed their ideas to prevent harm? Did they undertake risk assessment using a child-friendly tool?

(Also see www.acecqa.gov.au/resources/applications/sample-forms-and-templates)

REFERENCES

@annatheanxietycoach (2022). www.annatheanxietycoach.com

Australian Bureau of Statistics (ABS) (2019). www.abs.gov.au

Australian Childhood Foundation (n.d.). 'Safeguarding Children Foundational Knowledge.' www.vimeo.com/showcase/-safeguarding-children-foundational-knowledge

Australian Childhood Foundation (2020). 'Emma's Project.' www.childhood.org.au/emmas-project/?utm_source=Website&utm_medium=Banner&utm_campaign=Emmas+project

Australian Childhood Foundation (2020). 'Keeping Children Safe.' www.childhood.org.au/our-work/keeping-children-safe

Australian Childhood Foundation (2022). 'Emma's Project: Protecting children starts with listening and believing.' www.youtube.com/watch?v=5FMqZpMQIaw

Australian Childhood Foundation and Child Abuse Prevention Research Australia (2008). *Responding to child abuse and neglect in Australia*

Australian Children's Education & Care Quality Authority (ACECQA) (2009). 'Quality Area 2 – Children's health and safety.' www.acecqa.gov.au/nqf/national-quality-standard/quality-area-2-childrens-health-and-safety

Australian Children's Education & Care Quality Authority (ACECQA) (2010). 'National Law.' www.acecqa.gov.au/nqf/national-law-regulations/national-law

Australian Children's Education & Care Quality Authority (ACECQA) (2012). *What is the NQF?* www.acecqa.gov.au/nqf/about

Australian Children's Education & Care Quality Authority (ACECQA) (2018). 'National Quality Standard.' www.acecqa.gov.au/nqf/national-quality-standard

Australian Children's Education & Care Quality Authority (ACECQA) (2018). 'Quality Area 7: Reviewing Your Service Philosophy.' www.acecqa.gov.au/sites/default/files/2018-10/QA7_ReviewingYourServicePhilosophy.pdf

Australian Children's Education & Care Quality Authority (ACECQA) (2020) *Guide to the National Quality Framework.* www.acecqa.gov.au/sites/default/files/2022-03/Guide-to-the-NQF-compressed_0.pdf

Australian Children's Education & Care Quality Authority (ACECQA) (2021). 'Delivery of children to, and collection from, education and care service premises'

Australian Children's Education & Care Quality Authority (ACECQA) (2021). *NQF Snapshot: Q2 2022.* www.acecqa.gov.au/sites/default/files/2022-08/NQF%20Snapshot%20Q2%202022%20FINAL.pdf

Australian Children's Education & Care Quality Authority (ACECQA) (2021). *Providing a Child Safe Environment: Policy Guidelines.* www.acecqa.gov.au/sites/default/files/2022-03/Providing-a-childsafe-environment-policy.pdf

Australian Children's Education & Care Quality Authority (ACECQA) (2022). *My Time, Our Place.* www.acecqa.gov.au/sites/default/files/2023-01/MTOP-V2.0.pdf

Australian Government, Department of Education (2019). *Belonging, Being & Becoming: The Early Years Learning Framework for Australia.* www.acecqa.gov.au/sites/default/files/2018-02/belonging_being_and_becoming_the_early_years_learning_framework_for_australia.pdf

Australian Human Rights Commission (n.d.). 'Early Childhood Education.' www.humanrights.gov.au/our-work/education/early-childhood-education

Australian Human Rights Commission (n.d.). 'National Principles.' Child Safe Organisations. https://childsafe.humanrights.gov.au/national-principles

Australian Human Rights Commission (2014). *What does the Children's Rights Report 2013 say?* www.humanrights.gov.au/our-work/childrens-rights/publications/what-does-childrens-rights-report-2013-say?_ga=2.244472133.1799749640.1648437531-22834479.1648437531

Australian Human Rights Commission (2015). *Supporting young children's rights: Statement of intent (2015–2018).* www.humanrights.gov.au/sites/default/files/supporting_young_children_rights.pdf

Australian Human Rights Commission (2016). *All My Friends and Me – Building belonging: A toolkit for early childhood educators on cultural diversity and responding to prejudice (2016).* www.humanrights.gov.au/sites/default/files/buildingbelonging-eBook.pdf

Australian Human Rights Commission (2018). *Getting started on your child safe journey: Introductory self-assessment tool for organisations. Child Safe Organisations.* https://childsafe.humanrights.gov.au/sites/default/files/inline-files/CSO%20Introductory%20self-assessment%20tool%20for%20organisations_1.pdf

Australian Human Rights Commission (2018). *Introductory self-assessment tool for organisations.* www.childsafe.humanrights.gov.au/sites/default/files/inline-files/CSO%20Introductory%20self-assessment%20tool%20for%20organisations_1.pdf

Australian Human Rights Commission (2018). *National Principles for Child Safe Organisations.* https://childsafe.humanrights.gov.au/sites/default/files/2019-02/National_Principles_for_Child_Safe_Organisations2019.pdf

Australian Human Rights Commission (2018). 'Organisational self-assessment.' Child Safe Organisations. https://childsafe.humanrights.gov.au/learning-hub/organisational-self-assessment

Australian Human Rights Commission (2020). *Child Safety and Wellbeing Policy*

Australian Human Rights Commission (2020). 'National Children's Commissioner, Anne Hollonds.' www.humanrights.gov.au/our-work/commission-general/national-childrens-commissioner-anne-hollonds

Australian Human Rights Commission (2021). *A guide for children and young people to the National Strategy to prevent and respond to child sexual abuse 2021-2030.* www.humanrights.gov.au/our-work/childrens-rights/publications/guide-children-and-young-people-national-strategy-prevent

Australian Human Rights Commission (2021). *Guide for parents and carers.* Child Safe Organisations National Principles. childsafe.humanrights.gov.au/sites/default/files/inline-files/CSO%20Guide%20for%20parents%20and%20carers_1.docx

Australian Human Rights Commission (2021). 'Keeping kids safe and well – your voices.' www.humanrights.gov.au/safeandwell

Australian Human Rights Commission (2022). 'Updates from Australian and New Zealand Children's Commissioners and Guardians.' www.humanrights.gov.au/our-work/childrens-rights/issues/updates-australian-and-new-zealand-childrens-commissioners-and

Australian Institute of Family Studies (AIFS) (n.d.). 'I'm not a jigsaw puzzle.' www.aifs.gov.au

Australian Institute of Family Studies (AIFS) (2013). 'LGBTIQA+ glossary of common terms.' www.aifs.gov.au/resources/resource-sheets/lgbtiqa-glossary-common-terms#footnote-002-backlink

Australian Institute of Family Studies (AIFS) (2017). 'Risk and protective factors for child abuse and neglect.' www.aifs.gov.au/cfca/publications/risk-and-protective-factors-child-abuse-and-neglect

Australian Institute of Family Studies (2021). *Reporting child abuse and neglect.* www.aifs.gov.au/sites/default/files/publication-documents/2109_reporting_child_abuse_and_neglect_rs_0.pdf

Australian Institute of Health and Welfare (AIHW) (2019). 'Family, domestic and sexual violence in Australia: continuing the national story 2019.' Cat. no. FDV 3. Canberra, ACT: AIHW

Australian Institute of Health and Welfare (AIHW) (2020). *Australia's Children.* www.aihw.gov.au/getmedia/6af928d6-692e-4449-b915-cf2ca946982f/aihw-cws-69-print-report.pdf.aspx?inline=true

Australian Institute of Health and Welfare (AIHW) (2020). 'Australia's children: Justice and safety'

Australian Institute of Health and Welfare (AIHW) (2022). *The Aboriginal and Torres Strait Islander Child Placement Principle Indicators.* www.aihw.gov.au/reports/child-protection/atsicpp-indicators/contents/about

Berger, E, & Martin, K (2020). 'Why every teacher needs to know about childhood trauma.' The Conversation

Berry Street (2022). Berry Street's Education Model (BSEM) Clinical Conversations Child & Family Trauma Informed Practice. www.berrystreet.org.au/learning-and-resources/berry-street-education-model

Beyond Blue (2022). 'Build supportive relationships.' www.healthyfamilies.beyondblue.org.au/healthy-homes/building-resilience/build-supportive-relationships

Be You (n.d.). 'Educator wellbeing tools.' www.beyou.edu.au/resources/educator-wellbeing/tools

Bhathal, A, Chamberlain, C, Krakouer, J, Beaufils, JC, Gray, P, & Corrales, T (2021). 'First Nations children are still being removed at disproportionate rates. Cultural assumptions about parenting need to change.' The Conversation

Chief Parliamentary Counsel (2018). *Family Violence Protection (Information Sharing and Risk Management) Regulations 2018.* https://content.legislation.vic.gov.au/sites/default/files/2021-04/18-14sra003%20authorised.pdf

Child Welfare Information Gateway (2018). 'Supporting Brain Development in Traumatized Children and Youth'

City of Boroondara (n.d.). 'Advocate the image of the child – Nicole Talarico.' www.boroondara.vic.gov.au/media/video/advocate-image-child-nicole-talarico

City of Casey (n.d.). *Easy English Version Child Safety Policy.* www.casey.vic.gov.au/sites/default/files/user-files/City%20%26%20Council/Policies%20%26%20strategies/City%20of%20Casey%20-Easy%20Read%20Child%20Safety%20Policy.pdf

Coaston, J, (2019). 'The Intersectionality Wars'. Vox Media

Commission for Children and Young People (CCYP) (n.d.). 'Resources and support for the Reportable Conduct Scheme.' www.ccyp.vic.gov.au/resources/reportable-conduct-scheme/#TOC-2

Commission for Children and Young People (CCYP) (2017). 'About the Reportable Conduct Scheme.' www.ccyp.vic.gov.au/reportable-conduct-scheme/about-the-reportable-conduct-scheme

Commission for Children and Young People (CCYP) (2021). *Commission for Children and Young People Annual report 2020–21*. www.ccyp.vic.gov.au/assets/corporate-documents/Annual-report-2020-21.pdf

Commission for Children and Young People (CCYP) (2021). *Empowerment and participation: A guide for organisations working with children and young people*

Commission for Children and Young People (CCYP) (2022). 'Stronger Child Safe Standards come into force from today.' www.ccyp.vic.gov.au/news/stronger-child-safe-standards-come-into-force-from-today

Commission for Children and Young People (CCYP) (2022). V*ictoria's new Child Safe Standards*. www.ccyp.vic.gov.au/assets/resources/New-CSS/New-Child-Safe-Standards-Information-Sheet.pdf

Commissioner for Children and Young People (2021). *What can adults learn from children?* www.ccyp.wa.gov.au/media/4863/digime-what-can-adults-learn-from-children.pdf

Commonwealth of Australia (2010). *Educators: Belonging, Being & Becoming – Educators' Guide to the Early Years Learning Framework for Australia*

Commonwealth of Australia (2021). *National Framework for Protecting Australia's Children*

Commonwealth of Australia, Department of Social Services (2021). *Safe & Supported: The National Framework for Protecting Australia's Children 2021–2031*. www.dss.gov.au/sites/default/files/documents/12_2021/dess5016-national-framework-protecting-childrenaccessible.pdf

Department for Child Protection (2021). *Safe and well*. www.childprotection.sa.gov.au/__data/assets/pdf_file/0011/126497/19-070-Safe-and-Well-State-Reform_final.pdf

Desautels, L (2020). *Connections over Compliance: Rewiring our Perceptions of Discipline*. Wyatt-MacKenzie Publishing

Early Childhood Australia (ECA) (2016). *Code of Ethics*. www.earlychildhoodaustralia.org.au/wp-content/uploads/2019/08/ECA-COE-Brochure-web-2019.pdf

Early Childhood Australia Learning Hub (n.d.). 'eSafety Professional Learning Modules.' https://learninghub.earlychildhoodaustralia.org.au/esafety-early-years-program

endUP Movement (2021). *How We endUP: A Future Without Family Policing.* www.upendmovement.org/wp-content/uploads/2021/06/How-We-endUP-6.18.21.pdf

Farrugia, C (2022). 'Inclusive communication with LGBTIQ+ clients.' Australian Institute of Family Studies. www.aifs.gov.au/cfca/publications/inclusive-communication-lgbtiq-clients

Gandolfo, SL (2021). 'Mythbusting professional love.' *The Spoke – Early Childhood Australia's Blog.* https://thespoke.earlychildhoodaustralia.org.au/mythbusting-professional-love/

Gardoce, R (2022). *Fair Work Grants 10 Days' Paid Domestic Violence Leave In New Decision*, Sprintlaw. www.sprintlaw.com.au/articles/fair-work-domestic-violence-leave

Girraway Ganyi (n.d.). www.girrawayganyi.com.au

Governance Institute of Australia (2019). 'Building a child-safe culture with the child in mind.' www.governanceinstitute.com.au/resources/governance-directions/volume-71-number-10/building-a-child-safe-culture-with-the-child-in-mind

The Grace Tame Foundation (n.d.). 'The Harmony Campaign.' www.thegracetamefoundation.org.au/the-harmony-campaign

Hager, E (2019). 'Five approaches for creating trauma-informed classrooms.' Monash University. www.monash.edu/education/teachspace/articles/five-approaches-for-creating-trauma-informed-classrooms

Hager, E (2020). 'Is Child Abuse Really Rising During the Pandemic?' The Marshall Project

Hakansson, E (2022). 'Emma's project.' www.childhood.org.au/emmas-project

Haynes, J, & Blair-West, G (2022). *The Girl in the Green Dress*

Higgins, JR, & Butler, N (2007). *Indigenous responses to child protection issues.* 'Promising Practices in Out-of-Home Care for Aboriginal and Torres Strait Islander Carers, Children and Young People' (booklet 4). Melbourne: Australian Institute of Family studies

Hopper, J (2022). *Why Adults Fail to Protect Children.* www.jimhopper.com/topics/child-abuse/why-adults-fail-to-protect-children

Koori Curriculum (n.d.). 'Koori Curriculum Advisory Group.' www.kooricurriculum.com/pages/koori-curriculum-advisory-group

Lapointe, V (2020). 'The unavoidable necessity of the tantrum.' *Babyology.* www.babyology.com.au/toddler/behaviour-and-discipline/the-unavoidable-necessity-of-the-tantrum

Martin, H (2018). *Someone Should Have Told Me.* Safe4Kids

McCann, C (2007). *Zoli.* Random House

McLean, S (2016). 'The effect of trauma on the brain development of children: Evidence-based principles for supporting the recovery of children in care.' Australian Institute of Health and Welfare

McLeod, S (2019). 'The Zone of Proximal Development and Scaffolding.' Simply Psychology. www.simplypsychology.org/Zone-of-Proximal-Development.html

Melbourne School of Population and Global Health (2022). 'Child and Community Wellbeing.' www.mspgh.unimelb.edu.au/centres-institutes/centre-for-health-equity/research-group/jack-brockhoff-child-health-wellbeing-program

Milton, N (2019). 'Building a child-safe culture with the child in mind.' Governance Institute Australia

Morgan, C (2022). 'Australia facing "tsunami" of child abuse.' *The Sydney Morning Herald.* www.smh.com.au/national/australia-facing-tsunami-of-child-abuse-20220925-p5bku2.html

Moss, P (2001). *Beyond Early Childhood Education and Care.* www.oecd.org/education/school/2535274.pdf

NAPCAN (2020). *Commitment Statement to Children and Young People.* www.napcan.org.au/wp-content/uploads/2020/08/NAPCAN_CommitmentStatement_FINAL.pdf

National Children's Commissioner (2019). *Children's Rights Report for 2019.* Australian Human Rights Commission

National Office for Child Safety (2021). 'National Strategy to Prevent and Respond to Child Sexual Abuse 2021–2030.' www.childsafety.pmc.gov.au/what-we-do/national-strategy-prevent-child-sexual-abuse

National Research Centre for the Prevention of Child Abuse and Australian Childhood Foundation (2006). *The state of child protection: Australian child welfare and child protection developments 2005.* www.researchgate.net/publication/264546640_The_state_of_child_protection_Australian_child_welfare_and_child_protection_developments_2005

Northern Health (2020). *Cultural Safety and System Change: An Assessment Tool.* www.indigenoushealthnh.ca/sites/default/files/publications/documents/NH-Cultural-Safety-System-Change-Assessment-Tool-Jan-2020.pdf

NSW Government, Office of the Children's Guardian (2020). *Codes of Conduct: a guide to developing child safe Codes of Conduct.* www.ocg.nsw.gov.au/sites/default/files/2021-12/ChildSafeCodeofConduct_1_3.pdf

NSW legislation (2011). 'Education and Care Services National Regulations (2011 SI 653).' www.legislation.nsw.gov.au/view/html/inforce/current/sl-2011-0653

NSW Ministry of Health (2022). *Aboriginal Cultural Engagement Self-Assessment Tool.* www.health.nsw.gov.au/aboriginal/Publications/aboriginal-cultural-engagement-self-assessment-tool.pdf

The Orange Door (2019). 'About The Orange Door.' www.vic.gov.au/sites/default/files/2019-08/Fact-sheet-About-The-Orange-Door.pdf

PAPYRUS (2017). 'Is Abuse More Prevalent in Contemporary Societies?' www.papyrus-project.org/is-abuse-more-prevalent-in-contemporary-societies

Perry, BD (2006). 'Bruce Perry Quote & Video: Helping Children Heal From Trauma.' HeloiseRidley.com. www.heloiseridley.com/bruce-perry-quote-video-helping-children-heal-from-trauma

Perry, BD (2007). *The Boy Who was Raised as a Dog*. Basic Books

Perry, BD (2021). 'A Neurodevelopmental Approach.' www.bdperry.com

Pika, J (2019). 'The Strengthening Families Movement: Looking Back and Looking Ahead.' Center for the Study of Social Policy. www.cssp.org/2019/01/looking-back-at-the-strengthening-families-movement

Queensland Government, Department of Communities, Child Safety and Disability Services (2015). www.cyjma.qld.gov.au/resources/campaign/supporting-families/foundational-elements.pdf

Queensland Organised Crime Commission of Inquiry (2015). *Queensland Organised Crime Commission of Inquiry Report*. www.organisedcrimeinquiry.qld.gov.au/__data/assets/pdf_file/0017/935/QOCCI15287-ORGANISED-CRIME-INQUIRY_Final_Report.pdf

Queer Asterisk (2016, 2017). *LGBTQIAP+ Etiquette Guide and Glossary of Terms*. www.queerasterisk.com/files/LGBTQIAP-Etiquette-Guide-and-Glossary-of-Terms.pdf

Radley, JJ, Sisti, HM, Hao, J, Rocher, AB, McCall, T, Hof, PR, McEwen, BS, & Morrison, JH (2004). 'Chronic behavioral stress induces apical dendritic reorganization in pyramidal neurons of the medial prefrontal cortex.' *Neuroscience*, Vol 125, no. 1, pp 1–6

Rainbow Families (n.d.). *Understanding LGBTIQA+ Domestic and Family Violence*. #StrongSafeFabulous. www.strongsafefabulous.online/wp-content/uploads/2021/09/understanding-tipsheet-final.pdf

Raising Children Network (2021). 'Resilience: how to build it in children 3–8 years.' www.raisingchildren.net.au/school-age/behaviour/understanding-behaviour/resilience-how-to-build-it-in-children-3-8-years

Reggio Emilia Australia Information Exchange (2020). 'Reframing Learning: From Uncertainty to Hope.' www.reggioaustralia.org.au/reframing-learning-from-uncertainty-to-hope

Revell, J (2022). 'Grace Tame's Campaign Just Got the Legal Definition of Sexual Abuse Changed in the ACT.' The Latch. www.thelatch.com.au/grace-tame-act

Royal Commission into Institutional Responses to Child Sexual Abuse (2017). 'Final Report.' www.childabuseroyalcommission.gov.au/final-report

Safe4Kids (2019). 'Consent by Imanpa Kids.' www.youtube.com/watch?v=tyUCTG5k4nE

Sanders, J (2022). Body Safety – 'Empowering Kids to Stay Safe.' Hey Sigmund. www.heysigmund.com/body-safety-empowering-kids-stay-safe-safe-jayneen-sanders/

Scarlet, RR (2020). *The Anti Bias Approach in Early Childhood* (4th edition), p21

Secretariat of National Aboriginal and Islander Child Care (SNAICC) (2021). *Keeping our kids safe: Cultural safety and the National Principles for Child Safe Organisations.* www.snaicc.org.au/wp-content/uploads/2021/06/SNAICC-VACCA-OCS-ChildSafeReport-LR-with-alt-tags-May2021.pdf

Secretariat of National Aboriginal and Islander Child Care (SNAICC) (2021). 'Keeping our kids safe: Cultural safety and the National Principles for Child Safe Organisations.' www.snaicc.org.au/policy-and-research/child-safety-and-wellbeing/keeping-our-kids-safe

Star Health (n.d.). 'Being Equal.' www.starhealth.org.au/services-2/health-promotion/being-equal

Star Health (2021). *Being Equal Pilot Program: Stories of Change*

Strehmel, P, Heikka, J, Hujala, E, Rodd, J, & Waniganayake, M (2019). *Leadership in Early Education in Times of Change: Research from five continents.* Toronto: Budrich

#StrongSafeFabulous (n.d.). *Free to be me.* www.accesshc.org.au/app/uploads/AHC109_Book-Selection-Checklist_170607.pdf

#StrongSafeFabulous (n.d.). 'Resources for schools & childcare centres.' www.strongsafefabulous.online/resource_category/schools-childcare-centres

Taylor & Francis (2010). 'A1. Council of the European Union, Conclusions on the Middle East Peace Process, Brussels, 8 December 2009.' *Journal of Palestine Studies*, Vol 39(3), pp182–184. https://doi.org/10.1525/jps.2010.xxxix.3.182

Tsorbaris, D (2022). 'Protecting our children in chaotic times? We need more than a national framework.' Pro Bono Australia. www.probonoaustralia.com.au/news/2022/03/protecting-our-children-in-chaotic-times-we-need-more-than-a-national-framework

Turner, JJ (2019). 'LGBTQIAP+: We help you understand 23 gender terms.' News24. www.news24.com/parent/teen_13-18/development/lgbtqiap-we-help-you-understand-23-gender-terms-20190124

UNICEF (n.d.) 'United Nations Convention on the Rights of the Child' – children's version. www.unicef.org/media/60981/file/convention-rights-child-text-child-friendly-version.pdf

UNICEF Australia (2022). 'United Nations Convention on the Rights of the Child' – simplified version. www.unicef.org.au/united-nations-convention-on-the-rights-of-the-child

United Nations (n.d.) 'United Nations Convention on the Rights of the Child' – child-friendly language version. www.ccyp.wa.gov.au/media/1216/poster-united-nations-january-2008.pdf

United Nations (1989) 'United Nations Convention on the Rights of the Child' – full version. www.ohchr.org/en/instruments-mechanisms/instruments/convention-rights-child

United Nations (2015). 'United Nations Declaration on the Rights of Indigenous Peoples.' www.un.org/development/desa/indigenouspeoples/declaration-on-the-rights-of-indigenous-peoples.html

Unyte (2022). 'What Is Trauma?' www.integratedlistening.com/what-is-trauma

Urban, M (2022). 'Scholarship in times of crises: towards a trans-discipline of early childhood.' *Comparative Education*, pp1-19. Taylor & Francis. www.doi.org/10.1080/03050068.2022.2046376

van der Kolk, B (2020). Alliance Against Seclusion and Restraint. www.facebook.com/endseclusion/photos/our-brains-continually-form-maps-of-the-world-maps-of-what-is-safe-and-what-is-d/682653059272017/

Victoria Legal Aid (n.d.). www.legalaid.vic.gov.au

Victorian Government (n.d.). *Child Wellbeing and Safety Act 2005*. www.legislation.vic.gov.au/in-force/acts/child-wellbeing-and-safety-act-2005/037

Victorian Government (n.d.). *Family Violence Reform Rolling Action Plan 2020-2023.* www.content.vic.gov.au/sites/default/files/2021-04/Family%20Violence%20Reform%20Rolling%20Action%20Plan%202020%20-%202023%20-%20Combined%20Activity%20Summary%20%28Page%209%20to%20be%20updated%29.pdf

Victorian Government (2016). 'Spotting the Warning Signs of Child Abuse (Early Childhood).' www.education.vic.gov.au/Documents/about/programs/health/protect/EarlyChildhood_FactSheet_WarningSigns.pdf

Victorian Government (2017). *An analysis of exiting research: primary prevention of family violence against people from LGBTI communities.* https://media-cdn.ourwatch.org.au/wp-content/uploads/sites/2/2019/11/07031955/Primary-Prevention-of-FV-against-LGBTI-people-Report-Accessible-PDF.pdf

Victorian Government (2018). *Wungurilwil Gapgapduir: Aboriginal Children and Families Agreement.* www.dhhs.vic.gov.au/sites/default/files/documents/201804/Aboriginal%20Children%20and%20Families%20Agreement%202018_1.pdf

Victorian Government (2019). 'Building from strength: 10-Year Industry Plan for Family Violence Prevention and Response.' www.vic.gov.au/building-strength-10-year-industry-plan

Victorian Government (2019). *Ending Family Violence: Victoria's plan for change.* www.vic.gov.au/sites/default/files/2019-07/Ending-Family-Violence-10-Year-Plan.pdf

Victorian Government (2019). 'MARAM practice guides and resources.' www.vic.gov.au/maram-practice-guides-and-resources

Victorian Government (2020). 'Regulating the Child Safe Standards in early childhood services.' www.vic.gov.au/how-child-safe-standards-are-regulated-early-childhood-services

Victorian Government (2021). *MARAM Practice Guides: Foundation knowledge guide – Guidance for professionals working with child or adult victim survivors, and adults using family violence.* www.content.vic.gov.au/sites/default/files/2021-09/371%20VS%20Full%20Set_0.pdf

Victorian Government (2021). 'Who can share information under the information sharing and MARAM reforms.' www.vic.gov.au/ciss-and-fviss-who-can-share-information

Victorian Government (2022). 'About the information sharing and MARAM reforms.' www.vic.gov.au/about-information-sharing-schemes-and-risk-management-framework

Victorian Government (2022). 'Information sharing guides, templates and tools.' www.vic.gov.au/guides-templates-tools-for-information-sharing

Victorian Government (2022). *Monitoring Victoria's family violence reforms: Early identification of family violence within universal services, Family Violence Reform Implementation Monitor.* www.fvrim.vic.gov.au/monitoring-victorias-family-violence-reforms-early-identification-family-violence-within-universal

Victorian Government, Department of Education (2016). *Victorian Early Years Learning and Development Framework*

Victorian Government, Department of Education (2019). 'Teach Respectful Relationships.' www.education.vic.gov.au/school/teachers/teachingresources/discipline/capabilities/personal/Pages/respectfulrel.aspx

Victorian Government, Department of Education (2022). 'Understand your obligations to protect children'

Victorian Government, Department of Families, Fairness and Housing (2021). 'Children, youth & families'

Victorian Government, Department of Health (2017). 'Vulnerable children.' www.health.vic.gov.au/populations/vulnerable-children

Victorian Government, Department of Health (2021). 'Aboriginal and Torres Strait Islander cultural safety framework'

Victorian Government, Department of Human Services (2012). *Children with problem sexual behaviours and their families.* www.dhhs.vic.gov.au/sites/default/files/documents/201705/Children_with_problem_sexual_behaviours_-and-_their_families-2012_0.pdf

Victorian Government, Department of Justice and Community Safety (n.d.). 'Betrayal of trust fact sheet: The new organisational duty of care to prevent child abuse'

Victorian Government, Department of Justice and Community Safety (2022). *Department of Justice and Community Safety Annual Report 2021–2022*

Victorian Government, Family Violence Reform Implementation Monitor (2022). 'Monitoring Victoria's family violence reforms: Early identification of family violence within universal services.' www.fvrim.vic.gov.au/monitoring-victorias-family-violence-reforms-early-identification-family-violence-within-universal

Victorian Institute of Teaching (2021). *The Victorian Teaching Profession's Code of Conduct.* www.vit.vic.edu.au/sites/default/files/media/pdf/2021-07/Document_VIT_Code_of_Conduct.pdf

Victorian Institute of Teaching (2021). *The Victorian Teaching Profession's Code of Ethics.* www.vit.vic.edu.au/sites/default/files/media/pdf/2021-07/Document_VIT_Code_of_Ethics.pdf

Vijeyarasa, DR (2022). 'Three reasons why women leaders actually matter for women.' Women's Agenda. www.womensagenda.com.au/latest/three-reasons-why-women-leaders-actually-matter-for-women

White, EJ, Rooney, T, Gunn, AC, Nuttal, J (2020). 'Understanding how early childhood educators "see" learning through digitally cast eyes: Some preliminary concepts concerning the use of digital documentation platforms.' *Australasian Journal of Early Childhood,* Vol 46(1). Sage Journals. https://doi.org/10.1177/1836939120979066

Women's Agenda (2022). *New Commission unveiled to help combat 'national shame' of domestic violence.* www.womensagenda.com.au/latest/new-commission-unveiled-to-help-combat-national-shame-of-domestic-violence

World Health Organization (WHO) (2006). *Preventing child maltreatment: a guide to taking action and generating evidence.* www.who.int/publications/i/item/preventing-child-maltreatment-a-guide-to-taking-action-and-generating-evidence, p9

yourtown (2020). *Insights 2020: Insights into young people in Australia.* www.yourtown.com.au/sites/default/files/document/Kids-Helpline-Insights-2020-Report-Final.pdf

SUPPORT SERVICES

If you or someone you know is in immediate danger, **call triple zero (000)** and ask for the police.

You should also consider:
- Talking to your GP or another allied health professional
- Reporting historical or current experiences of abuse to the police
- Chatting to someone at www.lifeline.org.au
- Finding help and support on the following nationwide crisis lines:
  - QLife (LGBTI): **1800 184 527**
  - Blue Knot: **1300 657 380**
  - Lifeline: **13 11 14**
  - 1800Respect: **1800 737 732**
  - MensLine Australia: **1300 789 978**
  - Kids Helpline: **1800 55 1800**
  - Beyond Blue: **1300 22 4636**

A further list of national support services and groups and those specific to each state and territory is available via www.childabuseroyalcommissionresponse.gov.au/support-services

Some other organisations to contact include:

- Victorian Aboriginal Legal Service (VALS) – www.vals.org.au
- Safe Steps: Family Violence Response Centre – www.safesteps.org.au
- Queerspace – www.queerspace.org.au
- Child and Community Wellbeing – www.mspgh.unimelb.edu.au/centres-institutes/centre-for-health-equity/research-group/child-community-wellbeing

www.ingramcontent.com/pod-product-compliance
Lightning Source LLC
Chambersburg PA
CBHW070648120526
44590CB00013BA/880